Shaping Your HR Role
Succeeding in Today's Organizations

Shaping Your HR Role

Succeeding in Today's Organizations

William M. Kahnweiler, Ph.D.
and
Jennifer B. Kahnweiler, Ph.D.

ELSEVIER
BUTTERWORTH
HEINEMANN

AMSTERDAM • BOSTON • HEIDELBERG • LONDON
NEW YORK • OXFORD • PARIS • SAN DIEGO
SAN FRANCISCO • SINGAPORE • SYDNEY • TOKYO

Elsevier Butterworth–Heinemann
30 Corporate Drive, Suite 400, Burlington, MA 01803, USA
Linacre House, Jordan Hill, Oxford OX2 8DP, UK

 Recognizing the importance of preserving what has been written, Elsevier prints its books on acid-free paper whenever possible.

Library of Congress Cataloging-in-Publication Data
APPLICATION SUBMITTED

British Library Cataloguing-in-Publication Data
A catalogue record for this book is available from the British Library.

ISBN: 0-7506-7823-2

For information on all Elsevier Butterworth–Heinemann publications
visit our Web site at www.books.elsevier.com

05 06 07 08 09 10   10 9 8 7 6 5 4 3 2 1

Printed in the United States of America

Dedication

If we are lucky, every once in a while our lives will be graced with a compassionate, caring, and thoughtful person. Dr. Fred Otte was such a person for us and for countless others. He dedicated an exemplary career helping hundreds of people find their niche while advancing Human Resources as a profession. He was a colleague, friend, mentor, and consummate teacher in the truest sense of those words. He elicited the best in us while encouraging us to explore those parts of us that could be improved. Fred brought new meaning to the terms "growth," "development," and "helpfulness," and he loved toying with ideas and theories while maintaining solid footing in the practical. He gained joy from weaving an interconnected network of friends and colleagues. Although cancer took his body, his soul remains with us and with so many of the lives he touched in profound ways. It is with heartfelt gratitude that we dedicate this book to Fred, mentor and friend extraordinaire.

Epigraph

To be successful in Human Resources, you need to exhibit . . .

1. The exemplary intellect of Albert Einstein
2. The infectious charm and wit of John F. Kennedy
3. The creativity of Georiga O'Keefe
4. The profound charisma of Martin Luther King, Jr.
5. The keen business acumen of Jack Welch
6. The diplomatic skills of Madeline Albright
7. The vision of Steve Jobs
8. The courage of Helen Keller
9. The management wisdom of Peter Drucker
10. The humanitarianism of Eleanor Roosevelt
11. The insights into human behavior of Sigmund Freud
12. The deep compassion of Mother Teresa
13. The humor of Lucille Ball

    . . . and last but not least . . .

14.  (The hide of a rhinoceros)

Table of Contents

Preface and Acknowledgments

Who Should Read This Book and Why?

We wrote this book with four primary audiences in mind: (1) entry-level HR professionals, (2) mid-career HR professionals, (3) career changers who have decided they want to move into HR, and (4) undergraduate and graduate students in HR and related fields, such as management, industrial-organizational psychology, and organizational behavior. So if you identify yourself as belonging to one of these groups, this book is most definitely for you. Even if you don't fall into one of these groups, this book may, nonetheless, still be for you.

We consider entry-level to be up to three years of full-time experience in HR. If you are an entry-level HR professional as we define it, this book will help you learn about the profession's many options that lie ahead and guide you for positioning to advance in the field.

If you are a mid-career HR professional (we define this as roughly 3 to 10 years of full-time experience in the profession, including external HR consulting), this book will assist you in prioritizing the next steps to develop and enhance your marketability. It will also give you the tools to build upon the success you have already achieved and will maximize the likelihood of your continued success.

If you have decided you are ready to change careers and move into HR, you probably have already done a good bit of research about the field and the opportunities available to you. This book will add to your repository of knowledge about the field and provide resources to help you target specific kinds of HR jobs and organizations that are likely to be good fits for you. The book will also supply you with realistic views of HR in today's organizations that you may not have considered or uncovered in your career research up to this point.

If you are an undergraduate or graduate student in HR or a related field, full- or part-time, this book will be a helpful adjunct to other books and articles that are required reading in your classes. We view it as a particularly effective complement to readings that cover HR content knowledge (that is, specifics about what is involved in compensation, recruiting, labor relations, management development, etc.) and trends in HR and the workplace.

This book should also serve useful purposes for those of you who are (1) seasoned HR executives, (2) potential career changers, or (3) actual career changers who have not seriously considered HR as a possible next move.

If you are a seasoned HR executive (at least 10 years of increasingly responsible experience in HR), this book will enhance your ability to assist, mentor, and coach your staff in developing their HR careers. It will also give you some ideas to think about and act upon to increase your own effectiveness as an HR leader.

Are you thinking about changing careers, haven't decided what your new career will be, but HR is one of the possibilities you are contemplating? If so, this book should help you gain clarity about the suitability HR holds for you and thus will move you closer to deciding whether to pursue HR as your career change target.

Perhaps you are sure you want to change careers but have not up to this point seriously thought about HR as a possibility. Or more likely, your own experience with HR professionals has soured you on the field. This book will provide you with accurate and up-to-date information about what it is really like to have a satisfying and successful career in HR. You need this kind of information to make sound decisions. We know dozens of people who never thought they would ever work in HR (we are two of them). Down the road, they found themselves smack dab in the middle of HR and loved the work. Never say never! HR is certainly a very broad field and accommodates the career aspirations, values, and interests of diverse people at various stages of their lives. You could be one of these people, too.

How This Book Differs from Others

We provide tools, guidelines, ideas, and strategies for succeeding in a career as an HR professional. Our overall approach could be described as "thoughtfully pragmatic." That is, we avoid a pure "how-to" laundry list of "keys to success" as well as pure theory or lofty concepts that have intellectual allure but lack practical utility. We strike a balance between helping you think and helping you act. We draw upon empirical research and practical experiences to improve your thinking, formulate good decisions, and then execute those decisions. Such a balancing act is, we believe, necessary for HR professionals' success. This book walks the "balancing act" talk.

Our approach incorporates current issues and future trends in both the HR profession and the workplace. We want you to use both your head (making rational decisions) and heart (honoring who you are) in developing your role in this dynamic profession. To accomplish these ends, we offer a powerful model of HR career success that is based on understanding what critical knowledge is necessary to learn and then apply to achieve significant results. We hope that our combined 60+ years of human resources experience as well as interviews with 25 seasoned HR executives, consultants, and managers make this success model come alive for you.

We have yet to discover a book that charts a logical and thoughtful path on how to develop one's HR career. Most books that target HR professionals tend to be solely for senior HR executives or focus on very specific "hot" issues such as measuring the impact of HR. Likewise, although the market certainly has many books on career success, our research shows that none pertain specifically to the growing and dynamic HR field. In addition, these career books tend to take a cookbook approach or a highly conceptual/theoretical/philosophical one that makes it difficult for readers to apply to their daily lives. As noted above, we strike an uncommon middle ground. Readers will leave with a host of action steps they can consider as they strategize about ways to develop and perform in this expansive and growing profession.

We also think you will find that our focus on organizations (note the subtitle of the book) is fairly unique among books devoted to effective HR practice. HR does not exist in a vacuum. It is enacted in work organizations. And organizations have a significant effect on HR practice . . . and, we hope, HR practice has a significant effect on organizations. For us, organizational life is inseparable from HR practice and is thus a cornerstone of what this book is all about. As organizational life becomes more complex, stressful, and unpredictable, HR professionals are and will continue to be forced to move through multiple roles continuously and seamlessly throughout each day. This book is a roadmap to help you plan and implement these roles quickly, cost effectively, and creatively.

Our Research Methods

We drew upon four data sources for this book. We first researched published practitioner and academic literature that dealt with career development generally and career development for HR professionals specifically. We included relevant research findings and concepts from this review.

Second, we searched and then culled information from databases, websites, materials from HR professional associations, and information clearinghouses on the Internet. We generally discarded materials that were more than five years old unless they contained information and ideas that remain relevant to HR and organizations today.

Third, we reflected on our own experiences as HR professionals. We focused especially on the "lessons learned" from those experiences, the key issues those experiences highlighted, and the important questions we still ask ourselves when looking back over our HR careers.

Fourth, we interviewed highly successful HR practitioners for their thoughts, ideas, and experiences that, in their minds and hearts, contributed to their success in this field. We summarize below the methods we used with these people.

We spoke with 25 professionals who, to one degree or another and in one way or another, have clearly achieved success in HR. By "clearly achieved success," we mean they have been in HR for at least 10 years, have obtained increasingly responsible work throughout their time in HR, and have performed that work very competently. They also are very satisfied and fulfilled with the work they do. One of us spoke with 13 people, and the other interviewed the remaining 12. We knew most of these 25 people prior to asking whether they were willing to speak with us. We contacted the others through referrals by people in our professional networks.

One interview was conducted face-to-face at the request of the interviewee; the other 24 were conducted on the telephone. See Appendix C for the questions we asked each person. Although we told each interviewee at the outset that the interview would last no more than 30 minutes, all but a few lasted 45 to 90 minutes.

The 25 people in our sample represent a healthy cross section of HR roles (for example, some are generalists, others are specialists, some have been both), the kinds of industries they work in (for example, manufacturing, health care, high technology, federal and state government, banking, education, hospitality, utilities, energy), and organizational tenure (for example, some have spent their entire careers with one organization; others have moved around frequently). Both internal (employees) and external (contracted) consultants were represented, and for those who were full-time employees at the time of the interview, there was a sufficient mix of individual contributors, managers, directors, and senior-level HR executives. Our sample's gender and racial mix reflected proportions found in the general population. The shortest amount of time any of the 25 has been in HR was 10 years; most of our interviewees have been in the field for more than 20 years.

When we total the amount of experience our interviewees had at the time we spoke with them and then add to that our time in the field, we come up with roughly 600 years' worth of experience in HR. We think you, as a reader, will appreciate this experience. A book based on 600 years' worth of experience seems more credible and useful, at least to us, than one based on one author's 30 years of work in HR.

What did we do after we interviewed all the people who had agreed to speak with us? The process was fairly straightforward. Each one of us first looked only at the responses from the people we interviewed. Thus, initially there was "Bill's Data" and "Jennifer's Data," and Bill looked only at "Bill's Data" and Jennifer looked only at "Jennifer's Data." We took this approach to avoid contaminating each other's data with what each of us had heard from the people with whom we spoke. Each of us, in isolation, analyzed our 12 or 13 interviewees' responses on a question-by-question basis. We did not try to "force fit" responses into any particular category, thematic bucket, or our own biases of what was "truth." As we "let the data speak to us," certain themes emerged naturally from the responses. We also noted where and when interviewees' responses differed from each other on particular questions.

Subsequently, the two of us met and reviewed our data with each other, taking responses to one question at a time. We noted similarities and differences in the responses to each question between the people each of us interviewed. We then grouped the data from both groups of people on a question-by-question basis if, and only if, grouping people's responses into themes or categories was valid. In other words, if some people's responses to a certain question seemed to fall naturally into a theme or category one of us had come up with when we analyzed the data by ourselves, we noted this. We also noted if their responses did not fit into such groupings. Just as when we looked at "Bill's Data" and "Jennifer's Data" separately, we never tried to "force fit" what anyone had told us into a preconceived box when we looked at all the data from all 25 people. We simply let the data speak for itself.

Organization of the Book

The first three chapters of the book lay the groundwork and set the stage for the remaining chapters. In these initial chapters, we present an overview explaining where the field is now, the key opportunities and challenges HR is facing, and the roles HR adopts to capitalize on the opportunities and meet the challenges.

What you need to know that is driving the HR scene today is covered in Chapter 1.

Chapter 2 offers a complete picture of the many shades of an HR career. It serves as a "Realistic Job Preview" for those of you contemplating a career in HR. It also provides guidelines for those of you already in the field to map out your future and enhance your marketability.

Chapter 3 presents a breakdown of the varied settings in which you can work and describes the many possible roles you can play when working with your clients. It also examines the different hats that internal and external HR consultants wear to be effective.

Chapter 4 contains our HR Career Success Model and flows logically and naturally from the stage-setting first three chapters. It articulates how the three major legs of the stool—gaining knowledge, applying knowledge, and achieving results—work in conjunction to achieve HR career success. You can use the model as a diagnostic tool for you to assess yourself and then focus your development efforts. It can also serve as an excellent roadmap in setting goals and navigating your way around the HR profession.

Each of the next four chapters focuses on one piece of the HR Career Success Model in detail. Each of these chapters contains specific and doable strategies that enable you to put the model into practice in your day-to-day work in HR. Chapters 5, 6, and 7 break down the specific actions you need to take to gain competence and confidence. They provide tools, strategies, and guidelines for gaining self-knowledge, field knowledge, and organizational knowledge.

In Chapter 5, you will learn how to engage in honest self-appraisal. You will find important questions to ask in discovering what you need and want from your work. Approaches to filter and learn from your experience, assess your skills, know your traits and values, deepen your understanding of your personal style, and gauge your emotional intelligence are all addressed here.

In Chapter 6, you are provided with steps and tools to broaden and deepen your knowledge of the dynamic and varied field of Human Resources. This chapter also provides you with guidelines for learning about the trends in HR and how to keep abreast of them. Remaining current on trends is a key component of your becoming and remaining optimally effective in your HR role.

Chapter 7 focuses on how you can gain insight into the formal and informal ways organizations work, including the elements of cultural norms, power, and strategy. This chapter will help you become more "organizationally savvy" and thus increase your impact, exposure, and value on the organizational playing field.

Chapter 8 analyzes and presents numerous real-world case studies to illustrate how applying knowledge can be used to help solve important problems and create meaningful solutions. You will clearly see how actions such as earning trust and credibility, showing value, and selecting appropriate roles can make an impact on HR's customers. The barriers you face when applying your knowledge and how you can handle them effectively will also be presented.

The last chapter, Chapter 9, offers some ideas on where HR is likely to be headed in the future and where and how you can fit into that picture. It provides concrete steps for this journey. We look forward and identify five key HR trends that will impact the future roles HR professionals play. We will also look at ways to incorporate these trends into focused development planning, thereby leveraging these trends so that you can position yourself for success.

Finally, the Appendices will offer you additional tools and resources that will support you in shaping a successful HR career.

In Gratitude

When we look back and consider who has been instrumental in shaping us, we could write another entire book about them. We will attempt to recognize some of these people here. You would not be holding this book if it were not for all of them.

Our parents, Ruth and Louis Kahnweiler and Lucille and Alvin Boretz, gave used the confidence to explore our own unique paths. They have been remarkable role models who, through their actions, taught us the importance of family, laughter, and crafting meaningful lives. Their loving marriages of over 60 years each continue to inspire us.

Our two wonderful daughters, Jessie and Lindsey, have brought us indescribable joy. They have taught us about love, empathy, and patience, and we are so proud of them as they transition into their lives as young adults. Their accomplishments and resume items, while nice, are significantly less important to us than the self-assurance they display and the relationships they continue to build with others in the world. They are living proof that success is ultimately an inside job.

Arline Garson, aunt extraordinaire, has been one of our biggest cheerleaders and brings wisdom and a clear head to every situation.

Our siblings, Carrie, Nancy, and Kathy, their families, and friends from the different stages of our lives have all shaped us in profoundly significant ways. We are grateful for their love, honesty, and support. We owe a debt of gratitude to all our interviewees who gave their time and wisdom so freely and unselfishly. Their insights are laced throughout these pages and are an integral part of this book.

We have also been fortunate to work with hundreds of clients over the years. They have been excellent teachers, whether they intended to be or not. At times, we probably received more from our clients than they received from us. We can think of no greater gift from a client than when they trust us and have faith in the work we offer them. We are especially appreciative of those clients who showed resistance. From them, we learned the most.

To our peers in HR, we offer our sincere appreciation. Like our clients, they have challenged our thinking, asked probing questions, and helped to make this book a reality.

To our bosses, present and past, we thank them for their encouragement, mentoring, and confidence in us. Even those who were "negative role models" helped us to clarify our values when it came to managing, leading, and developing people at work.

We would be remiss if we did not thank the thousands of students and training program participants we have been so fortunate to cross paths with over the years. Like our clients, many of them have been outstanding instructors, stretching and challenging us in the teaching and learning processes. They remind us how life can be unfair at times, for we have learned so much from our students and trainees and we get paid for this learning while students and trainees pay to be in our presence. Something about that seems at least slightly unfair. We sincerely thank them all.

Ailsa Marks and Dennis McGonagle, our editors at Elsevier/Butterworth-Heinemann, have demonstrated the highest levels of professionalism, competence, and confidence throughout the duration of this project. From the beginning, their faith in our ideas, and in us, gave us the fuel to keep going to the finish line. We also wish to thank Jennifer Pursley Jones, Sarah Hajduk, and Chuck Hutchinson at Elsevier for their invaluable assistance.

Last but not least, we wish to thank each other. In many ways, this project has been a living testament to the adage that "valuing diversity is a wonderful concept that is not always easy to execute." We suppose that, like many couples, opposites indeed attract. The two of us are opposites in many ways, and we knew our personality and work style differences going in. Nonetheless, it was not until we actually underwent the writing process that the concept of "valuing diversity" transcended the world of ideas and became real.

In the final analysis we simply allowed each other to be who we are. This book is a product of that acceptance, tolerance, respect, and patience.

Introduction

Making This Book Work for You

Whether you have toiled in HR for three decades or have yet to devote one hour of work to HR, we recommend you read the first four chapters in sequence. By doing so, you will be able to put the subsequent chapters in context and will thus gain more from them. You can read the "gaining knowledge" chapters (5, 6, and 7) in any order, depending on your needs. For example, you may want to read the chapter on gaining self-knowledge (Chapter 5) first if that is the area of knowledge necessary for HR success that you think is in most need of your attention. Similarly, if you believe organizational knowledge represents a clear and important gap in your knowledge base, you may want to read Chapter 7 first before taking on 5 and 6. We suggest you read Chapters 8 and 9 in that order after you have finished with the first seven chapters.

We designed this book to have sufficient shelf life. Although rapid changes in organizations, the HR field, and one's own career goals and priorities are relentless, we nonetheless believe many of the concepts and tools in the book can serve you well for some time. After your first read, we urge you to refer back to parts of the book again and again as your needs and interests evolve over time. We are not so arrogant to claim every part of this book will "absolutely stand the test of time." We are, however, confident that at least parts of the book will stand the test of some amount of time for some of you.

A Few Points on Language

We have avoided using overly complex or highly theoretical language. We have also avoided using overly simplistic (and thus inaccurate) portrayals of the realities HR people face in today's organizations.

Our intent is to help you think and to stretch your thinking. We want you to reflect on your current and future HR roles, perhaps in ways you haven't thought about already. We want you to consider some ideas and strategies you either never thought about or did think about but dismissed outright. We offer perspectives of HR that may be new or different for you. We have tried to use language that invites you to think and explore—both on your own and with colleagues.

Yes, we want you to think. And we do not want you to overanalyze to the point of not taking action and staying stuck in the land of inertia. So we also want you to act. And we do not want you to act impulsively or do something simply for the sake of doing something or to stay busy. We have used language to help you make sound decisions and take useful actions that are based on sufficient dosages of forethought. This book has been written in ways that encourage you to consider various options and their likely consequences and then act on that thinking.

For the sake of readability, we have chosen the term "we" when referencing ourselves. We do this even when describing a personal opinion or thought that one of us holds.

We use the terms "client" and "customer" interchangeably throughout the book. We recognize that organizations use different terms when referring to those who are the recipients of HR services (for example, end user, associate, and managerial partner, to name but a few). We chose to use "client" and "customer" because for us these terms imply much of what HR is about—serving and helping people in valuable ways.

We use the term "business" generically throughout the book. So if you are employed by or consult with a nonprofit or government agency, do not view our use of the word "business" as being irrelevant to you and your situation. On the contrary, it is just another way of saying "organization."

We also use the terms "internal consultant," "internals," "external consultant," and "externals" in many parts of the book. We define the first term as someone who is employed by one organization and part or all of his or her job involves the provision of consulting services to that organization. This person may be employed full- or part-time by that organization. "External consultant" refers to someone who is engaged on a temporary basis (usually for an agreed upon project) by an organization for consulting services. This person is not employed in the technical and legal sense by that organization. He or she may be self-employed or employed by a consulting firm. Keep in mind that the term "client" does not apply solely to the recipient of services provided by external consultants. Internal HR consultants have clients (or customers), too.

We refer to those we interviewed for this book as "interviewees." At times, we refer to these 25 people collectively (for example, "Most of our interviewees told us . . ."), and at other times, we reference specific individuals when we believed their point was compelling enough to highlight.

Some interviewees granted us permission to use their names and their current employer's name in the book. Others granted us permission to reveal their names but not their employer's identity. Still others did not want us to reveal either in the book. Thus, sometimes an individual interviewee's name and current employer will appear in the book, while at other times, we kept these identities anonymous.

Concluding Remarks

We welcome your feedback, comments, and suggestions. You may contact us at www.myhrsuccess.com.

We have planted the seeds in this introduction. It's now time to get to work and reap the harvest.

Are you ready to shape your HR role? Are you seeking ideas and tools to help you be as successful an HR professional as possible in today's organizations? Then let's get started.

Laying the Groundwork
for Success

Have you been in Human Resources for a while and unsure how to get to the next level? Have you neglected your development? Are you considering HR as a career? If so, we wrote this book for all of you.

We wrote this book to help you take charge of your career. We want you to take away ideas, strategies, and insights. This isn't a "how-to" book. It is a thinking book. We believe that careers are much too varied to be boiled down to a few uniform steps. However, we also think having certain bodies of knowledge about you, organizations, and the HR profession are important for you to succeed. Those lessons have been culled from our more than 60+ years of experience and from interviews with successful and seasoned HR professionals.

We want this practical advice, these insights, and these "lessons learned" to serve as a type of mentor. Good mentors allow you to pick their brains. They also permit you to translate their knowledge into what fits your situation. And most importantly, they ask the right questions. Consider this book your personal mentor in a pocket as you stop to focus on your career. Make sense? If so, read on.

Help Wanted: Competent and Confident HR Professionals

It's a new day for HR! The Human Resources profession today is a force to be reckoned with. It is growing in stature and importance as organizations increasingly recognize people as their most important asset. HR has a more predominant place in the decisions and strategies of organizations than ever before. HR professionals also have to fill some very large shoes. For internal HR professionals (those working inside organizations), juggling multiple compliance issues with their roles as business partners has made their days long and their plates extremely full. External, or outside consultants, who make up an increasingly larger proportion of the profession, also face this balancing act with a host of diverse clients.

A recent Society of Human Resource Management (SHRM) conference brochure stated: "Different, unique and often perplexing issues arise each day in the workplace. As a respected business partner, you provide the important link between workforce and stockholder by influencing policy and by using your expertise to create policy and practice elements that affect the overall success of your organization. Why? Because they affect your organization's most important asset—its human resources" (Society of Human Resource Management conference brochure 2003). Individuals of the highest caliber, competence, and motivation are needed to fill these large shoes. We wrote this book so you can become that person.

The Opportunities

What a difference you can make! Whether you are an HR generalist or specialist, are experienced or just starting out in a large or small organization, you sit at the crest of the wave of opportunity—the opportunity to make a significant contribution to your organization, your field, and the people you serve.

You get to engage in problem solving, partake in continuous learning, experience tremendous variety, and change and achieve results. When you help a manager hire a new team that hits the ground running or redesign a rewards program that results in retaining key people, you make a difference and impact organizational performance. As technological changes and more transactional HR functions are outsourced, HR professionals continue to take on more strategic consulting roles. In the book *Execution* (2002), Larry Bossidy, a Fortune 100 CEO, and Ram Charan, a leading management scholar, make the case that linking people processes with strategy and business processes is critical to execution success. In the best organizations, HR walks side by side with its leaders. You will see plenty of examples of this approach in our book.

The Challenges

The HR picture is not all rosy. HR is not just "the soft stuff." It is not a black-and-white function, nor is it paint by number. Because HR involves people and organizations, it exists in the real world of grays, neither of black nor white. Our career suggestions are designed to help you in that world. For instance, what do you do when you are pulled in numerous directions with multiple clients who all see their needs as having the highest priority? How do you manage horrendous workloads and keep your stress level under control? How do you assist people and organizations whose goals are often at odds with one another?

We will also help you answer the question, How do I keep my career thriving in a climate of uncontrollable economic fluctuations? Once considered a safe haven, HR positions have fallen prey to downsizing. The authors have both been downsized at one time or another, and we know what a humbling experience it is. We also believe that the best insurance policy for protecting yourself is to keep your skills fresh and vibrant. If you are let go or experience changes on your job, you will bounce back. This book will help you to be resilient and weather these inevitable cycles.

This book will also help you manage how others perceive you. Even though titles have changed from "personnel" to "HR," HR professionals can be viewed with distrust. In a recent class we taught, a suggestion was made to a participant that he consult with his HR rep on a difficult employee situation. The student shrugged his shoulders and said, "I am not sure what help they will be." It is of great concern to us that HR is viewed in this negative light. The Dilbert cartoon strip has had some success making fun of Human Resources. It's "Catbert: Evil Director of Human Resources" provokes recognition in many of its readers (see Figure 1.1).

We want to help you learn ways to build trust and establish relationships with your clients. We will provide many examples explaining how you can be seen as the "go to" person for a host of challenging and important issues that occur in organizational life today.

Figure 1.1 Your Position Has Been "Excessed." Reprinted with permission.

Making Development a Priority

"The cobbler's children have no shoes." We use this expression to say that HR professionals often spend much of their time on the development of others while unfortunately neglecting their own learning and growth. You need to also turn the spotlight on yourself. Otherwise, your development is surely left to happenstance. What happens as a result? You will get stale and lose your edge.

All professionals, including accountants, engineers, and psychologists, must continually develop their skills and stay at the top of their game. In fact, they are required to do so to maintain their credentials. Aside from the formal credentialing practices that are now in place in HR, we believe it is imperative that you continue to understand the changing workplace and its trends. You avoid obsolescence by doing that. Can you imagine a doctor who is not aware of the latest and most effective treatments for diseases she is treating? She would quickly lose her credibility if she weren't up on the latest medications and approaches to treating disease. You, too, must learn new skills, trends, and approaches. In this way, you keep yourself viable and up to meeting the challenges of your jobs. Every professional we interviewed for this book resoundingly spoke of the need to engage in this continual learning.

Consider this story from a colleague who ran the local division of an HR consulting firm. Each month she scheduled breakfast forums where professionals from similar industries could meet, network, and learn from each other. Another purpose was to discuss changing industry trends.

The group of sales reps she convened were involved in lively, well-attended monthly exchanges. These sales professionals sacrificed potential sales to attend and viewed this networking opportunity as an important investment, ultimately paying off in increased sales.

Not so the HR forum—last-minute cancellations and weak turnouts forced our colleague to end the group. When asked why they didn't show up, most of the HR managers cited pressing concerns back at work. They saw their presence on the job as critical and subject to last-minute crises. By taking a more shortsighted view and by not putting development as a true priority, the HR professionals missed out on a beneficial growth and learning opportunity.

In this book, you will read many examples illustrating how successful HR professionals put a premium on this kind of learning. Bringing outside perspectives into their world is an integral part of the HR professional's success.

Bringing Who You Are to What You Do

As professionals who specialize in both HR and career development, we are well versed in the opportunities and challenges described in the preceding section. For the past 15 years, Bill has been a Professor of Human Resources at Georgia State University. During the prior 17 years, he worked as an internal HR consultant for General Electric and as an External Consultant for Hay Management Consultants. Jennifer has been an HR practitioner for more than 30 years. She has owned her own consulting business specializing in career development for 20 years and has held internal and external consulting roles at several private and public sector organizations including General Electric and the U.S. Department of Homeland Security.

Both of us have passion for a profession that has a richness, variety, and an ability to bring who we are to what we do. In talking about work recently with some friends, we were each asked whether we enjoyed our jobs. We didn't hesitate long and both shared that we love what we do and don't think of it as work. Is this true every minute of every day? No, of course not. But there is no doubt that we have been and continue to be energized by this fascinating profession. We want the same for you—to be stimulated and excited by your work.

This book is presented to you as a labor of love. We hope that in its pages you will sense how much we care about HR as a profession and the people who practice it. We also have a profound desire to assist you in becoming a more effective, competent, and confident professional, whether you have been in HR a while or are contemplating a new career in the field. Ultimately, we want this book to serve as a catalyst for your bringing who you are to what you do for a living.

We have seen it countless times as we interviewed people for this book and with others in the field. "It" is the tremendous energy, commitment, and results that transpire when you bring who you are to your work. We only hope that this book can bring you closer to that reality. We are confident that it can.

How This Book Works

We want you to be able to invigorate your career and find your place in Human Resources. To do this, we have created a practical framework called the *Career Success Model*. This model will help you plot your course. You will understand (1) what steps you can take to move your career forward and (2) how you can achieve results for the clients you serve—now and in the future. And although we said in the Preface that this is not a prescriptive cookbook, you will find many helpful tools. Numerous examples are provided to illustrate the major components of the model. We drew these examples from our career experiences and those of thousands of individuals with whom we have worked. In addition, we have summarized the highlights of more than 25 interviews that we conducted with successful HR professionals from across the globe.

You will also find professional resources such as websites and professional organizations.

We wrote this book to help you take charge of your own career. We will provide you with a practical framework to better understand what steps you can take to find your place and grow your career with satisfaction and confidence against the dynamic backdrop of today's organizations.

So what will you take away specifically from reading this book? You will learn (1) what an HR career looks like today—both the opportunities and the challenges, (2) the varied settings in which you can work, (3) the key roles you can play, (4) how to take targeted actions to make sound decisions in your HR career, and (5) the resources available to help propel your career forward and make you more resilient in this changing world economy.

As you can see, this book can serve as your new portable mentor. As such, we hope you find value and validation in its pages. Congratulate yourself for putting the focus on you. In so doing, you are serving your clients and your organization in the best way possible. You are achieving the kinds of results that shape a successful HR career.

References

Society of Human Resource Management Conference Brochure, Orlando, Florida, June 22–25, 2003, 3.
Bossidy, L. and R. Charan. 2002. *Execution*. New York: Crown Business.

What Does an HR Career Look Like Today? Opportunities, Appeals, and Challenges

Now is a very interesting and exciting time to be an HR professional. Never before have we witnessed the rate and scope of changes in organizations and in the HR profession itself. Few HR professionals we know say they are bored, plateaued, or unchallenged.

Not very long ago, many organizations placed sub-par employees into HR (and back then this department was usually referred to as "Personnel"). For example, one of our friends, who was a senior executive at AT&T and is now retired, told us that there used to be two basic career paths for people in the company: (1) perform adequately (and not necessarily superbly) for a period of time, and then get promoted to a management position, perform that job adequately, and remain in management until retirement; or (2) perform adequately, get promoted into management, perform as a manager less than adequately, and then be transferred to HR. For many organizations, especially large ones, this situation seemed to be the norm. In essence, many, if not most, who toiled in HR (or "Personnel") in those days were there by default. HR was not seen as a career; it was a dumping ground.

Fortunately, this situation has changed drastically. The professionalization of HR is real and continues to evolve. People are choosing HR as their craft or moving into it after doing other kinds of work. New opportunities exist for HR external consultants like never before. HR is no longer where organizations place people who have no clearly viable role. Thankfully, being in HR no longer means a professional's career is in trouble. Quite the contrary!

Being a member of a bona fide profession is one appeal of a career in HR. Those who succeed in HR find many aspects of the field quite attractive, exciting, and meaningful. This chapter will describe the many and varied appeals of being an HR professional in today's ever-changing and dynamic organizations.

Part of the excitement of being in HR today is the myriad challenges that are part of the HR landscape. This explains why we never hear HR professionals complain that minutes seem like hours or hours seem like days. Rarely, if ever, do we hear HR professionals complain that they don't have enough to do or what they do is busywork or meaningless. Many, if not most, of the challenges confronted by HR people require much energy, skill, creativity, and resilience. This chapter will provide an overview of these challenges. Knowing them will enable you to decide whether HR is a good career move for you, or if you are already in the field, being aware of the challenges should help you formulate some viable career plans within the profession.

Let's look at the opportunities, appeals, and challenges that come with the HR territory. There are many to consider.

The Opportunities: A Multitude of Options in Crafting an HR Career

As you shall soon see, having options in your career is generally a very good thing. Why? Well, for one, market conditions change. What's "hot" today can be downright "freezing" tomorrow. For another, people (and that includes you) change. Your interests, values, priorities, and what you seek from work often change over any period of time. Therefore, a career that provides options can accommodate your changing needs, preferences, and circumstances as you go through life. In addition, the needs and wants of organizations change. These days, such changes are the norm.

Thus, if you are in a career that offers a multitude of choices about what you do, where you do it, and how you do it, you will be well positioned to remain in and thrive in that career, no matter what personal, organizational, and environmental changes come down the pike. HR offers such choices and flexibility.

Sometimes people see choices as black/white, yes/no, go/no go, either/or issues. Nothing could be further from the truth when it comes to HR careers today. If anything, you can become overwhelmed with the nature and scope of choices to shape an HR career. But even if you are the kind of person who tends to feel besieged when many options are at your disposal, isn't it better to have too many than not enough choices? And no choice is final. In fact, HR is one of those occupations that allows practitioners to make career choices that open up additional future options. That is, you are not relegated to stay on rigid, inflexible career paths. Let's look more specifically at three major dimensions of HR and the plethora of options within each one that are at an HR professional's disposal throughout his or her career.

1. **Do I become a specialist or a generalist?** Many HR professionals, particularly at mid-career, ask themselves if they should become a generalist or a specialist. For example, suppose you have some solid experience in EEO practices, management development, and incentive compensation. Should you deepen your knowledge and experience in one of these areas, thereby enabling you to be the organization's authoritative resource in that one specialty? Alternatively, should you try and gain knowledge and experience in some HR areas in which you have had little, if any, exposure (in this example, it could be HRIS, benefits, staffing, OD, or other HR subfields)? To specialize or generalize? Many HR professionals wrestle with this question at some point in their careers, and sometimes at many points.

   Ghosh (2003) argues that HR cannot afford to be both a specialist and generalist profession and that the HR function should organize around projects rather than by subfunctions within an HR department. Although we believe this idea has some merit, it still doesn't address what individuals should do in planning their career moves.

   The results of our interviews with more than 25 highly successful HR practitioners do not offer definitive, cookbook answers to the issue. When asked to look back and state what the biggest mistake has been in their career to date, several told us that they wished they had specialized earlier in their career. They believed if they had done so, they would have become more marketable. Maybe so. On the other hand, others told us they wished they had been more focused on being a broad generalist earlier on in their careers to enable them to make better, more informed decisions concerning the next steps in their career progression. It seems to us that both arguments have merit. The bad news is there is no clear, irrefutable answer to the generalist-specialist question. The good news, and we believe it is very good news, is that making this decision probably doesn't matter as much as you might think. That is, you can always decide to specialize in one or more HR areas; conversely, there is rarely if ever a wrong time to get off the specialist track and acquire experience in HR areas that are new to you. Our interviewees are living proof that success can and does happen for generalists and specialists equally. Some of them started off as specialists and have remained so. Others have zigzagged back and forth between specialties and more general HR jobs.

We think it's helpful to view the issue not as an either-or but rather as a continuum. So rather than view the issue this way

→ Specialize <u>OR</u> Generalize

consider viewing it this way

→ Specialize_____Generalize

The preceding diagram conveys that there are different degrees or gradations of specialization as there are generalization. For example, HR professionals could concentrate on 2 or 3 subfields of HR or devote all their time to one of them. Likewise, they could be in a job that requires some knowledge and experience in 6 or 7 HR areas, whereas another job could call for a similar level of knowledge and experience in 10 HR areas. Even at the most senior levels, incumbents rarely possess specialized knowledge and skills in more than a handful of HR areas. Otherwise, the minimum age to qualify for such jobs would be 80!

So, rather than look at the specialist-generalist issue as a dilemma, and an either/or one at that, view it as representing abundant opportunities in shaping and reshaping an HR career over your entire working life. Your success is not 100 percent contingent on making "the right specialize or generalize decision" (as if there was one right decision to make in the first place). And it may not ever be contingent on this issue at all. Remember that no choice is final and irreversible. Even if in hindsight you determine you made a poor decision in the past, that decision does not necessarily mean it was a career-ending mistake.

2. **Which function (or functions) do I work in?** The functions of HR are as diverse as the people who perform them. While all HR functions are, by definition, connected in one way or the other to "the people side" of the organization, the kind of work each entails is very different. Thus, the skills, preferences, personalities, values, and interests of the people performing these various HR functions tend to be very different.

Think for a moment about being a compensation analyst for the organization. In this role, the incumbent is expected, among other things, to conduct salary surveys and interpret the results, perform detailed analyses of job requirements, and recommend salary structures to management. Across the hall is an employee relations representative whose major job is to listen to employee and management concerns and try to help resolve various disputes that arise among people in the workplace. Down the hall from them is a benefits coordinator whose job it is to process health claims, assist individuals to decide which insurance plans to enroll in, and create newsletter briefings that inform employees on upcoming changes in the plans. Across from them sits an organizational effectiveness consultant who works with managers and executives in formulating and implementing organization-wide change efforts. And across the hall from them is an instructional designer who creates web-based training programs for the organization's salesforce.

While these job descriptions are admittedly cursory, imagine what each person would be doing at a given point in time. You would likely see each person performing very different tasks in very different ways. And the above is just the tip of the HR iceberg! There are many other functions and types of jobs within the profession. And don't forget that all these people have managers, directors, and vice presidents in their chain of command as well.

Our point is that there are a multitude of HR functions and a great variety of jobs within each of those functions that can and do have great appeal for virtually anyone throughout his or her career. Some functions and jobs emphasize specialized knowledge and skill; others draw on more generalized competencies, including those HR professionals in small businesses who usually must be generalists partnering with outside vendors. Some functions and jobs appeal to introverts, whereas others are an extrovert's dream. Do you have a knack for analytical thinking? There are plenty of HR jobs for you. Do you prefer to rely on your interpersonal skills rather than analytical ones? No problem. Do you seek variety in your day-to-day tasks? HR has abundant opportunities to satisfy such a need. Likewise, if you prefer work that is more structured and less variable, HR can fill that bill, too. And remember that jobs within a particular HR function—be it staffing, employee relations, HRIS, or OD—vary a great deal. Add to this the multiple degrees of specialization (or lack thereof) among jobs we referenced earlier. Can you now imagine the range of options you have as an HR professional? It is huge!

3. **What kind of organization should I work in?** A benefit we have reaped in our own careers has been our 60+ years of experience in a wide variety of organizations, as employees and external consultants. We have also studied many organizations over this period of time. We have found that the kinds of organizations within which HR is practiced are almost infinite. In fact, the amount of variety in HR jobs pales by comparison to the number of orga-

nizational variations available to us. As you know, organizations come in all sizes ranging from a 2-person business born in a garage to global corporations employing hundreds of thousands of people. We know HR professionals who toil in 15-person social service agencies and multibillion dollar corporate behemoths and everything in between. Although all organizations share some common characteristics, suffice it to say that size affects the climate and culture of workplaces and the way work is performed in them.

HR occurs on a daily basis in the three major sectors of workplaces: for-profit, government, and nonprofit. Generally speaking, each has its own way of doing things, including the way HR is conducted.

Organizations differ in many other ways. Take, for example, the life stage factor. Organizations in a start-up mode tend to have very different needs, priorities, and strategies than ones that are mature. Those that are experiencing exponential growth are different from those that are facing market share decline, downsizing, or hanging on to survive. HR work in these organizations tends to be very different, even when job descriptions covering the HR work sound very similar.

Like nations, organizations have cultures—those norms, values, and ways of going about things that make them unique. Some organizational cultures are parental, whereas others emphasize individual responsibility. Still others emphasize teamwork, whereas in others the hierarchy drives most, if not all, behavior. Similarly, leaders of organizations typically have profound effects on cultures. Sometimes those leaders define the organization's culture. Leaders, and the leadership styles they employ, come in all varieties as well.

How HR is practiced across industries varies a great deal as well. For example, an employee relations job in a unionized manufacturing environment bears little resemblance to an employee relations job in a high-tech start-up or a 300-bed hospital.

The bottom line is organizations come in all sizes, shapes, flavors, tastes, and textures. They are like the multitude of colors and hues on an artist's palette. And although HR jobs across organizations share some common elements, they tend to be more different than similar when comparing them on an organization-to-organization basis. Add to this diversity the fact that most organizations these days are changing significantly, have just emerged from a major change, or are anticipating undergoing one, and you have the recipe for a very profound range of options to shape an HR career.

Taking all these factors into consideration, we are confident in stating unequivocally that you can find "a comfortable fit" in HR. If you are entering the field or have been in it for decades, have worked in one sector or all three, or if you have been a deep and narrow specialist or a broad generalist, we believe this is true. If you are interested in HR, abundant opportunities are available for you to find HR work that fits you and is conducted in the kind of organization that fits you (WetFeet 2003). And if anything, we foresee the future as presenting even more and not fewer options for you, as an HR professional, to conduct meaningful and impactful work throughout your life.

The Many and Varied Appeals of an HR Career

What draws people to HR? If you are already in the field, what drew you to it in the first place? What may draw you if you are contemplating going into it? What has drawn people who have shaped very successful careers in HR?

The reasons people gravitate to HR are as varied as the people themselves. Here are six of the major reasons we have uncovered:

1. **Helping people.** Many people are motivated to be helpful to others. As an old saying goes, one of the best ways to help oneself is to help others. Assisting people and organizations is a cornerstone of the HR profession; thus, HR professionals can find abundant opportunities to satisfy their desire to be helpful. When asked why they went into HR in the first place, many of our interviewees mentioned a desire to help others. And some remain motivated in this way. Jonathan Dawe, Director of Safety, Training, and Development for Simmons Company, asks himself at the end of each work day how helpful he has been with every person he has seen that day. He then asks himself how he can be more helpful tomorrow. When tomorrow comes, he goes through the same process again. Gary May, formerly a line executive and a Chief Learning Officer at a major corporation and now a professor of business at Clayton College and State University, believes that a key competency that HR professionals need today to succeed is a desire to help people. Many others told us that their most gratifying moments in HR occur when they can see their efforts are helpful to other people. We hope you can understand clearly the basis of our claim that helping people is a cornerstone of the HR profession.

2. **Experiencing continued growth.** The HR profession is expected to grow in size and stature. According to WetFeet (2003), the number of HR jobs is expected to increase 12.7 percent between 2000 and 2010 compared to the previous decade. Even more encouraging is recent data from The Bureau of

Labor Statistics (2004) that predict employment for HR professionals is expected to grow faster than the average for all occupations through 2012— at a rate of 21 to 35 percent! There are and will continue to be many ways HR professionals can develop, both personally and professionally. So while the profession itself is growing, the people in it are able to seize many opportunities throughout their careers to expand their professional and personal capabilities.

3. **Enjoying endless variety.** Not only is HR a very diverse field, as we described in the previous section, but HR jobs in and of themselves are characterized by a high level of variety. For most if not all HR jobs, no two days are the same. HR professionals work on diverse job tasks and projects as well as with a diverse array of people on a daily basis. For those who seek variety in their work, HR can and does certainly fill the bill. Our interviewees told us over and over that "each day is never the same in HR" and that this attracted them to the field initially and keeps them motivated to remain in it.

4. **Being oneself.** HR, perhaps more than many professions, allows individuals to honor and express their values in their work (and get paid for doing so!). As such, HR affords you abundant occasions to bring who you are to what you do and to shape a successful career in the process. Indeed, several of our interviewees told us that one of the main reasons they went into the field and have stayed in it is that they can be themselves at work. They value authenticity in themselves and others, and HR is a viable avenue in which to enact this value. Art Blake, a retired internal Organization Effectiveness Consultant with a large utility, told us that being honest with himself and with clients was necessary for him to succeed in his career. Art said that HR was the only kind of job he had ever had that fostered and at times demanded his being true to himself and his clients.

5. **Being influential.** As HR's status and importance as a profession grow, there are increasing opportunities for the HR professional to influence how the organization operates. HR can and does have an impact on all major functions and operations of an organization—or at least it should! So, for those who are motivated by "making a difference," you can satisfy such needs in an ongoing way when performing HR work. Whether it is assisting shop floor employees to perform their job more effectively via training or job aids, exploring career options with a financial analyst, or advising a senior executive on the long-range human resource strategy the organization needs to formulate, HR professionals make a difference—to organizations and to the people employed by them. John Courtney, Manager of Learning

Technologies Manager for InterContinental Hotels Group, told us his primary motivation for leaving the field of education and going into HR was not, as some might assume, the greater earnings he could accrue in HR compared to teaching but rather the greater opportunities HR afforded him to make a difference. John sought to have more impact on more people than he felt he was having as a teacher, and HR seemed as though it would be a good fit for him when he was contemplating what to do if he stopped teaching.

6. **Having flexible career paths.** As alluded to earlier, you are not locked into a specialist *or* generalist career path in HR. In the vast majority of organizations we know and have worked in, HR career paths avoid a rigid, "our way or the highway" structure. Thus, HR provides a flexible and responsive career path that accommodates people's changing values, priorities, interests, and career goals throughout the course of their careers. In addition, many HR professionals decide to take "time out" from their HR work for one reason or another and perform other functions (for example, becoming a line manager) for a period of time and then return to HR. Thus, you can find options within HR career paths as well as flexibility in getting off and on the HR career path throughout your career. Meredith Hodges is currently an operations manager at Georgia Power, a large utility based in the southeastern United States. Up until this time, she had occupied various HR jobs for about 10 years. She thought her credibility and effectiveness as an HR professional would be enhanced if she took a line management job for a while and then moved back into HR. Her manager in HR and the head of operations were both willing to have Meredith engage in this developmental assignment for a specific time period, so Meredith left HR temporarily. Although she has not yet returned to HR, Meredith, her current manager in operations, and her manager in HR all are confident she will bring even more value to the organization after her stint as a line manager is over than she did when she was in HR (and she was seen as a consistently outstanding performer the entire time she was in HR, too). Another interviewee went about this process a little bit differently than Meredith but achieved similarly distinguished results for her HR career. She started out in operations and spent about 5 years in it despite knowing in her heart that HR was the place she wanted to be. She believed such a foundation in the line organization would serve her well when she transitioned into HR. And her prediction came true. And then some. After 10 years in progressively responsible HR positions, she now is responsible for the training and development of all employees and managers in one of the world's largest and

most well-respected hospitality companies and leads a staff of about 100 HR professionals.

Be sure to note what has *not* been listed as an appeal of an HR career. That is, what don't you get from choosing HR as a career that's considered by many to be appealing? Three things come to mind: (1) fortune, (2) power, and (3) fame or celebrity status:

- **Fortune.** Although you can certainly receive very lucrative compensation packages as an HR professional, more likely than not, money in and of itself is not the primary or sole motivator in this field.
- **Power.** Likewise, those who yearn to acquire power and authority and to continually expand their power base are typically not attracted to HR as a career pursuit. Yes, HR professionals can and do influence, often with those in power and who have the authority to exercise that power. However, we know very few souls who seek power for its own sake and find HR an appealing career. Conversely, we know very few souls who find HR a very appealing way to make a living who also seek to acquire and increase their power and authority in organizations.
- **Fame.** If you are the kind of person who seeks fame (as well as fortune), HR is probably not a good fit for you, either. There may be a select few, but most of us in HR have not achieved celebrity status nor do we seek this in the future. The love we have for the work, along with the aforementioned appeals, amply rewards us.

What did our interviewees tell us when we asked each of them why they've stayed in the field? The vast majority of responses spoke of the benefits we presented above, particularly with regard to simply loving the work. Several people stated that HR is their calling and passion. Others noted the many opportunities for continuous growth, skill acquisition and development, and learning that HR affords them. Still others said, as we noted earlier, that one of the main reasons they have remained in the field is its endless variety and the way it fits so well with who they are as individuals. No one said HR is ever boring; on the contrary, many told us how stimulating HR is, how it stretches them because it always presents them with tough challenges that draw on their problem-solving skills. Three HR senior executives told us that the money has been a key factor in their retention. But note they said "a key factor" and not "the key factor." Note also that money was not a factor in their decision to enter the profession, either.

You might be thinking at this point, "If HR is such a great profession, why isn't everyone on earth clamoring to get into the field?" Well, for one reason, despite its many and varied appeals, HR, like every other profession, is not for everyone. Second, like life itself, being an HR professional has some potential downsides. We prefer to call them "challenges," however, rather than downsides or problems. The next section will address the major challenges that come with the HR territory.

The Challenges of an HR Career

Let's say one or more of the appeals we listed in the preceding section are indeed appealing to you right now. And amassing vast wealth, obtaining much power, and achieving celebrity status aren't in your game plan. What else about HR should you consider?

An HR career, like life, is not solely a bed of roses. There are many obstacles to face. They are not insurmountable problems but rather are challenges that can help bring out the best in you. Here are the major ones HR professionals are confronted with on a regular basis:

1. **Power (or relative lack thereof).** As an internal or external HR professional, many of your clients/customers will occupy positions that are higher in the organizational hierarchy than yours. Thus, there is usually a differential in position power between you, the HR professional, and the people you serve. This differential can sometimes create challenges in influencing clients/customers to do what you want them to do, listen to your ideas, or even get on their calendar. Paradoxically, in some organizations HR is given too much power. This situation can result in HR professionals taking power trips (as well as assuming total responsibility for tasks that should reside with managers, such as hiring decisions), being seen as obstacles by managers, or simply having too much work to do. It is helpful to keep in mind that power is relative, not absolute (and we say this absolutely!). WetFeet (2003) advises HR professionals to gauge how important the HR function is in an organization relative to other functions when job hunting. We agree. If the HR function is relegated to performing "administriva," paper pushing, and other mundane tasks, more likely than not this is a sign that HR is not highly valued in that organization. On the other hand, if "the HR point of view" is represented at senior-level meetings and decision processes, managers in general utilize HR for important issues, and the expertise and services of

HR professionals are used on a regular basis, it's likely that HR as a function is fairly important in that organization. So what can you do if you are looking for a new job in another part of your current organization or in a different organization to gauge HR's status in the organization? Or if you are an external HR consultant, what can you do to assess this? Ask questions when interviewing and even at the "exploring options" stage. Ask the kinds of questions behavioral interviewers ask to elicit specific, concrete examples of how HR is viewed in the organization and to what degree it is or isn't valued. If you find promising opportunities where all evidence points to HR being highly valued or you are fortunate to be in that situation already, just remember that there is almost always a position power differential between HR professionals and the positions of those they serve. This situation requires that you employ different forms of power (which we will discuss in a subsequent chapter) other than purely position power.

2. **The Tightrope Act.** Most, if not all, HR work is a constant act of balancing the employee advocate role while serving management. In other words, you attempt to assist the individual and the organization. There is an automatic tension between individual employee and management agendas, even when the employee relations climate is open, honest, and trustworthy. A classic example can be found in most compensation systems. In general, employees want a compensation system that is fair (as they define that term), equitable (as they define that term), and highly competitive (if not generous); and management, in general, wants a compensation system that is easy to administer and explain and is cost effective (as they define that term). In general, individuals want to maximize their compensation; HR professionals representing management (or the organization) want to help minimize costs, especially fixed costs, such as compensation. HR professionals are thus often smack dab in the middle of this tension. To complicate matters, it is management, not individual employees, who pay HR professionals for their work. Thus, HR professionals are often faced with dual allegiances, and, at minimum, this situation can become very confusing. Clearly knowing "the right thing to do" when walking on a tightrope is rarely easy and simple. And you can certainly fall off it from time to time.

3. **Skeptical clients/customers.** Some people, especially managers, are inclined to distrust staff or support functions such as HR. If there is not outright distrust, there can be a devaluing of those functions that are seen as disconnected from "bottom-line contributions." This skepticism of staff or support functions extends to the people who perform them. Getting

buy-in from such people is certainly a challenge. Several of our interviewees told us this, too. When asked what their biggest challenge was throughout their HR career, they said things such as "lack of influence or respect" and "having to prove my competence, credibility, and the value of what I offer." We have worked with and observed many HR professionals who, at one time or another, personify the comedian Rodney Dangerfield's tag line, "I don't get no respect."

4. **Poor image.** HR's reputation, however inaccurate it may be, can be a curse if it is viewed as a superfluous, bureaucratic, paper-pushing (i.e., useless) function. A less-than-stellar reputation of HR in an organization, be it deserved or not, can be tough to overcome in some instances. A survey of 425 senior- and mid level HR managers conducted by Katcher (2003) found that 48 percent of them thought senior management respected them and their contribution to the organization. Forty-one percent believed HR plays an important role in the development of the organization's strategy. Is the glass half full, half empty, or something else? Although the results of one survey cannot be interpreted to represent all HR professionals' beliefs about what senior management thinks of them and their role in formulating organizational strategy, there certainly seems ample room for improvement. We think it is fair to say that at least in some organizations and with some managers and employees in some organizations, the image of HR professionals is tainted simply because they are in HR. These sorts of perceptions are, by definition, over-generalizations and often are simply stereotypes. Nonetheless, they are real in the eyes of the perceiver.

5. **Vulnerability.** These days, few, if any, jobs and organizational functions are immune to the prevalent practices of downsizing, outsourcing, acquisitions, and restructuring. The term "job security" is an oxymoron now, and it appears unlikely this will change in the foreseeable future. At the same time, HR jobs and the professionals who occupy them are particularly vulnerable victims of job loss. By definition, a staff/support function is relatively less valued than line functions; thus, HR is more vulnerable when resources are scarce. This vulnerability can take many forms—for example, downsizing of HR staff, HR initiatives receiving inadequate or no funding, and outsourcing of some HR functions. Even when resources aren't scarce and HR is valued by the organization, you often have to sell your services to get the chance to perform them. HR services often entail intangibles and are thus hard to measure. This can make selling them to decision makers (the owners of the checkbook) a profound challenge.

6. **A sense of becoming overwhelmed.** HR professionals can take on too much work, responsibility, or both. This can easily happen, especially if you are the kind of person who loves being helpful to people and being needed. People in HR can seem particularly prone to burnout. In other instances, the HR function (and thus the HR professionals who comprise it) can unknowingly be held accountable for tasks that others (most notably managers) don't want to bother with, such as administering reward programs. HR can also unknowingly be held responsible for outcomes that are outside its control (and perhaps even its sphere of influence). A prime example of this is turnover. Is this an HR issue? What about management's part in the ownership of the turnover issue? If management does not take some responsibility for turnover (claiming, for example, unwanted turnover is HR's job to deal with and solve), HR can, consciously or not, agree to take total ownership of "the turnover problem we have." Add to this mix the fact that many clients of HR are becoming more demanding (Ghosh 2003), expecting more and better service at less cost and delivered more quickly. In the aforementioned survey of benefits managers (Katcher 2003), 83 percent said their work is often emotionally draining. Several of our interviewees stated that their biggest challenges as an HR professional are managing time, constantly prioritizing and reprioritizing tasks, and dealing with people's problems and emotions all the time. When asked what their biggest mistake had been, several of our interviewees commented that the urgent tends to drive out the important; that is, they were consumed with fighting fires and lost sight of the big picture, only to discover this when the fires died down. And then new fires erupted that consumed their attention.

   All of these dynamics, singly and collectively, can lead to a feeling of being overwhelmed at minimum and burnout at worst. Certainly, nothing is wrong with being needed nor in being busy. Even very busy. Stress can lead to productivity and satisfaction if it is manageable and then managed. However, sometimes HR professionals can become overstressed to the point where they feel helpless and hopeless.

7. **Elusive impact.** By definition, HR deals with a variety of "people issues." Human beings are complex creatures. Thus, accurately measuring the impact of HR initiatives, programs, and other efforts is challenging at best. Some great work is being done in this area. However, compared to functions such as sales, production, operations, or even finance, the impact of HR, at the individual, group, and certainly at the organizational level, is tough to quantify accurately and validly. This can add to HR's already

vulnerable status as described in item 5 above, especially when managers in the organization "go by the numbers" to make decisions about allocating scarce resources. The challenge of measuring the impact of HR professionals can also feed the negative stereotypes and generalizations depicted in item 4 above. We have heard all too often comments like, "You HR people are just touchy-feely types who don't know squat about this organization and how it works."

John Courtney, the Learning Technologies Manager at InterContinental Hotels Group we referenced earlier, has found that he really cannot assess the ROI of his efforts at the organizational level because, for one, it is impossible to isolate his work from other factors that contribute to the same organizational-level outcomes. For example, he says that if he claims his sales training programs increase sales revenue, he is ignoring other factors that contribute to increased sales revenue, such as new product features, a customer's increased budget, or just plain luck. John stays very current on HR evaluation trends and says he has yet to see a case in which the effects of HR can be isolated from everything else and thus is skeptical about being able to make a case that HR has results that can be precise, valid, and quantifiable. You may not be as cautious or skeptical as John is about measurement of HR impact. Just consider how difficult it is to measure what you do and how well you do it, especially if you are trying to measure organization-wide effects. And as John told us, even if you think you can make this case, you better believe the marketing, finance, sales, operations, and other function heads are beating a path to the CEO's door (and checkbook) just as people in HR are doing. By the way, in case you are curious, John says he uses a "perceived value" measure with his customers that does not attempt to quantify the results he produces nor isolate them from other factors, and he claims it has worked very well. From what we can see, it certainly has helped him achieve ongoing success in the HR craft.

8. **Delayed gratification.** Related to item 7, when it is hard to accurately assess the impact of what you do, you often don't know whether you have made an impact at all or when the signs of an impact emerge. "People Professions" like HR must often take a leap of faith when it comes to determining if and how it has been helpful. In many instances, the effects of what HR people do can lie dormant for months if not longer. Delivering training is a common example of these realities. For sure, you can measure how satisfied participants of a training program were at the end of the program. But does that really tell you much that is important in terms of

the impact of the program on outcomes important to the organization? Furthermore, training program participants often do not even realize the impact the program had on them and their work unit until long after the program was delivered. Most HR professionals are gratified to learn that what they did made a difference on some level. Many of our interviewees told us that "making a difference" was a key factor in their entering the profession and staying in HR—whether that difference was helping individual employees perform their jobs better, helping a manager lead more effectively, or helping an entire organization run more efficiently. The challenge is that you often do not learn this for some time after you have done the work, if at all.

Concluding Remarks

Several years ago, Dave Ulrich, a noted researcher, consultant, and writer about the HR profession and HR trends, claimed that there was never a better time to be in HR (see MacLachlan 1998). We agreed with him then and agree with him now. If we were writing this book in the 1980s, we could not and would not say this. Why? Because the appeals and opportunities of a career in HR were not as abundant and pronounced as they are now. Working in HR is very exciting, fulfilling, and meaningful, and it appears highly likely it is only going to get even more so in the future.

At the same time, as we have noted here, there are many challenges ahead. Indeed, as Wiscombe (2001) declared, HR is not all about feel-good work with people and having fun. It is not, never has been, nor will it ever be all about giving out warm fuzzies and making other people happy. In fact, at times people may despise you.

For sure, there are easier, less challenging ways to make sure you have a roof over your head and a full stomach. But many people are thrilled to be in HR and find it an excellent vehicle to shape their careers. So can you. If the many appeals of HR don't appeal to you, then you probably should explore other career options. Likewise, if the challenges we have described sound like insurmountable problems to you, look for other ways to make a living and a life. If the real opportunities in HR sound like obstacles to you, by all means consider other profession paths that do have opportunities you value. And if you are already in HR, but going to work is a daily struggle, perhaps it is time to reassess what you want and how to get it and whether continuing in HR is the best strategy to achieve your goals and satisfy your desires.

But if you thrive on solving problems, love tackling tough issues, want variety in your work, get a kick out of helping others, and seek a flexible career path that offers many diverse options, HR is likely a good fit for you. Indeed, this is a great time to be in HR as the profession continues to grow and mature. As you, organizations, and the world change, your HR career can be shaped to capitalize on whatever those changes bring to your life.

References

Bureau of Labor Statistics. U.S. Department of Labor. 2004. *Occupational Outlook Handbook, 2004–2005 Edition,* Human Resources. Washington, D.C. Also available at http://bls.gov/oco/ocos021.htm (accessed June 9, 2004).

Ghosh, G. 2003. *HR's Evolving Role.* www.HR.com (accessed August 11, 2003).

Katcher, BL. 2003. *HR Pro's Express Job Dissatisfaction.* www.careerjournal.com (accessed June 11, 2003).

MacLachlan, R. 1998. "HR with Attitude." *People Management* 4, no. 16 (1998): 36–39.

WetFeet. 2003. *The WetFeet Insider Guide to Careers in Human Resources.* San Francisco, CA: WetFeet, Inc., 15, 22.

Wiscombe, J. 2001. "Your Wonderful/Terrible HR Life." *Workforce* 80, no. 6: 32–37.

3

The Many Hats HR Professionals Wear

Think about a movie or play you saw recently. How would you describe, in three or fewer words, the role that the main character played? Heroine? Villain? The hero's lieutenant? Tragic victim? Bumbling fool? Crafty detective? The town's misanthrope?

Think about some people in your high school graduating class. Who was the "well-rounded person"? The "class clown"? The person who was "always in trouble with authority"? The "biggest flirt"? The "big time jock"? The "eccentric artist"? The "defiant protester"? The "comedian"?

Shakespeare suggested the world is a stage and we are merely actors on it. And like the characters in a well-acted play or film, each of us has a role to play in the world. And more than likely, we enact multiple roles on the world's stage throughout each day—worker, manager, parent, child, friend, citizen, and HR professional among them.

As you saw in Chapter 2, one of the appeals of an HR career is that it offers great variety in the work itself, the range of customers/clients, and the kinds of organizations in which HR services are needed. This chapter offers an overview of another aspect of HR that offers a good deal of variety: the different kinds of roles HR professionals can and do play.

Several writers have provided frameworks and descriptions of HR's roles. For example, Ulrich (2001) says that HR needs to assume five key roles to be effective: (1) coach, (2) architect, (3) designer, (4) facilitator, and (5) leader. Wiscombe (2001) claims that, as an HR professional, you take on varied roles such as party planner, social worker, change agent, and many more. The work of Peter Block (2003) describes three basic roles of consultants whose work focuses on staff/support functions (including HR): (1) pair-of-hands, (2) expert, and (3) collaborator. Heathfield (2003) states that HR is in a process of significant transformation as it embraces the roles of strategic partner, employee advocate, and change mentor. A retired line executive from AT&T believes that HR professionals have two choices when it comes to the roles they play: implementers or initiators.

We do not take issue with any of the preceding conceptualizations. However, we think they are somewhat limited. Why? Because they do not adequately capture the depth and breadth of this dynamic and growing field.

Knowing the various roles HR professionals have at their disposal will enable you to be of maximum service to your clients. Those clients have diverse needs and challenges that require you to employ diverse roles in order to help them.

In this chapter, we will present an HR role framework that builds upon the preceding ideas and extends them to reflect the realties of HR practice today and the way it will likely play out tomorrow. This framework contains nine different roles that HR professionals assume at virtually any point in their careers (and at any given time during any one day at work!). We will describe all nine roles, provide examples illustrating how each one works in practice, and highlight the key skills needed to enact them. We will also provide some guidelines for choosing which roles to play when.

Following our role framework, we will discuss HR's role as a consultant. Because the consulting role has many facets and variations, we decided it deserves to be treated in a separate section. Thus, you can consider HR taking on nine roles plus a consultative one.

We want to emphasize that one key role HR professionals play is the foundation for all the roles HR assumes—and that is the role of being helpful. So when you learn about the roles HR professionals assume in this chapter, also think about this overarching role of being helpful to clients/customers. That is, indeed, the ultimate purpose of HR, isn't it?

Role Framework

One way to visualize the variety of HR roles is through a two-factor matrix—one factor being the degree of emphasis a role has on building and maintaining relations with people and the other concerning the relative emphasis a role has on achieving results. A similar, though not equivalent, way of conceptualizing role options was first introduced by Champion, Kiel, and McLendon in 1990 and directed to Organizational Development (OD) consultants. It contained nine roles incorporating two factors: client needs for growth and client needs for results.

The framework we are proposing likewise has two factors: the HR professionals' emphasis on relationships and their emphasis on results. Our framework can be illustrated as shown in Figure 3.1.

Let's first look at what we mean by "relationships" and "results" and how these terms are to be used (and not used) in the framework.

"Relationships" have to do with support, encouragement, empathy, and other so-called "soft stuff." We say "so-called" because often the process of building and maintaining effective relationships with people is anything but soft—it is hard! Furthermore, because HR is, by definition, a people-oriented craft, the quality of relationships HR professionals have with others is a key component of their success.

By "results," we mean the achievement of some outcome, either through your own efforts, through others' efforts, or in some combination. As Ulrich (2001) argues, HR has for too long overemphasized the activities it performs and has underemphasized the results it produces.

The arrows in the role framework denote that both relationships and results exist in varying degrees in each HR role. Thus, when performing as a collaborator, the HR professional provides relatively high levels of relationship skills and results-driven behaviors. At the opposite end of the spectrum, a relatively low level of emphasis is placed on both results and relationships when performing in a process-consulting capacity. When the emphasis is on producing results and there is relatively little need for relationship building, the HR professional would employ the director role; conversely, if the need for results is relatively low but the need for support, encouragement, and other human relations skills is high, a helper role is called for.

RESULTS ⟶

Helper	Guide	Collaborator
Feedback Provider	Trainer	Model
Process Observer	Expert Advisor	Director

RELATIONSHIPS ↑

Figure 3.1 HR role framework.

A Few Caveats

Before we describe each role in detail, a few caveats are in order. You might be tempted to conclude that the collaborator role is the single "best" role for HR professionals to employ because it requires high levels of relationships and results. This is simply not true, despite repeated calls for the HR profession to "partner" with clients, collaborate with line managers, and seek out and develop 50-50 relationships with customers. Collaborating is, in our framework, but one role professionals play and in and of itself is no more important nor inherently helpful than any of the other eight roles. Each role is situation-specific. That is, different situations will call for different roles. We also caution you to avoid making the assumption that low levels of relationships and results means that no emphasis is placed on these factors when assuming roles that call for low levels of these factors. For example, when acting as a director, the HR professional still needs to emphasize relationships to some degree, though not to the degree he or she would need to when taking on the role of, say, a guide. In other words, per the worn-out cliché, everything's relative. It is not an all-or-nothing affair.

Role Descriptions

In this section, we describe each of the nine roles in our role framework. Examples will accompany each role to help make these roles more real so that you can understand and gain clarity on what each role entails. Realize that these descriptions are for illustrative purposes only. Rarely do HR professionals perform any single role at the exclusion of all the other eight. They also move in and out of roles quickly, so that in "the real world," distinguishing what role you are playing at a given moment can be tough. You can be a director one minute and a supporter the next.

1. **Process Observer.** Edgar Schein, a noted authority on organizational change and career development, created the term "process consulting" (1987, 1990, 1999). He defines it as "a set of activities on the part of the consultant that help the client to perceive, understand, and act upon the process events that occur in the client's environment" (Schein 1987, 34). Typically, process consulting focuses on how human interactions take place within the organization. When HR professionals act as process observers (see Figure 3.2), they are watching how people interact with each other. This includes

RESULTS ⟶

Helper	Guide	Collaborator
Feedback Provider	Trainer	Model
Process Observer	Expert Advisor	Director

RELATIONSHIPS ↑

Figure 3.2 The process observer role.

attention to nonverbal behaviors as well as what is said among people. Put simply, a process observer looks at what is going on among people who are interacting with one another. It is, in its pure form, a data collection role (Kahnweiler 2003).

Being a process observer can occur in a formal or informal context. Often HR professionals are asked to observe meetings attended by client personnel, not so much to pick up on the content of the meeting but rather the process of how the meeting is being conducted. This is an example of a formal context. Another formal context for process observation occurs whenever you are meeting with a client. You can observe how you and your client are interacting by "stepping out of your shoes" for a moment and noting the process that is going on between the two of you. Many examples of informal contexts occur, or should occur, just by your being in the organization's system. Because you are an HR professional, human interactions of all sorts take place in your presence all the time. They are rich opportunities to observe the processes of those interactions.

Typically, when acting as a process observer, you want to be unobtrusive. You do not want your acting as an observer (whether in a formal or informal context) to influence how the people you are observing are behaving.

Remember that you are simply observing people. You are neither advising them about what they might consider doing nor are you telling them what they should definitely do. You are just watching them. Thus, there is little, if any, feedback or intervention when you act as a process observer. This is why we have placed this role in the low relations–low results cell. Despite process observation being a relatively low key–low impact role, do not assume it is unimportant. On the contrary, you might be surprised at how much you can learn simply by watching people in your organization interact with one another, be it in the hallway, at a meeting, in the cafeteria, on the shop floor, or in the executive suites. Most HR professionals do this all the time, and the seasoned ones probably do not even realize they are doing it frequently. This behavior has become second nature.

2. **Feedback Provider.** Moving one cell up on the left-hand column of Figure 3.3, we come to the role of feedback provider. In this capacity, HR professionals use the data they obtained as a process observer and feed it back to the client in a supportive and nondirective manner. As is the case when enacting the process observer role, the feedback provider role occurs in both formal and informal settings. Say you are sitting in on a client's staff meeting because the client asked you to observe and provide feedback on the process of the meeting. Suppose the manager who is leading the meeting is dominating the conversation, allowing little chance for others to make comments or ask questions. As a process observer, you see that the manager is talking 95 percent of the time, and when others talk during the other 5 percent, the manager is preoccupied with her notes, looking at her watch, and tapping her fingers on the table. It seems the manager is not really listening when others speak. As a feedback provider, you tell the group what you observed. In this case, you have observed the manager talking most of the time, and when others speak, the manager is perusing her notes, glancing at her watch, or tapping her fingers. You say this in a matter-of-fact, nonjudgmental tone as a feedback provider. Then you allow the group, particularly the manager in this case, to respond to the feedback.

Note that when you give feedback, it is behavioral and not evaluative. You could have said something like, "You know, Mr. or Ms. Manager, you seem to be a lousy listener. Is this a long-standing problem you have? Or are you even aware of this?" More likely than not, such feedback, if you can call it that, will cause the manager to be overly defensive or offensive, and nothing productive will be accomplished.

RESULTS →

Helper	Guide	Collaborator
Feedback Provider	Trainer	Model
Process Observer	Expert Advisor	Director

RELATIONSHIPS ↑

Figure 3.3 The feedback provider role.

During the HR professional's work day, there are, as we noted earlier, numerous opportunities for process observation of an informal nature. There are also numerous opportunities to share those observations with those you are observing. A simple example could be when you run into a client, Tom, with whom you have done some work before. Tom is yawning, hunched over, and has large bags under both eyes. (Note: This example assumes you have a good enough relationship with Tom that it's likely he would not be offended by your comments about his appearance.) As a feedback provider, you could say something like, "Tom, nice to see you. You look kind of tired today" and then see what transpires, if anything, between you and Tom. As in our formal example, note that you are using nonjudgmental language when giving Tom feedback. You are simply reporting an observation you have made. You are not saying, "Tom, my, you look awful. Maybe you should catch up on some sleep." The purpose of feedback is to open up dialog, not close it down. That is why being supportive and nondirective (not giving advice, avoiding leaping to conclusions about the causes of the behavior you observe, and not judging people) is a central tenet of being a feedback provider. And as with all nine HR roles, being helpful is at the root of providing feedback.

3. **Helper.** When HR professionals act as helpers (see Figure 3.4), they are drawing upon the highest level of human relations skills possible. They are sensitive to the needs and wants of the people they are trying to help at all times. When you act as a helper, the client is typically in a highly emotional state. He or she likely needs ample amounts of encouragement, empathy, and support from you. Directive interventions such as giving advice, asking probing (and sometimes irritating) questions, or confronting the client are not part of the helper's repertoire (though these directive tactics can be helpful at times). Because the helper role emphasizes relations and de-

RESULTS ⟶

Helper	Guide	Collaborator
Feedback Provider	Trainer	Model
Process Observer	Expert Advisor	Director

RELATIONSHIPS ↑

Figure 3.4 The helper role.

emphasizes results, it is typically not used in situations requiring immediate action, quick decisions, or easily verifiable results.

You likely have experienced situations in which people simply need a sounding board, a trustworthy person to whom they can vent, or a sympathetic (or even better, an empathetic) ear. No decisions or actions need to be taken then (or possibly ever). They just want to be heard and to feel supported. This is an ideal time for HR professionals to step into the helper role.

HR professionals are not therapists—ditto counselors, psychologists, psychiatrists, and social workers. Without question, unless you are licensed to practice a helping profession such as psychology, counseling, law, medicine, and social work, you should not attempt to mimic these highly trained and specialized professionals. At the same time, we view Human Resources as a helping profession in its own right. When HR plays the helper role, it is, we think, acting in ways that are at the core of the profession. No, HR professionals are not therapists in the legal sense. No, you can't and shouldn't hold yourself out as a provider of "therapeutic services." But, surely you hope, through your work with other people and in service to other people, that your work is beneficial to them.

4. **Expert Advisor.** Let's now take a look at the middle column of our role framework—guide, trainer, and expert advisor. All three roles emphasize results more than the three roles in the far left column, but they have less emphasis compared to the three roles in the far right column. Let's begin with the expert advisor role (see Figure 3.5).

This role is probably one of the most familiar ones to those who have been in the HR field awhile. It is also probably very familiar to those who have used HR's services. Being an expert advisor involves drawing upon

RESULTS ⟶

Helper	Guide	Collaborator
Feedback Provider	Trainer	Model
Process Observer	Expert Advisor	Director

RELATIONSHIPS ↑

Figure 3.5 The expert advisor role.

knowledge and skills in one or more specialized areas of HR to advise and counsel clients/customers on issues pertaining to those knowledge areas and skills. Common examples are abundant. Suppose a manager is trying to decide who to hire among three top candidates for an open position. As an HR professional who provides services to this manager, you may offer your opinions to assist the manager in making this decision. Your decisions will likely be based on each candidate's qualifications vis-à-vis the job's requirements, your assessment of each candidate's potential, and your knowledge of what the manager's goals are and how this open position intersects with those goals. Or, perhaps employees want some help deciding which health care plan is most cost effective for them among several choices. Note that when you act as an expert advisor, you do not make decisions for others. You draw upon your expertise to assist others to make those decisions.

5. **Trainer.** When you act as a trainer (see Figure 3.6), you are, in effect, a teacher. Obviously, when you lead a classroom-based training session, you are enacting the trainer role. You can also serve as a trainer in less structured learning situations—for example, when you are helping a new manager understand and apply the nuances of an HR policy or procedure with a messy employee relations issue or when you are assisting an employee in exploring long-range career options. When you are in a training mode, you are assisting clients to formulate and implement solutions based on theories, concepts, and principles germane to the situation. You provide people with new tools with which to view and deal with situations. In this context, you are not lecturing at people, nor are you telling them what they should do. Training requires more human relation skills than this. In fact, it typically requires somewhat more relationship skills compared to the expert advisor role. The situations that call for your serving as a trainer are more

RESULTS ⟶

Helper	Guide	Collaborator
Feedback Provider	Trainer	Model
Process Observer	Expert Advisor	Director

RELATIONSHIPS ↑

Figure 3.6   The trainer role.

complex, ambiguous, and/or challenging compared to those in which the expert advisor role is appropriate.

6. **Guide.** The role of guide requires the most human relations skills among the three that require the mid-range emphasis on results (see Figure 3.7). Being a guide is similar to being a trainer; however, situations that call for the guide role require a higher level of human relations skills than those addressed via a trainer role. As a guide, you offer more support, encouragement, and understanding of the client's needs on an emotional level than you do as a trainer. For example, you may be working with an individual who has just found out his job has been eliminated. As a guide, you need to offer ample amounts of empathy and compassion while also being mindful that the person needs to also address the realities of the situation (explore and look for alternative means of employment). Thus, a high level of interpersonal skills and a moderate emphasis on results are in order.

Here's another example that illustrates when being a guide is appropriate: Say you work with a group of coworkers who are not getting along (and presumably want to improve the situation). There is some need for positive results to be achieved and a greater need to address some delicate interpersonal dynamics. Addressing these dynamics primarily or solely by teaching (that is, employing the trainer role) the coworkers concepts and tools for "how to get along" will probably be insufficient. Likewise, simply advising them on "how to get along better" will likely fall short of the mark, as would running the group through an off-the-shelf team-building exercise. As a guide, you might, for example, first try to see whether each coworker thinks there is a problem. If they all agree there is a problem, a guide would then ask each coworker to describe, in his or her own words, what the problem is. A guide would then use this data to gauge if and to what degree each

RESULTS ————————————————————————►

Helper	Guide	Collaborator
Feedback Provider	Trainer	Model
Process Observer	Expert Advisor	Director

RELATIONSHIPS ▲

Figure 3.7 The guide role.

member is willing and able to commit to do something about the problem. You would then use the coworkers' responses to the commitment issue as data to guide each member and the group as a whole through a process of enacting those commitments. Such a process would likely be more than "a one-time event," especially if the group's lack of cohesion, trust, and productivity were pronounced and long standing. Can you now see how the level of human relations skills here are of a higher order than teaching the group members what to do or telling them what they should do? Can you also see how, as a guide, you don't push hard for results, while at the same time you avoid being completely nondirective or laissez faire?

Note that we have deliberately avoided the word "coach" here, though the guide role is more akin to coaching than any other. We have found that coaching in the workplace has gained tremendous popularity in recent years while being one of those terms that can be misunderstood and misapplied. Some see coaching as cheerleading; others see it as armchair psychotherapy. We see it as neither of these.

7. **Director.** When you use specialized knowledge, skills, and experience to solve a problem, you are acting as a director (see Figure 3.8). Unlike the expert advisor, you are taking matters in your own hands as a director. There is little, if any, need to involve your clients/customers in the issue when you act as a director. This is why there is relatively low emphasis on relations in the director role. In our experience, there are few instances when the director role is needed or desirable because there are few instances when involvement of our clients/customers is not needed. Contrary to some unfortunate perceptions among some of HR's customers, HR professionals are, by and large, not police officers in the sense of enforcing "the law" (for example, HR or other organizational policies). There are, however, times when you

RESULTS ⟶

Helper	Guide	Collaborator
Feedback Provider	Trainer	Model
Process Observer	Expert Advisor	Director

RELATIONSHIPS ↑

Figure 3.8 The director role.

need to put on your law enforcement uniforms. For example, if you observe a breach of safety policies, you are obligated, ethically and legally, to see that this situation is corrected immediately. Likewise, when you discover that a manager is not following hiring or termination policies, you need to be directive with that manager.

You need to direct very cautiously if you are to maintain credibility in service to your customers. Remember that the cornerstone of all HR roles is to be helpful. Most people are not motivated by being told that what they are doing is wrong, nor are they generally energized and productive when they are told what to do by someone in authority. So you need to put on your director hat (or cop uniform) very judiciously.

There is another reason to employ the director role with care. Some of your customers would just prefer you take on their people problems and issues so they can devote time and energy to other matters. HR issues are not the sole province of HR professionals (unless you are willing to take on this responsibility, and that creates a whole host of other problems for you, such as potential burnout).

8. **Model.** You know what models are. Here, we are not referring to people who walk down a runway with stylish new clothes, of course. When HR is acting as a model, it is showing others how to act (see Figure 3.9). You can learn a great deal simply by observing someone who has the knowledge and skills that you lack. When you act as a model to others, they too can see what certain actions look like and eventually learn to incorporate them in their own repertoire.

Effective models know when to model and to whom. They also know what behaviors to display when modeling. This is why this role requires more human relations savvy than the director role does. In countless situ-

RESULTS ———————————————————▶

Helper	Guide	Collaborator
Feedback Provider	Trainer	Model
Process Observer	Expert Advisor	Director

RELATIONSHIPS

Figure 3.9 The model role.

ations, modeling is appropriate. When you are working with a team to improve the way members listen to each other's ideas, you should model the very behaviors you want those members to emulate and eventually display themselves. In another example, say you are helping managers conduct performance review discussions with their employees. Suppose you are discussing with them how to deliver "bad news" to an employee who has been judged to be a sub-par performer the past year. In addition to providing the managers with some concepts and tools pertaining to this task (training), you can also show the managers what those concepts and tools look like in practice. This approach can often be a much more powerful and effective learning strategy than merely training someone in the principles of "good listening skills" or "giving negative feedback skills."

Some would argue that HR needs to be a role model 24/7/365. A "do as I say not as I do" approach will only undermine any respect and trust you may have earned. We do not take issue with this argument. However, in the context of HR roles, in some circumstances the single most effective way to be helpful is to show your clients/customers what you think is in their best interests to do by doing those very things yourself.

9. **Collaborator.** We have come to the last role in our nine-role framework. It is here that the need to enact high levels of human relations skills on issues when results need to be bought into and achieved collaboratively. Ideally, when you collaborate, you are acting in a 50-50 relationship with others, who, by definition, own the remaining 50 percent of the bargain. Another term that we have seen with increasing use (and, like "coaching," is an increasingly overused and abused term) that is akin to collaborator is "partner." Unlike a guide, a collaborator has more responsibility for helping to achieve results (see Figure 3.10). Unlike a model, a collaborator needs to

RESULTS ──▶

Helper	Guide	Collaborator
Feedback Provider	Trainer	Model
Process Observer	Expert Advisor	Director

RELATIONSHIPS ▲

Figure 3.10 The collaborator role.

utilize the highest levels of interpersonal competence to establish and maintain a 50-50 partnership with the client/customer. In some ways, being a collaborator is like being a spouse—at least in its textbook form! Each party has equal responsibility for making the relationship work and for the results that relationship produces.

When are 50-50 collaborations needed? Often you run into (or will be thrown into) situations in which both you and your client lack the necessary knowledge, skills, abilities, and time to tackle the situation on their own. But the situation calls for both parties to be equally involved in the "tackling" process. Put another way, both your customers and you need to "own the issue" equally as well as need to own the solution equally. Perhaps senior management requires some assistance in formulating long-term organizational strategies, including "people strategies" and where and how those link with other substrategies. Because "people strategies" are not the sole province of HR (or at least they shouldn't be), collaboration with senior management by HR on this task is appropriate. Perhaps a department or subsidiary wants to devise a new incentive plan that departs from an existing plan in other parts of the organization, and that department needs to draw on your expertise in incentive plan design and administration to accomplish this goal. A collaboration is needed because you have expertise the client lacks, whereas the client knows the organization and its needs, goals, and people better than you do. Furthermore, when the new incentive plan is up and running, you may be called upon to monitor and administer the plan while the client executes it. Thus, at both the design and implementation stages, a 50-50 collaborative arrangement (or partnership, if you want to call it that) is merited.

Primary Skills Required of Each Role

To list each and every skill that is required for all nine roles is beyond the scope of this book. At the same time, we think it will help you to get a grasp of the primary skills that are needed to perform these roles. By "primary," we mean those skills that can be categorized as "make or break." That is, these skills are the ones that are imperative for you to possess and deploy to perform a particular role effectively; without them, no matter what other skill sets you bring to the role, it is unlikely you will enact that role with success.

Figure 3.11 displays these essential skills.

HELPER	GUIDE	COLLABORATOR
*Interpersonal Sensitivity *Make It Easy For People To Open Up *Use "Third Ear" (listen and read between the lines)	*Well-Developed Interpersonal Skills *Knowing What Works When and Why *Knowing When To Push and Hold Back	*Highly Developed Interpersonal Skills and HR Area Knowledge *Strategic Thinking *Analytical Problem Solving
FEEDBACK PROVIDER	**TRAINER**	**MODEL**
*Interpersonal Sensitivity *Judgment (when to give and withhold feedback) *Acting Nonjudgmentally	*Knowledge of Principles and Theories *Able to Explain Concepts and Tools in Simple Terms *Awareness of Interpersonal Dynamics	*Able and Willing To Walk One's Talk *Self-Awareness *Helping Others Develop New Skills
PROCESS OBSERVER	**EXPERT ADVISOR**	**DIRECTOR**
*Being Nonthreatening *Being Keenly Observant *Knowing What To Observe	*Deep, Specialized Knowledge and Experience *Determining Where and When Specialized Knowledge Is Needed *Imparting Knowledge Clearly	*Specialized Knowledge Base *Willingness To Get Hands Dirty *Able to Explain Why Action Is Necessary

Figure 3.11   Primary skills required for HR roles.

Some Guidelines for Choosing One's Role

If you have ever observed seasoned HR professionals in action, you probably have noticed that they seem to slip in and out of roles seamlessly and effortlessly. If you are a seasoned HR professional yourself, you have likely experienced a similar dynamic. On some level, HR professionals choose among various role options many times a day, though this process can and usually is unconscious or subconscious.

Those newer to the field may wonder how they can effectively enact the "right" role from the nine we have presented at the right place at the right time with the right people. This is a legitimate issue. Unfortunately, it is not a paint-by-number process (if you arc in situation X, choose role Y). Most of us learn how to choose our roles through trial and error, especially (and we hope) after our errors! We can, however, offer some guidelines to assist you in choosing the viable roles to adopt.

First, ask yourself if you have a choice. Sometimes your role options are fairly limited—for example, if there is truly an immediate need or crisis. In most cases, however, you do have a choice—if you are willing to see it as your choice.

After you consider whether the situation is a real emergency, we recommend you take a hard and honest look at your skills because HR roles are deeply inter-twined with the skill packages the HR professional possesses. You can't perform a role if you don't have the requisite skills to enact it. Link your current skills to each role in our framework. Doing this should help you see which roles you can adopt today and which skills you need to acquire and develop tomorrow to expand your role repertoire. In general, those roles that require the most relations skills will call for the most well-developed interpersonal competence; likewise, the roles that are most focused on results will require you to possess the skills that facili-tate and achieve results if you are to succeed in that role.

In addition to skill sets, it will help you to determine and distinguish between client needs and client wants. All too often people come to HR with all sorts of issues and problems, and they also come with the solution they want you to imple-ment. More often than not, HR needs to question the client's diagnosis and solu-tions before jumping to action. Helping professionals are not order takers. Although your clients may indeed have assessed a situation accurately and com-pletely, more often than not they cannot simply do so because they are too close to the action. Or, they may have diagnosed the problem well but then concluded that what is called for is the most convenient, least risky, or cheapest solution, none of which are necessarily the best solution. Suffice it to say here that often your correct role should be driven by the needs of your clients and not solely by their wants. And it is up to you to determine their needs and to try to convince them that sometimes what they want is not what they truly need.

Training requests are a common example illustrating how wants and needs can and should be distinguished. Suppose the Manager of Customer Service comes to you and says his reps need a refresher in that great customer service course you delivered to them several months ago. Is such retraining the solution? What, indeed, is the problem? If the reps lack sufficient knowledge or skill, then perhaps a refresher is what is called for. However, maybe the reps possess sufficient knowl-edge and skill but aren't motivated to use what they know and can do on the job. Maybe they don't trust the manager. Perhaps the technology used in the customer service operation isn't working. Maybe the reps are burned out or bored. Or there could be numerous other plausible reasons the reps' performance is less than satisfactory to the manager. The point is that you must do all you can to distinguish client wants and client needs to be of maximum assistance. Wants and needs are often very different.

As we mentioned previously, rarely does HR assume one pure role in any given circumstance. You mix and match, jump from one to another, and often change roles at a moment's notice. You can likely relate to a time on a project when you started out, say, performing primarily as the expert advisor, and as the project unfolded, different client needs emerged, causing you to expand your role from an expert to a guide, helper, and/or collaborator.

Thus, all things being equal, you will be most effective when you have the skills, experience, and confidence that will enable you to perform as many roles as possible because situations that need your help rarely require you to perform one or even a few roles. And after you have gained experience in multiple roles, you should be able to more clearly see which ones are the "right" ones at a given point in time with a given client on a given issue. You will thus become "role clear." You will also more clearly see which role or roles are most appropriate at the outset of a project, based on your understanding of the project and the client needs when the project is launched. And after you have some understanding of the project at hand, you can begin to formulate the roles you want and need to employ, at least at the outset of the work. In this way, you can state the roles your customers can expect you to assume at the start of your work with them. Being "role clear" up front will help avoid misunderstandings and disappointments that can occur later on between you and your customers. Who isn't for that?

Consulting Careers

One of us has taught a graduate-level course in HR consulting for the past 15 years. One thing that continually amazes us is how many students, some of whom have been in HR for a decade or more, view consulting as an expert from the outside who comes into an organization, gives advice, and leaves. We think this is an extremely narrow and myopic perspective of what HR consulting is about. Such a restrictive perspective ("I either have a full-time HR job, or I'm a self-employed consultant") leads many of these students to conclude they have never consulted and probably never will. Consulting can be and is performed by virtually any HR professional. If you are involved at all in distinguishing client needs from client wants (and we are encouraging you to do that per the previous discussion on role choices), then you are probably consulting. If you provide thoughtful recommendations to clients, then you are probably consulting. Like many students in the aforementioned HR consulting course, you probably already act as a consultant and may not have realized it. Realize it now. And embrace the role and improve your performance in it.

Just what is consulting anyway? Of course, definitions vary. We view it as a process that typically begins with the HR professional distinguishing client wants from client needs. Based on this diagnosis, the HR professional then works with the clients to address those needs. It often entails "selling" the clients to buy into what their needs are. That is, clients come to the HR professional usually thinking they know what the problem is, but often, or at least sometimes, the clients' diagnosis reflects what they want and not what they truly need. Thus, client wants and needs often differ. When a client and HR professional reach agreement on client needs (reflecting what the real and not the apparent problem is), the HR consultant works with the client to address them. Typically, the HR professional will employ the nine roles we presented in this chapter throughout the consulting process.

Perhaps it will help to distinguish consulting from nonconsulting. Consider the following two dialogs between a manager of customer service and an HR professional.

> *Manager: Hi. How are you doing? I wonder if you can give my people a refresher in that customer service training program you put them through three months ago. They're a little rusty and need some retraining.*
>
> *HR professional: Sure. When do you want to schedule it? OR*
>
> *HR professional: I think I can do that. Do you want to have them go through the entire course again or just selected parts? OR*
>
> *HR professional: I can help with that. Do just some people need retraining, or do you think your whole group needs to go through it?*

> *Manager: Hi. How are you doing? I wonder if you can give my people a refresher in that customer service training program you put them through three months ago. They're a little rusty and need some retraining.*
>
> *HR professional: Thanks for coming by to talk about this. What leads you to believe your people need retraining?*
>
> *Manager: Well, I've seen some slippage in their performance, starting about three weeks after you trained them. They just need some reminders about how to approach certain customers.*
>
> *HR professional: What leads you to think the performance drop is caused by your people forgetting some aspects of the training?*

Manager: Well, I don't know if they all forgot some things. It just seems they have.

HR professional: It sounds as though it's tough to really know what is causing the performance slippage. Is that right?

Manager: Yeah.

HR professional: OK. I think, then, it makes sense to try to uncover what is really driving the performance drop, and to do that, I am going to need to ask you a lot more questions about that, and I will probably need to talk with your people as well and perhaps observe them on the job, too. I could give a refresher course, but I'm concerned that will treat the symptoms of the performance issue at best. What do you think?

The first dialog is really order taking. The HR professional reacts to the client's request to "jump!" with "how high?" or "when do I jump?" The HR professional's intent in this example is probably noble—he or she wants to be of service. We question how effective this person will be in this scenario.

By contrast, the second dialog shows how the HR professional also has the intent to be helpful but in a much different way. This person really wants to be sure the problem has been correctly identified before jumping to solutions. The HR professional shows the client that he or she cares about the performance issue and wants to help, but in ways that avoid simply complying with the client's initial presentation of that issue. In this example, the drop in customer service rep performance may in and of itself be a symptom of a larger issue. At this stage, you simply do not know. Thus, when consulting, HR professionals are, in many ways, acting as organizational detectives. They distinguish symptoms from root causes through questioning, observation, and other means of data collection just as detectives would on a case.

Suffice it to say at this point that consulting broadens the HR professional's role package considerably. You can think of consulting as superceding the nine roles in the role matrix. It uses all nine to one degree or another on a given project.

We have witnessed an increasing call for HR professionals during the past 15–20 years to "act like consultants." This most certainly includes those of us who are full-time employees in one organization. Thus, consulting has been viewed, and we will view it here, as an HR role that is not the exclusive province of outside experts who work on projects in our organizations. We strongly urge you to view it this way.

More recently, some have argued that if HR professionals don't break out of their silos (areas of HR knowledge and expertise), they are very vulnerable to being undervalued, laid off, or at least seen as being marginal players in an organization (Gay and Labonte 2003; Green 2002). Sartain (2003) drives home the point that those in HR advise and hopefully influence decision makers on a host of issues, but generally are not the ones who make the final call when it comes to such things as hiring, promotions, and compensation decisions. This is consulting! Why? Because you are helping (yes, there's that concept again) people address their needs, solve their problems, and make good decisions. You are not doing these things for them. You are helping them do those things.

We foresee the 15- to 20-year-old call for HR professionals to start acting like consultants to increase in the coming years. We think this is a positive trend in the profession, for when you act like a consultant, you work on real needs of clients. When you work on clients' real needs, your value increases.

Why do we keep seeing authors and consultants (as well as customers) urging HR professionals to be consultants? There are many reasons. For one, technology has replaced people performing the more transactional or administrative HR functions. Many organizations are outsourcing those kinds of HR functions as well. Many HR professionals who have worked full-time in one organization have been "forced" to take on a consulting career because they have left the organization involuntarily and cannot find another full-time HR job. But we think this shift goes beyond these fairly recent marketplace dynamics and economic realities.

When you consult, you are market-driven and avoid being product-driven. Your career identity as consultants (whether you consult virtually all the time, 5 percent of the time, or something in between these two extremes) allows you to really try to be responsive to your customers' concerns, needs, and challenges. When your career identities are enslaved by a rigid job title ("I am a benefits specialist II) or a line of products ("I provide managers with lists of viable job candidates" or "I help resolve disputes between middle managers and employees on the shop floor"), you are limited in what you offer to clients and organizations. Your value is limited to the "products" you say you offer, whether it is benefits information, dispute resolution, or something else. When you are market-driven, by definition, you respond to marketplace conditions and trends, often with a whole host of "products" that meet real needs and demands your clients are facing. Your market can be described as your clients' issues, problems, and challenges pertaining to people. That is often quite a large (and lucrative) market to target.

Look at this situation from your customer's point of view. Say you have a problem or challenge and go to an HR person for help. That person has an array of products to offer. But what if none of them really addresses your problem or challenge? Then what? More likely than not, you will not engage the HR person for help, and you'll seek help elsewhere or try to deal with the issue yourself. When you are the customer, your perception of the HR person's value to you is probably minimal, at least in this instance. On the other hand, if your HR person employs a consultative role, chances are he or she will really spend time and effort working with you to uncover what the real problem is, and then work with you to address it. And if the HR person doesn't have the products (knowledge, skill, or both) to address your issue, he or she will help you find someone who has the best products for your particular issue. That's being market-driven! What do you, as the customer, think your perceived value of the HR person (and perhaps the HR function as well) is now?

Has HR been slow to adopt this role? If so, why? Since we have seen the call for HR professionals to act like consultants for so long, it certainly seems HR has been slow to adopt the consulting role. One important question you should ask yourself, if you don't see yourself as a consultant (yet) is, "Do I have the skills, temperament, and interest to add consulting to the repertoire of services I offer?" We hope you have the interest or will soon find a way to develop it. The skills needed to be an effective consultant could take up three books, so we will not go into detail on them here. Suffice it to say for now that as a consultant you are anything but an order taker. You are market-driven and not product-driven. The market is the needs of clients and your organization, not what you happen to know well or what you like to do the most. This necessitates skills in organizational diagnosis, among others. Temperamentally speaking, the consulting role is considerably easier to do if you have healthy amounts of tolerance for ambiguity. Some would say this is imperative if you are to act consultatively. Remember that order taking requires little, if any, such tolerance. So if a client comes to you and says, "Find me three good candidates for this open position" or "Tell me what the OSHA requirements are for this job" and you say, "OK" and then follow through, you are executing an order, not acting consultatively.

Consulting for HR professionals takes two basic forms: internal and external. Let's look at each one, with all the variations and permutations within each form.

Internal HR Consulting

As an internal, you typically will be a full-time employee of one organization. You can be an internal consultant as a part-time employee as well. The key is you are an employee, not a contractor. Perhaps the best way to describe the role of an internal HR consultant is to distinguish it from "having an HR job" in an organization.

Although HR jobs are as varied as the people who occupy them and the organizations where those jobs are housed, some fundamental and consistent differences exist between an HR job that incorporates consulting from one that does not. Keep in mind that an HR job that incorporates consulting can, in itself, come in many forms. For example, the HR job may require consulting 20 percent of the time, 5 percent of the time, or all the time. Generally speaking, here are the major differences between an HR job that entails some consulting and one that does not:

1. Consulting is more ambiguous than other forms of HR work. The problems are rarely clearly visible, defined, and straightforward—ditto the solutions to the problems.
2. Consulting is project-based, whereas other aspects of HR work tend to be more or less routinized. That is, the tasks involved tend to occur over and over again, whereas consulting projects have a finite beginning and end.
3. Some internal consultants act as their own P&L center. That is, they charge managers in the organization for their services and are expected to continually bring in new business that exceeds the cost the organization pays for employing them (salary, benefits, office space, etc.). A key expectation of internal HR consultants at Southern Company, a leading energy provider in the United States, is that they make and not lose money in their work with clients (managers and employees of Southern Company) over a year's time. Such structures in nonconsulting HR jobs are rare.
4. Consulting work provides even more variety than other HR jobs do (and as we've noted, many HR jobs come with truckloads of variety). Because consulting tends to be project-based rather than job-description driven, variety is the name of the consulting game.
5. Most HR jobs require considerable skill to perform them well. When you add consulting to the mix, even more skills are required, be they technical, managerial, interpersonal, business, or functional.
6. Consulting is prone to fueling false pride in you and unhealthy dependencies on you by those you serve more than being in an HR job. What sounds more impressive? Being a trainer or consultant? A recruiter or consultant? A benefits specialist or consultant? And as you gain consulting experience and competence, you will often witness clients actually agreeing to and implementing your advice. That can be a huge ego boost to the point of engendering grandiosity. Consulting, more than many HR jobs, can also fuel clients' dependency on you, which can feel seductively wonderful but at the same time contribute to unhealthy overreliance on you. You are then

asked (or told) to identify and solve every problem a client has. Because every HR role is about being as helpful as possible, when you take on work for clients and do it all yourself and not involve them in the process, you may earn more money, status, and prestige—for yourself. But what are the clients getting? You know the bit about teaching people to fish versus doing the fishing for them. When you take on work or responsibilities that your clients have some ownership in, you deprive them of developmental opportunities. In that way, you are not helping your clients.

Green (2002) and others argue that one reason HR doesn't take on a more consultative role is that it doesn't have the capacity to do so. It's not that some professionals don't want to assume an internal consulting role; it is more that they don't know how to do it nor what is really required. We want to encourage those of you who haven't tried on the consulting hat to be open to the idea, even if that idea scares or overwhelms you. Consulting takes many forms, and there are myriad ways to do it and do it well. As noted consultants Geoff Bellman (2002) and Peter Block (2003) note, consulting offers opportunities to bring who you are to the work as opposed to trying to force fit yourself into a prescribed (and perhaps rigid) job description. That being said, some signposts will make your transition to a consulting role (even if it entails only 5 percent of your job) more challenging than it already can be. Challenging? Yes. Impossible? No way!

We can boil down these signs to three:

1. How high is your tolerance for ambiguity? (That, in itself, is an ambiguous question, isn't it?) Per the above, we can state without ambiguity that consulting, by its very nature, is ambiguous.
2. How high is your tolerance for delayed gratification? Consulting is often more fuzzy than other forms of HR work. So obtaining quick feedback on your performance as a consultant is illusive … and elusive.
3. How accustomed are your clients/customers to you acting in a consultative way? When you take on a new role or posture with people who have worked with you in other ways, they may be confused at best. Be prepared to deal with this and to explain to your clients what you are trying to do and how this will ultimately help them and the organization. And be a little concerned if these people are not confused initially as you try on a new role. If they aren't at least slightly puzzled, you still may be doing too much hand holding or falling back on your tried-and-true way of working with clients (for example, the product-driven methods you have used for years with con-

siderable success). If clients you have worked with before don't see a change in the way you come across to them, chances are you are thinking you are taking on a consulting role when you really are not.

External Consulting

Many aspects of "consulting from the outside" are similar to the internal HR consulting role. Both are ambiguous, project-based, and full of variety in terms of clientele, issues addressed, and outcomes achieved. Both forms of consulting also entail being accountable to two bosses—the client and the manager to whom the consultant reports (an exception is when you are self-employed as an external). There are, however, some definitive differences between internal and external consulting. There are also key differences among the several forms that external HR consulting can take. As we cover these differences, keep in mind we are making generalizations. Like you would with any generalizations, take them with some dosage of salt because exceptions do exist.

As a general rule, external consultants travel more than internal ones. The reason is that an external's clients usually come from numerous organizations at a given point in time, whereas an internal's clients, even if they are spread across the globe, are in one organization. Although some internals do have profit-loss accountabilities, many do not. They are employees first and consultants second. The vast majority of external consultants are measured by the revenue they produce or help to produce. Many are expected to market themselves. Certainly, if you are self-employed, you are either out there trying to bring in new business or are billing clients on current projects. Again, generally speaking, it is easier to market yourself and your wares when you are inside one organization compared to trying to get your toes in many organizations' doors. Externals generally enjoy more autonomy than internals, at least in terms of the scheduling of work with clients. Many internals claim that externals enjoy more respect and status than they do. Internals have told us countless times that they make recommendations that management doesn't buy into, whereas someone from the outside makes the same recommendations and management buy-in somehow magically happens. Of course, internals enjoy having more knowledge of the organization's operations, politics, and culture and can more readily see the long-term impacts of their efforts compared to externals. At the same time, because they live in the client organization full-time, internals can suffer from myopia and blind spots more readily than externals. Externals can also more readily apply what they have learned from one organization to the next, whereas internals are focused on the organization in which they are employed. Finally, in most instances, externals' occupational identity is usually that of "consultant," whereas many internals see themselves as an "employee" first and a "consultant" perhaps second, or even lower on the identity pole.

Table 3.1 summarizes the major differences between internal and external consulting. As you review this table, don't forget to take your salt.

You can effectively shape an HR career performing either as an internal or external, or both. We know many people, including ourselves, who have woven back and forth between these two basic ways to consult. One is not inherently "better" than the other. They just have some differences—usually. Prestige, respect, credibility, compensation, and other forms of rewards can be accrued in both venues.

Some signs indicate that external HR consulting is growing, no doubt fueled by the waves of downsizing, outsourcing, restructuring, acquisitions, and other cost-containment strategies that have left many HR professionals jobless, including those with decades of experience at the highest levels. Often organizations can purchase HR services and expertise on an as-needed basis with externals, thereby avoiding the fixed costs of employing that expertise full-time (as well as the costs, time, and energy necessary to recruit, hire, and train people for HR positions). Obviously, organizations of all kinds find such cost savings and flexibility attractive. All indicators we have seen suggest such trends will continue, and therefore the market for competent external HR consultants will continue to grow.

There are four basic ways to perform external consulting. Although describing the nuances of each one is beyond the scope of this book, we have listed the essential elements of each venue in which external consultants operate:

Table 3.1 Major Differences between Internal and External Consulting.

Factor	Internal	External
Travel	None or Moderate	Frequent
Accountability for Revenue	Little to None	High
Marketing Oneself	Relatively Easier	Relatively Harder
Autonomy	Moderate	High
Perceived Status	Relatively Less	Relatively More
Knowledge of Client Organization	Extensive	Moderate
Risk of Myopia	High	Little to None
Professional Identity	Employee	Consultant

1. **Large firms.** While it is debatable what constitutes "a large consulting firm," we consider a firm composed of more than 50 consultants to be large. Of course, some are considerably larger, such as TPF&C, Hay, Mercer, Hewitt, and Accenture. Other large professional service firms, such as Deloitte, have separate units devoted to HR consulting. In some ways, large firms are like any large organization. Numerous procedures, policies, and a wealth of resources are at your disposal. Often, especially if you're a beginning consultant with a large firm, it is not expected that you start bringing in clients right away. Furthermore, the name of the firm is often so well established that it serves as a brand. This enables consultants to work on projects that they likely would not be able to obtain had they tried to get the work themselves. Usually, though not exclusively, working in a large firm involves working on several projects for different clients at any one time. Often, large consulting firms serve large organizations. That is, their clientele are disproportionately housed in the Fortune 100.

2. **Mid-sized firms.** We consider consulting firms with around 10 to 50 consultants to be mid-sized. Mid-sized firms often target specific industries and/or geographic locations to gain an edge in the marketplace. They may employ some specialists, though not nearly as many as larger firms. Although their clients come from the largest organizations, mid-sized firms often serve mid-sized clientele. All things being equal, unless you operate at the top in a large consulting firm, you will likely have more access to the executive suite of mid-sized clients working in a mid-sized firm than you would working in a large firm serving large clients.

3. **Small firms.** Consulting firms with fewer than 10 full-time consultants can be considered small. Members of small firms typically enjoy closer working relationships with one another than those in larger firms. Certainly, small firms do serve large clients, including large government agencies and behemoth, global corporations. Generally speaking, however, small firms have lower fixed costs than large firms do, and therefore their fees are often lower and thus hold more appeal to smaller organizations looking for some outside help. Small firms often get work that the bigger firms either don't want or can't compete with price-wise. Smaller firms also tend to target clients on a local or regional basis. Thus, any travel involved will be less time-consuming compared to the travel time consultants endure when working in larger firms.

4. **Me, Inc.** Of course, you can be an external consultant in the smallest venue possible—a firm composed of you and you only. When you work for your-

self, you enjoy levels of freedom that no job— even those in the most autonomy-driven cultures of consulting, start-up, or freewheeling high-tech firms—can match. You are also responsible for everything—marketing, arranging travel, buying paper clips, sending out invoices, paying bills, filing taxes, gaining web presence, and the list goes on and on. Being a self-employed consultant means you are literally selling yourself to clients, whereas as a member of a firm, be it small, medium, or large, you are also selling and representing the firm that employs you. We have heard many people, especially those who see themselves as employees first, say, "I will never work for myself." We would caution you to never say never. Almost anything is possible . . . literally. However, if the idea of marketing and selling yourself doesn't hold high appeal right now, chances are now is not a good time for you to transition into the Me, Inc. role. At the same time, we know many "Me, Inc.'ers" who hire people full- or part-time to do their marketing and some of their selling for them. Many independent consultants also partner with other independents on projects, with marketing efforts, and on sales leads. So if you are having trouble envisioning yourself as an independent, keep in mind that you do not have to do everything all by yourself. However, marketing and sales are a huge part of being an independent consultant, whether you hire people to perform those tasks for you or collaborate with your peers on them. Unless your name and reputation are fairly widely known, chances are marketing and sales will be part and parcel of your "Me, Inc." career.

Concluding Remarks

One of the wonderful aspects of being in HR is the multitude of roles you perform. You serve as an expert at 9 a.m. and at 10:30 you shift to helper mode. By 11 a.m. you have switched roles again to a process observer, and before lunch you find yourself performing consultatively. And all this may be with the same individual client!

Varying roles means you have options and the freedom to choose which ones to employ. Along with such freedom is considerable variety—one of the cornerstones and key appeals of being a member of the HR profession. Having multiple roles at your disposal allows you to be responsive to the ever-changing dynamics of the organizations in which you practice your craft, the fluid markets in which these organizations operate, and the incessant changes that you

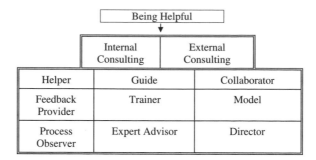

Figure 3.12   Expanded view of HR roles.

experience as an individual. Virtually every one of our interviewees told us these very same things.

So as organizations change, and as you change and grow, you have many hats to try on to be successful. Viewing HR roles in this expansive way will also help you formulate a self-identity that is much broader, more responsive to customer expectations and requirements, and more satisfying to you than identifying yourself by a restrictive job title and description that was likely created by someone other than yourself. You are more—considerably more—than "a benefits specialist" or "an HR manager" or "an instructional designer Level III."

Take a look at Figure 3.12 for a visual portrayal of the major points we have made in this chapter.

We hope this chapter has given you some ideas about how to escape from traditionally rigid, narrow identities that have been imposed upon you to a new world that contains a broad array of identities that you define for yourself. In doing so, you will, in Shakespeare's terms, be able to act competently and confidently on many different stages playing the different roles that are called for. You will avoid being typecast or stereotyped by others into a small box that has no room for more than one or two characters on one or two stages.

References

Bellman, G. 2002. *The Consultant's Calling.* San Francisco: Jossey-Bass.

Block, P. 2003. *Flawless Consulting.* San Francisco: Jossey-Bass.

Champion, DP, DH Keil, and JA McLendon. 1990. "Choosing a Consulting Role." *Training and Development Journal* 44, no. 2: 66–69.

Gay, DL, and TJ LaBonte. 2003. "Demystifying Performance: A Roadmap." *Training and Development* 57, no. 5: 64–75.

Green, ME. 2002. "Internal HR Consulting: Why Doesn't Your Staff Get It?" *Public Personnel Management* 31, no. 1: 111–119.

Heathfield, SM. 2003. *The New Role of the HR Professional.* http://humanresources.aboutyou.com/libraryweekly/aa051400a.htm (accessed October 15, 2003).

Kahnweiler, WM. 2003. *Process Consultation: A Cornerstone of Organization Development Practice.* In *Organization Development: A Data-Driven Approach to Organizational Change,* ed. Waclawski and Church. San Francisco: Jossey-Bass, 149–163.

Sartain, L. (with Martha Finney). 2003. *HR from the Heart.* New York: AMACOM.

Schein, EH. 1987. *Process Consultation* (volume 2). Reading, MA: Addison-Wesley.

———. 1990. "A General Philosophy of Helping: Process Consultation." *Sloan Management Review* 31: 57–64.

———. 1999. *Process Consultation Revisited: Building the Helping Relationship.* Reading, MA: Addison-Wesley.

Ulrich, D. 2001. "Adding Value." *Executive Excellence* 18, no. 8: 18–20.

Wiscombe, J. 2001. "Your Wonderful/Terrible HR Life." *Workforce* 80, no. 6: 32–37.

4

The HR Career Success Model

We have made a strong case that HR is a dynamic, growing field that has abundant opportunities for you to grow professionally and personally throughout the life span of your career. We hope you can readily see that you can shape your HR career in a multitude of ways in all kinds of organizations and that you can meet those organizations' needs, meet your own needs, and make a real difference. At this point, you may be wondering just how to proceed. This chapter will help you do that. It provides the foundation for shaping your HR career, whether you are just starting out in the field or have toiled in it for decades.

Like a building or house, your career needs a solid foundation in order for it to work. You need a career-shaping foundation throughout your work life to be optimally effective. Such a foundation helps you focus, stay on track, set new goals, and make sure you are striving for the right things at the right time in the right ways. Without such a foundation, shaping your HR career is left to chance. We have found most people benefit by being thoughtful and deliberate in shaping their careers.

In this chapter, we present our HR Career Success Model as such a foundation. Subsequent chapters will go into more depth on each aspect of the model, along with concrete actions you can take to make the model work in your career and life.

Why a Model?

We are confident you have been in many situations that could be described as confusing or baffling. Think of one such situation. Maybe you were in unfamiliar territory, got lost, and didn't have a map to find your way out. Perhaps you were trying to get in touch with and understand something about yourself or a loved one. Maybe something happened at work that really confused you. Were you ever confused about something and tried the same strategy repeatedly to get unconfused? Have you ever repeated the same behaviors over and over and each time expected different results? (By the way, some people have claimed this to be an operational definition of insanity. We leave it to you to agree or refute that theory.)

Dealing with people (including yourself) and organizations can become pretty confusing. Sometimes it is very confusing. Life is confusing. Other than waving a white flag and giving up the quest to get more clarity on confusing situations and what to do about them, what else can you do?

Models, at least helpful ones, provide frameworks that simplify complex phenomena. Career success in general and career success in HR in particular can become quite complex when you consider all the factors involved. First, the issue of what constitutes HR career success is anything but unilateral and clear-cut. And as you've seen in the preceding chapters, the HR field is dynamic, broad, and ever changing. What you, as an individual, consider "success" can and often does change over the life span of your career, too. Add to this the fact that HR is a field applied in organizations. We have not witnessed too many organizations that we would characterize as "simple" and "easy to understand." Furthermore, we believe that any view of career success must incorporate some sort of learning, growth, and development. Enacting these concepts can also tend to be quite complex.

Dealing with complex issues and phenomena can become quite confusing. It can also be frustrating. This can easily lead to inertia or simply giving up unless you can somehow simplify what you are trying to understand and act on. So first, a model provides a roadmap. The roadmap helps you to minimize confusion and inertia and maintain your focus. Second, in the context of career development and success, a model allows you to benchmark where you are at a given point in time. Third, a model can facilitate your honing in on your strengths and development needs, setting important and achievable goals, and then taking specific actions to develop your HR career and yourself. In this process, a model can help you formulate sound strategies targeted to specific dimensions of success that you need to work on and improve.

A good model can help you think about and act on those elements of success pertaining to your work, your organizations, and yourself that merit attention at a given point in time. This is a much more efficient and effective way of going about developing yourself and your career versus taking a hit-or-miss, random approach to development.

What else does a good model do for you? To achieve the results just described, a model ought to be easily understood. After all, if you can't understand the elements of a model and their relationship to one another, what good is the model? A good model also ought to strike a balance between thoroughness and simplicity. It should not be so simplistic that it lacks substance (such as lists of "follow these 10 bullet points and you will achieve career success forever"), nor should it be so complex that even renowned scholars struggle with understanding and using the model. Lastly, a good model ought to be more than "Uncle Harry's Opinion." In other words, a good model ought to be based on solid research and the experiences of many people—in sum, there needs to be a sufficient amount of good data as a basis for the model.

Of course, you are well equipped to use your own judgment as to whether and to what degree our HR Career Success Model meets these criteria of "a good model." We think you will find that it does.

The model contains three major building blocks or elements:

1. Gain Knowledge
2. Apply Knowledge
3. Achieve Results

Pretty simple, right? You gain knowledge in some area, use it, and then live happily and successfully thereafter. Of course, this process does get more involved than this. But consider these three major elements, depicted in Figure 4.1, as "the foundation of the foundation."

We will describe the three major building blocks and the components within each one in some detail. But first, we want you to know our assumptions that underlie the entire model. This information should assist you in fully understanding all the dimensions of the model, the way they interconnect, and most importantly, the ways you can use the model as a framework and a roadmap to enhance your success in the HR craft.

Underlying Assumptions of the HR Career Success Model

- Anyone can achieve results. The important thing is the kinds of results that are achieved. Assuring the right results are achieved in a given situation requires that certain knowledge is acquired and then applied to that situation.

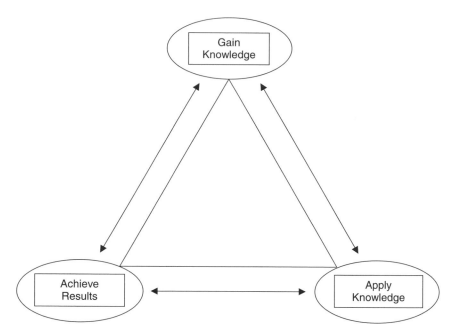

Figure 4.1 The major elements of the HR Career Success Model.

- How knowledge is acquired is irrelevant, be it from experience, other people, reading, seminars, school, introspection, or other sources. The important issue is that HR professionals have acquired knowledge in some key areas; otherwise, achieving important results is left to chance and other factors beyond their control or influence.
- Knowledge in and of itself has little use. Applying that knowledge in different situations is what matters. And knowing which knowledge to apply to which situations (i.e., using good judgment) is important. A hallmark of a profession, including HR, is that judgment is required. A paint-by-number or cookbook approach will be insufficient to tackle the issues and problems faced in that profession.
- Although the model deliberately avoids an overly simplistic, cookbook recipe view (and therefore an unrealistic view) of career success, it intends to portray pathways to success in digestible, practical pieces.
- Success means different things to different people. Success also means different things to you at different stages of your career. The career literature is replete with definitions of success. For example, Judge and his colleagues

(Judge and Bretz 1994; Judge, Cable, et al. 1995) distinguish between objective (for example, upward mobility, pay) and subjective (for example, job and career satisfaction) measures of career success. Deer (1986) claims five factors comprise career success: (1) upward mobility, (2) autonomy, (3) excitement, (4) balance, and (5) security. Schein (1990) offers the idea that professionals' work must satisfy their strongest career value (what he terms "career anchors") to be successful in their career. Many other factors and typologies of career success exist. So how do you define success? We think it is up to you to decide this definition throughout your career. The effective use of our model today requires that you are fairly clear on what success means to you today. What does success as you define it look like now? How might it look 10 years from now? In other words, our model does not embrace a particular definition of career success. That choice resides within you. The model is sufficiently flexible and adaptable so that it can be applied with virtually any view of success in mind. This assumption of the model highlights the importance of self-knowledge, which is one of its three major elements. Self-knowledge is covered thoroughly in the next chapter.

The Model

Let's now look at each of the three major elements of the model in some detail. Our goal is to lay out what we have found are checkpoints along the path you take in shaping your HR role. Subsequent chapters will outline specific actions you can take to broaden yourself in these areas.

Gain Knowledge

HR professionals must possess three major areas of knowledge to shape a successful career in the field. These areas are (1) knowledge of self, (2) knowledge of the field, and (3) knowledge of the organization in which you work (or multiple organizations if you consult externally).

Knowledge of Self

Because HR professionals, by definition, work extensively with and on behalf of others, it is important, and some say imperative, that you possess ample supplies of self-awareness. This is true of all helping professions, and we view HR as such. So what aspects of yourself do you, as a successful HR professional, need to be knowledgeable about or at least aware of? There are several. Six to be exact. These aspects are covered more fully in Chapter 5.

- **Experiences.** They include both professional and personal experiences as well as the mistakes you make along the way and what you learn from them. Everyone knows that experience is the best teacher. We would add that it's the best teacher if you bother to reflect thoughtfully and honestly about your experiences in order to take important lessons with you to future experiences. Your experiences also give you clues about the skills you need to acquire and those you already have but need to improve upon. Some of these development needs could be "blind spots" (unknown to you), and therefore help from others to uncover them is needed before you can work to address them.

- **Core skills.** If you are not aware of the skills you possess, it is difficult, if not impossible, to deploy them. Each HR professional probably possesses a multitude of skills in many different arenas. For purposes of this discussion, core skills for HR professionals can be grouped into three large buckets: (1) functional skills (that is, the "technical" areas of HR, such as compensation, employee relations, staffing, etc.), (2) analytical skills (that is, problem identification and problem-solving capabilities, distinguishing symptoms from causes, etc.), and (3) interpersonal skills (such as listening, influencing, negotiating, empathizing, etc.). In our experience, many people tend to underestimate the level of their skills, their portability, or both. This is often the result of having talents that have become second nature, so they are taken for granted. Or you know certain skills that you possess but can't imagine how you can take them with you to new jobs or different organizations.

- **Traits.** Everyone brings certain characteristics to situations, and these characteristics tend to be very stable and resistant to change. Consider traits as a way to define your personality. Your traits play a key role in determining person-job and person-organization fit. If you have ever toiled in a job or organization where you felt you didn't belong, the reason was probably that there was a poor fit between the job or organization and your key traits. Traits also drive your preferences for the kind of work environment that fits you best. This pertains to the kind of work environment (not only the physical environment, but the social one as well) in which you perform your best work. For example, do you perform at your best in large, complex environments; hard work/hard play ones; relatively calm ones; or ones that are characterized by crises? Here's a quick story about traits: One of us was giving an overview of the Myers-Briggs Type Indicator, a well-known and widely used personality assessment tool, in a class on being an HR leader. One of the students, who was working in HR, told the class that her boss uses this instrument to help her HR team communicate and collaborate with one another. The student then started crying. We asked what the tears were about. She said her boss called her in recently to review and discuss her Myers-Briggs results. In that meeting, her boss supposedly told the student she "had no business being in HR because of her Myers-Briggs Type." We told the class this is an excellent example of how not to use this assessment tool as well as an excellent example of how not to view traits or personality as they pertain to an HR career. Why? Because for one, traits are not skills. For another, no type of personality or package of traits unequivocally suggests that a person with that package should avoid HR as a career. On the contrary, HR is a career that can provide an excellent fit for virtually anyone with any personality or combination of traits. However, it is important to know your traits so you can shape your HR role in ways that capitalize on those traits and not conflict with them.

- **Values.** What are your top priorities that must be satisfied on the job to maximize your performance, job satisfaction, and emotional investment in the work? Helping others? Making a difference? Contributing to others' success? Doing work that is highly meaningful to you? What would you really fight for? These sorts of questions can help you uncover the values that you bring to work.

- **Key likes and dislikes.** Everyone has many of these. What do you want and not want in terms of the work itself that you do, the nature of the management climate in which you perform it, the skills you enjoy using the most, etc.? What energizes you? What deflates you? Key likes and dislikes also include your preferred roles. Which HR roles (see Chapter 3) do you prefer to use most often? Which ones do you want to use more than you do now? Which ones would you like to avoid or use minimally?

- **Emotional intelligence.** This aspect of self-knowledge includes knowing your limits, being in touch with others' emotions as well as your own, and responding in ways that let others know you know and appreciate how they are feeling. Managing relationships and managing yourself in those relationships are also part of emotional intelligence. People who have high emotional intelligence are very personally and socially competent. Emotional intelligence also includes knowing your major stressors and what to do about them. Every job, career, and occupation has stressors. What are your "hot buttons," or those issues and circumstances that get your blood boiling? What can you do about them and/or your reactions to them? Good stress management is a key to anyone's success, and HR work is certainly no exception. Having adequate reserves of emotional intelligence helps you manage stress effectively rather than it managing you.

Self-knowledge is a key component for anyone's career development. Because HR, by definition, deals with people, there are endless ambiguities, judgment calls, unprecedented situations, and shades of gray to deal with all the time (as opposed to jobs that deal primarily with data or things). Inadequate levels of self-knowledge will make it impossible to handle these realities. Furthermore, talk is cheap. By knowing yourself and conveying to others your self-knowledge, you model what you ask others to do. For example, suppose you are providing counsel to a manager on her management style. Perhaps you are trying to help the manager become aware of how she comes across to employees. Imagine trying to do this if you do not have sufficient knowledge of the ways you come across to others.

As helping professionals, what you do not know or don't acknowledge in yourself can hurt you (and others, too). Self-knowledge is a life-long pursuit for successful HR professionals. It is not a program from which you graduate. Virtually every one of our interviewees told us they like learning about themselves continuously and have every intention of staying on the path of self-discovery. Is this kind of learning always pleasurable? Indeed not. In fact, and as our interviewees corroborated, often it is painfully difficult to face up to some things about yourself. At the same time, it is always helpful to do so. You can't do something about yourself unless you first are aware of what it is about you that may need some attention.

Knowledge of the Field

What aspects of the field do you need to know? These aspects encompass two broad areas:

- **The functional areas of HR (e.g., recruitment and staffing, OD, compensation, etc.).** Note: The depth and breadth of knowledge required for success in any given area will depend in part on whether you seek to be a generalist or specialist.

- **Issues and trends in the HR profession.** They include new developments, techniques, concepts, and tools as well as directions the field is heading in or seems to be heading in the future. Keeping abreast of these aspects is essential in today's rapidly changing workplaces.

Knowledge of the Organization

Ulrich (1999) and Sartain (2003), among many others, cite HR professionals' lack of organizational knowledge as one of the field's greatest weaknesses. This shortcoming has been expressed by our customers in a number of ways, such as "You HR people don't know our business" or "HR doesn't really understand my needs" or "The people in HR have good intentions, but they have no idea how to really help my people because they don't know the business of our business." Sometimes, this lack of organizational knowledge (whether real or imagined) can be expressed by a customer in very simple terms—"My HR person just does not understand business." What are the major organizational elements the successful HR professional needs to know about and understand? (Very likely, you will need to know about more than one organization if you consult externally.) Organizations are complex, fascinating, and confusing "creatures." We have identified the following six key elements on the organizational landscape that HR professionals need to know about:

- **The fundamentals of how the organization works.** What is the business of the business? How does the organization go about this business? What are its major functions and operations? How does the organization achieve its mission? How does it make money (or not lose money if it is a nonprofit or government agency)?
- **Issues and trends affecting the organization, its industry and market sector, and the people employed by the organization.** These issues and trends include societal demographics and their impact on workplaces and workforces, competitive pressures faced by the organization, likely future scenarios that will affect how business is conducted, and the like. What keeps the CEO up at night? Why?
- **Organizational culture.** In its simplest form, an organization's culture is "the way things are done around here." Culture is composed of the underlying, often unspoken yet powerful norms the organization expects its members to embrace and enact consistently. What does the organization

really value? Clues to culture are what the organization does and does not do that reflects its values; sometimes this is not congruent with what the organization says it values. What systems and processes are in place that encourage and reward people to enact these values?

- **Power.** How is power acquired and kept? Who has it and who doesn't? How are important decisions made and by whom? To what degree is power shared downward and across from the top? How much autonomy do people have? What decisions do people make on their own? In consultation with others? What are the issues or decisions over which people have no say or input?

- **Customers.** How does the organization acquire, satisfy, and retain them? Who does the organization serve? What do customers expect from the organization, and how does it try to meet and perhaps exceed those expectations? What plans, if any, does the organization have for acquiring new customers? What are the organization's customers wrestling with and worried over?

- **Business strategy.** What are the key goals of the organization in the next six months? A year? Five years? How are these goals to be achieved? Where and how are people figured into the equation? What systems support the strategy? What new processes need to be created to help drive the achievement of the organization's strategy?

We have merely touched upon "the basics" here. Academic disciplines, shelves full of books, and entire lifetimes have been devoted to the study of a single element within one of the three broad areas of knowledge described above. When you add it all up, HR professionals need to know much about many things. Figure 4.2 shows "the basics."

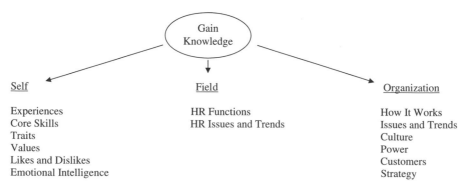

Figure 4.2 Areas of knowledge needed for HR success.

Apply Knowledge

Our model avoids the dictum of "knowledge for knowledge's sake." We question the value of knowledge, however acquired, unless it is applied in some way, at least in the context of being successful in HR. Thus, the second component of our success model involves deploying knowledge in some fashion (versus just talking or thinking about it). This is where you put your knowledge to the test. It is where you live every day.

You might be wondering what two Ph.D.s know about applying knowledge or if they even apply knowledge in the first place. Both of us are, at heart, practical people. Bill's approach in his university classes has always been about the practice of HR and not solely the theories, concepts, and models of HR that can inform that practice. He is, by nature, a "pracademic" and has been accused by some of his more intellectually purist colleagues as "too practical" or "anti-intellectual." He considers these attributes compliments. Jennifer's approach with adult learners is similar in that she always ties course materials to the realities her participants and clients are dealing with all the time. Likewise, her career counseling firm is in business to help clients take concrete actions to solve whatever career dilemmas they are facing. Yes, we want you to continue thinking as you read this book. And more than that, we want you to apply that thinking to the realities you face every day. Shaping an HR career is not a purely intellectual pursuit!

What, then, does applying knowledge entail? There are five major components: (1) accessing knowledge, (2) choosing appropriate roles, (3) showing value, (4) earning trust and credibility, and (5) honoring boundaries. Next, we will explore what each of these components entails.

Accessing Knowledge

What you know will be useless if you can't access this knowledge. It is thus important for you, as an HR professional, to keep your repositories of knowledge in all three areas (self, field, organization) easily accessible at all times. Often, much of this knowledge will be in your head. Sometimes, you will need to lean on sources outside yourself (for example, literature and other people) to access the knowledge. Just the other day, Meredith Hodges, one of our interviewees, called to seek Bill's ideas for books, articles, and other resources before she contacted an outside vendor about a training course it had designed. Another interviewee, Dianne Smith, leaned on external consultants for a framework to use in her work on an organizational change initiative. Whether you tap into your own knowledge base or that of others, you need to be organized so that whatever knowledge you need is available quickly.

As we have already noted, much of the important HR work you face is difficult, complex, and challenging. Thus, you need to be able to easily combine and integrate areas of knowledge when tackling such issues. For example, you may be faced with a compensation issue that likely has talent retention, motivation, and cost-benefit ramifications. Facing the compensation issue from a strictly technical standpoint (that is, access compensation system knowledge) will therefore likely be inadequate and possibly harmful. If you view issues narrowly (from one perspective using a single base of knowledge), then you are enslaved by the "hammer in search of a nail syndrome." When you are a hammer and only a hammer, every problem, challenge, and opportunity looks like a nail. Everyone knows this is rarely the case.

Another very critical component of accessing knowledge is an important part of self-knowledge—learning from mistakes. In fact, making mistakes can often be the most helpful way to learn and retain what you've learned. So when accessing your knowledge, don't forget to draw upon the critical lessons you have learned (and perhaps relearned) from the mistakes you and others have made. Yes, you can learn much from others' mistakes as well as your own, and the process is often less painful with the former!

Choosing Appropriate Roles

Choosing appropriate roles ultimately results in making sound decisions about which role or combination of roles (see the nine-celled matrix in Chapter 3) to apply at the right time with the right people in the right situations. HR is anything but a paint-by-number profession. No true profession really is. When applying appropriate roles, you know, or at least have a pretty good sense of when to act as an expert, guide, director, or helper. Experience (including those inevitable mistakes) is the single best way to aid you in making good role choices. At the same time, solid judgment, intuition, and a willingness to try on new roles will aid in this process. Choosing appropriate roles also involves applying your knowledge to problems and opportunities that matter to the organization, its customers, and its future.

Have you ever decided to work on a project primarily because you thought it would be fun, interesting, and meaningful to you, only later to find out its value to the organization was minimal at best? We are not recommending you always take on work that is un-fun, un-interesting, and un-meaningful to you. Your performance will suffer and no one, including you, will benefit from that. We are recommending you apply your knowledge on selected projects that are valued by the organization and by individual customers, even if the work may appear initially to hold less than optimal levels of fascination to you personally. We realize some of you may not have a real choice when you are assigned and not asked to work on a project. Still, we think you can be more strategic in your work and what and how you do that work. In addition, you should leverage your knowledge in ways that align with the culture of the organization. Otherwise, you run the risk of beating your head against the proverbial wall, and the wall will win. So if your organization's culture values exceeding customer expectations, enact the roles that will likely produce that outcome for you. If your culture emphasizes thoughtful analyses before taking risks, make sure your role or roles reflect this behavior. At times, it may be appropriate for the HR professional to challenge the existing culture. You can still act in ways that recognize the current culture while pushing for culture change.

Showing Value

Like any enterprise, HR must identify its customers' needs and then tailor its products and services to meet those needs. Thus, when you apply your knowledge, you need to do so in ways that your customers understand and value. As a customer (or consumer) yourself, don't you expect a service provider to explain what the service can and cannot do for you in ways you can easily understand? And isn't your choice whether to purchase that service from that person contingent, at least in part, on your being confident that the provider understands and appreciates your needs and priorities? We strongly believe HR's customers are no different. So in addition to showing customers you understand and appreciate them, you also need to apply your knowledge on those things that your customers worry about. This means that you must be market-driven rather than product-driven. When you say you are "a defined-contribution benefits consultant," you are being the latter. When you say you "identify your client's defined-contribution benefits needs and then design tailor-made solutions to those needs," you are acting in a market-driven manner.

To identify your customers' real needs, you must do all you can to make it easy for them to tell you what is really going on in their organization and with themselves. Being market-driven in the initial stages of working with a customer (sometimes referred to as "the needs identification stage") means you really try to understand and appreciate what you hear clients tell you while holding off on trying to convince them how valuable you can be. Your clients should not have to expend much effort to determine whether you understand and appreciate their needs.

Showing value also entails a genuine willingness to help clients even when you should not be involved with them on some task. Suppose a manager comes to you for help with a concern he has about the performance of one of his direct reports. As you try to understand the issue and uncover the manager's real needs, it becomes apparent that you lack the knowledge, skills, and/or abilities required to help the manager directly. You can, however, refer the manager to other people who you think can help him. In that way, you are taking an ethical path and doing your client a service. Showing value often entails employing consulting competencies such as those suggested by Green (2002). These competencies include but are not limited to managing relationships, providing advice and counsel that is influential, employing process skills, uncovering real client/customer needs (rather than simply being an order taker based on what clients say they want from you), and possessing a genuine desire to be helpful.

Earning Trust and Credibility

The adage that trust and credibility can take years to acquire and seconds to lose applies to HR as well. *All* your actions count. So whether you are applying self-knowledge, HR field knowledge, or organizational knowledge, how they are applied is critically important in establishing and maintaining credibility with others. All the knowledge in the world will mean little if you fail to apply it in ways that enhance others' trust and belief in you. Obviously, this means, at minimum, that you deliver on your commitments. And it goes beyond this. Nearly every one of the successful HR practitioners we interviewed said, in one way or another, that their relationships have been keys to their success. Like a garden, if your relationships aren't cultivated, nourished, and cared for on a constant basis, they will wilt and eventually die. So when you apply your knowledge, you must do so in ways that expand your network and grow what Bozionelos (2003) terms your "social capital."

All the HR functional skills in the world cannot compensate for poor or even mediocre relationships with customers. And your customers simply must know what you offer and have faith that you will be helpful. A considerable amount of work on your part is needed. (And sometimes a little humility is needed as well; for example, when Bill worked as an HR professional in a manufacturing environment at GE, the interviewers told him during the interview process that they would hire him if he agreed not to tell anyone he had a Ph.D. It was thought that his credibility with people on the shop floor would be jeopardized and his educational credentials would threaten the managers he was to serve.) And like a garden that grows weeds when you have not spent enough time caring for it, you cannot put off tending to your relationships "when you have more time." If you prefer the term "networking" to relationship management, then we suggest you network all the time and not just when you smell trouble brewing in your career or when you need customers more than they need you. In Chapter 8, we will provide many concrete actions you can take to expand your networks inside and outside the organization and improve the quality of the relationships you already have.

Honoring Boundaries

While engaged in expanding your networks, increasing your credibility, and enhancing others' trust and faith in you and your services, you must also be mindful that you cannot, and should never try to be, all things to all people. Even the most talented and successful HR professionals probably cannot even be some things to some people. This statement implies that you need to know your limits. Certainly, everyone has limits in terms of skills. But knowing your limits also means being clear about how far you are willing to go in service to others and then respecting yourself by respecting these boundaries. So when you enact a cornerstone of the HR profession, that of helping others, you should never, ever abuse yourself by overcommitting. Honoring yourself by having a high regard for yourself requires that you

- Judge when to push for your ideas and when to back off.
- Know when to hold them and when to fold them.
- Learn to say "no" and not feel guilty.
- Make it easy for customers to do business with you and hard for them to abuse or take advantage of you.
- Be clear what you are and are not responsible for (e.g., help with solutions rather than full accountability for solutions)—that is, determine who has ownership of the process or issue and how much responsibility you are willing to take on.
- Serve others and not be subservient to them.

Several of our interviewees affirmed these points. For example, when asked if they could turn back the clock and do one thing differently, what would it be and why,

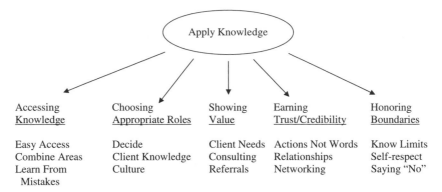

Figure 4.3   Areas of applying knowledge needed for HR success.

a VP of HR said, "Set and honor boundaries." Why did this person say this? Because she had become bogged down with too many tasks for too many customers and ended up not satisfying any of them. Honoring boundaries is often easier said than done. For one, a desire to help is noble. And many people have gone into HR because they valued helping other people. But too much of a good thing is not a good thing, for yourself and for your customers. You cannot help people when you are overextended, doing work others should be doing, and taking on too many commitments.

Figure 4.3 summarizes the key elements in applying your knowledge.

Achieve Results

Acquiring knowledge and applying it effectively as our model suggests will produce results that are valued by both the HR professional and the organization. Although the definition of "success" varies among people, your experience, coupled with the experiences of other seasoned HR professionals, frames "success in an HR career" as a win-win situation between the individual and the organization.

For example, we know of many individuals who have worked long and hard at the HR craft, often achieving the top HR executive position in their organization. Unfortunately, they are not satisfied. They describe their work as an endless series of frustrations, obstacles, and discouragements. Are such people really "successful" despite their six-figure incomes, impressive titles, and significant responsibilities?

On the other hand, we know of others in HR (as well as in other fields) who love their work and have fun doing it. They tell us that overall they are pretty satisfied. However, the organization (particularly influential and powerful managers) does not place a high value on what they are doing in HR, nor do those managers see these HR professionals' contribution as being a critical piece of the organization's goals. Are these HR folks really successful? Are they really as successful as they could be?

So the third major element of our HR Career Success Model, Achieving Results, is really about individual HR professionals deriving benefits they value (be it finding fulfillment, achieving satisfaction, helping others, making money, having autonomy, being creative, something else) and delivering benefits the organization values (be it problems solved, money saved, headaches avoided, productivity increased). Let's take a closer look at what such win-win situations look like.

As Ulrich (1999) notes, successful HR professionals must deliver results. We agree with him that HR has been hampered for too long by its focus on activities and programs with little, if any, attention paid to the results produced by those efforts. For sure, it is very difficult to precisely measure the results of what HR professionals do. And as Ulrich chastises, those in HR often measure what is easy to measure (for example, the number of programs initiated, the number of people participating in the programs) rather than what is right to measure (for example, money saved, effects on productivity). Furthermore, as Sartain (2003) admonishes, one of the surest ways to achieve ineffectiveness is to package your efforts as "an HR program." Such packaging reflects your customers' lack of involvement in and ownership of what you do. Little true success can be achieved in these instances.

Huselid and his colleagues (Becker and Huselid 2003; Beatty, Huselid, and Schneier 2003) studied the effects of HR initiatives on organizational outcomes and found some promising results. For example, they found that those organizations where various HR programs and activities are bundled (that is, integrated into a cohesive, tight package where each HR component is linked to the others) enjoy a 33 percent higher market value compared to organizations without bundled HR practices. Similarly, Caudron (2003) recently discovered that 15–30 percent of an organization's value is linked to the quality and effectiveness of its HR practices. She also found a relationship between the number of effective HR practices in public corporations and the value of their stock shares. In other words, the better an organization's HR practices are, the higher its return to shareholders will be and vice versa. Other studies, such as those conducted annually by The American Society for Training and Development (ASTD), have found a link between the amount of money spent per employee on training and development and the organization's overall performance in the marketplace. A recent stream of research (Bassi and McMurrer 2004) confirms this through empirical evidence showing that those companies that invest in employee development above industry averages in a given year enjoy higher than average shareholder returns the following year.

Although these quantitative approaches to measuring HR success are laudable, and future work on developing and using metrics in HR is certainly warranted, there are additional ways that you can gauge your success on the organizational side of the equation today. Most of our interviewees told us that their success, as measured by their boss, their clients, and themselves, is often achieved through "soft data." For example, such data can be as simple as the kind of feedback received from a client at the end of a project, how often clients come back to you for repeat business or to bounce ideas off you. Another gauge is whether clients see you as a valuable source of referrals on issues on which you cannot and should not assist. Our success model does not, therefore, limit the measurement of success, on the individual side of the equation as well as the organization's side, to quantitative indicators.

Here, then, are the results HR professionals can achieve (however measured) by gaining knowledge (however acquired) and applying it in the ways that our model suggests:

- Expertise is sought (versus you thrusting yourself onto customers). If customers come to you for help, it is likely that they value your expertise and the results you can help them achieve by leveraging that expertise. If you find yourself looking for business more often than customers are looking for you, chances are you need customers more than they need you.
- Satisfied customers do your marketing for you (versus your having to constantly justify what you do and sell yourself). As the saying goes, nothing achieves success like success. When you deliver what you promise and your customers gain benefits from your services, they become satisfied customers of HR. They then tell others what you have done for them and will recommend you. This is a much more powerful marketing strategy than if you are the only one pitching your wares. If you find yourself spending inordinate amounts of time justifying what you do, defending the need for your services, or promoting the benefits of HR, and you are the only one doing these things, chances are you are not achieving the results the organization values.
- You are seen as a valuable resource (versus overhead/an expense). As Schein (in Coutu 2002) notes, deeply held assumptions people have are very

stubborn. They resist change above all else. This implies that you must challenge the assumption, held by some managers and employees, about HR in general and yourself in particular, that you are simply a cost to be minimized rather than an investment to be optimized. Some people will probably never let go of this assumption, wrong as it may be. You must then capitalize on those instances in which your customers do see HR as a wise investment. If everyone in the organization sees you as an overhead item, not appreciably different from a piece of furniture, then you are probably not achieving results that are valued. Conversely, if HR's budget is adequate compared to other functions, and if it reports to the CEO or other titled top job, chances are HR is valued by the organization, as are the people employed in the HR function.

- You are satisfied with yourself and the job you do (versus approaching or falling into burnout, disillusionment, angry cynicism, or discouragement). As we noted previously, if you somehow achieve results that the organization values but are not enjoying the work, ask yourself whether you are achieving success. If you do not gain a sufficient level of satisfaction in the HR work you do, we wonder whether you have achieved results that are signposts of success. We want you to wonder about that, too.

- You are in the loop in important meetings, decisions, and projects (versus wishing you were or finding out about them after they have taken place). When you are seen as a valuable resource, a wise investment, and helpful expert, you are included in important discussions and decisions, especially those that are strategic in nature. If you are not invited, you must ask why and then do what it takes to get an invitation. Then, as Sartain (2003) suggests, you must be involved in important ways in these meetings and discussions by bringing "the HR point of view" into the room. At times, you may need to educate the other participants about the human implications of pending decisions; at other times, you may need to be more confrontational to get your points across. As Sartain notes, your getting an invitation to sit at the table is necessary but insufficient. It's what you do when you are there that matters.

- Customers truly "partner" with you (versus dumping work on you or, worse yet, ignoring you). When we say "truly partner," we mean that at least some of your customers are invested in and involved with the work you are doing on their behalf. If all your work is of the "garage mechanic variety" (that is, you are told to go fix something without the customer working with you to fix whatever it is that needs repair), chances are you are not achieving results that are truly valued by the organization over the long term.

- Customers are demonstrating what they learned from you in their work (and if they are managers, in their subordinates' work). This is, perhaps, the single most valuable "sign of success" that HR professionals can achieve. This sign goes beyond "repeat business." Your clients are actually using what you have taught them. In this way, HR is not just something performed by HR professionals. It is infused throughout the organization. For example, managers are managing employee performance in ways you have taught or advised them. Or employees are being mentored, developed, and led in ways that bring the best out in them and increase their contribution to business results. Your clients see the value of HR to the business of the organization, not just a "nice to have" or "something those HR people do." More than 75 percent of our interviewees stated this outcome as a sign of their success, as measured by hard data, soft data, or a combination of the two. Making a difference in the line organization (your customers' lives and ultimately your customers' customers' lives) is at the heart of this yardstick of success.

- You are seen as an important component of the organization's success (versus being seen as a "nice to have"). Whether the organization measures its success by profit margins, efficiency, customer loyalty, employee retention, or other means, you are seen as contributing to those outcomes in meaningful, significant ways. A clear line of sight exists between your efforts and these organizationally valued outcomes.

- You believe passionately that what you do matters to yourself, to the organization, and to the people you serve (versus seeing yourself as a "nice to have"). If you do not have passion for your work, chances are your customers won't either. If your customers cannot see your passion and feel it, chances are they won't either.

- You encounter values conflicts between you and your customers (versus relationships characterized by outwardly cordial exchanges but deep-seated, unspoken conflicts between you). Having values (or other types of) conflicts as a signpost of success may seem counterintuitive. Consider that if you do not encounter values conflicts on a fairly regular basis, this is likely a sign that either the work you are doing is not highly valued by your customers or you are compromising your own values by being overly compliant toward your customers. For example, one of our customers, a "high middle" level manager, told us (he didn't ask us) to "go get me three minority female engineers. And quick!" The organization had huge federal government contracts, and there were rumors that vast sums of revenue could be lost if the organization did not increase the racial diversity in its

Figure 4.4 Signs of achieving results for HR success.

engineering workforce swiftly. Apparently, this manager's organization was deemed as a target. Although we certainly wanted to be of maximum service to our customer and help avoid very costly ramifications that would result if federal contracts were to go away (not to mention the many people who would become unemployed as a result), we also had a deeply seeded value that the right thing to do is hire the best person for a particular job regardless of race, creed, color, ethnicity, gender, and other job-unrelated demographic factors. We thus had a pretty serious values conflict after being told to find three engineers who were members of a particular racial group and gender. HR professionals face similar values conflicts frequently as they navigate the organizational landscape. Does your organization profess that people are its most valued asset? Does the mission statement say or imply this? How does that compare to the way the organization behaves toward people on a day-to-day basis? If you see some disconnect between the talk and the walk, chances are you, as an HR professional, are going to be facing values conflicts with your customers relatively often. And that is OK. It means you are dealing with important stuff! As mentioned in Chapter 2, values conflicts are part of the HR territory because the agendas of staff and line functions are often in conflict. Remember the tightrope act metaphor?

An overview of the Achieving Results component of our Success Model is illustrated in Figure 4.4.

Additional Considerations

One more aspect of our HR Career Success Model merits attention. You'll note in Figure 4.1 that arrows go in both directions between all the paired components of the model. There are six such pairings: (1) gaining knowledge and applying it,

(2) applying knowledge and achieving results, (3) achieving results and gaining knowledge, (4) applying knowledge and gaining it, (5) achieving results and applying knowledge, and (6) gaining knowledge and achieving results. What does all this mean? Are we adding complexity unnecessarily here? Are we contradicting ourselves when we said earlier that a good model is one that strikes a balance between simplicity and complexity? Obviously, we hope not!

We trust it is fairly evident how the model works when you move within the components in a linear fashion. That is, you gain knowledge, apply it, and then achieve results. However, our own experiences, coupled with what our interviewees told us, suggests that viewing HR career success solely in this way is limiting and does not completely reflect reality in the day-to-day work in HR.

Our model is thus fluid and dynamic rather than rigid and linear. So, when you achieve results, we hope you have gained some knowledge in the process! This knowledge could be self-knowledge, organizational knowledge, or field knowledge. Or two of the three. Or all three. The cycle may then continue by applying this new knowledge to achieve results. Furthermore, applying knowledge in the ways we have described can in and of itself be a vehicle to gain new knowledge (about yourself, the organization, and the field). Likewise, when you achieve valuable results, part of what you take from this experience is learning how to apply knowledge in various situations as well as adding to your repository of knowledge. And when you gain new knowledge, it can be, and often is, the kind of knowledge you need to have to achieve desirable results.

Thus, a key element of our Success Model is learning. And learning from experience. And using that new learning to apply to different situations to achieve results, all of which adds to your learning. Thus, there are six pathways to success, not just one!

Concluding Remarks

The responses we received from our interviewees highlight the many hues of success. When asked to comment on a mistake they had made in their career, several pointed to elements of the Success Model, such as setting and honoring boundaries. When asked to recall a turning point in their career, they gave a variety of responses ranging from "building bridges with top management" and "learning that learning never stops" to "getting line management experience" and "being influential with people who sit on the bottom rungs of the ladder as well as with those who sit in plush chairs in the boardroom." We also heard a range of comments concerning the competences, traits, and qualities HR professionals need today and in the future. Most of these issues are housed somewhere in our model. Examples include knowing the business, using good judgment, being flexible, being customer-focused, having thick skin, being authentic and true to yourself, having integrity, being a strategic thinker, having well-honed diagnostic skills, and being both highly influential and empathic in your multitude of relationships inside and outside the organization.

In revisiting the question "What is success?" that we posed at the beginning of this chapter, we trust our model helps you decide the answer for yourself. We recognize that getting your arms around the question can be confusing at times. Even researchers whose own careers involve the study of career success are often at odds with one another. For example, a study of personality and career success (Siebert, Crant, and Kraimer 1999, 2001) found that political know-how is critically important to achieve success in organizations, while Judge and Bretz (1994) found that one can easily become too political, whereby self-promotion can lead to career failure.

Ultimately, you must decide what constitutes success in your HR career at a given point in time. Use the model throughout your HR career to help you discover what success means and what it looks like to you. What are the results you are going for? Do you want to influence a cultural change in the organization? Do you want to get managers to take more ownership of the hiring process? Be clear and specific about what outcomes you seek that spell success for you, your customers, and your organization. Then decide what knowledge you need to tap to get the job done. Look at what new knowledge you need to acquire and the parts of your current knowledge base that you need to expand. You can then move into action mode. Never stop learning.

Despite the fact that HR is a helping profession and is inherently linked to what other people do (and don't do), consider that in many ways success in HR is "an inside job." You can always find people who think you are not successful. That is their opinion. You needn't be enslaved to it. You certainly don't need to agree with it.

In addition, don't tie success to perfection. All of our interviewees, highly successful by most definitions, currently have development needs. And they always will. Lifelong learning and development are cornerstones of being successful and continuing on the path of success for HR professionals. And yes, sometimes that learning is not fun at all. It can be painful (Coutu 2002).

If you never consider yourself successful until you have mastered everything there is to learn in HR, your success will be illusive and elusive. What matters is that you are willing to recognize your shortcomings and then do something about them. That is what the next three chapters are all about—putting our Success Model to use in shaping your HR role. In so doing, there will be good fits between you and an HR job, you and your HR career, and you and the organization in which you practice your craft.

References

Bassi, L, and D McMurrer. 2004. "How's Your Return on People?" *Harvard Business Review* 82, no. 3: 18.

Beatty, RW, MA Huselid, and CE Schneier. 2003. "New HR Metrics: Scoring on the Balanced Scorecard." *Organizational Dynamics* 32, no. 2: 107–120.

Becker, B, and M Huselid. 2003. "Measuring HR?" *HR Magazine* 48, no. 12: 56.

Bozionelos, N. 2003. "Intra-organizational Network Resources: Relation to Career Success and Personality." *International Journal of Organizational Analysis* 11, no. 1: 41–66.

Caudron, S. 2003. "HR Is Dead. Long Live HR." *Workforce* January: 23–26.

Coutu, DL. 2002. "The Anxiety of Learning." *Harvard Business Review* March: 2–8.

Deer, CB. 1986. "Five Definitions of Career Success: Implications for Relationships." *International Review of Applied Psychology* 35, no. 3: 415–435.

Green, ME. 2002. "Internal HR Consulting: Why Doesn't Your Staff Get It?" *Public Personnel Management* 31, no. 1: 111–119.

Judge, TA, and RD Bretz. 1994. "Political Influence Behavior and Career Success." *Journal of Management* 20, no. 1: 43–65.

Judge, TA, DM Cable, JW Boudreau, and RD Bretz. 1995. "An Empirical Investigation of the Predictors of Executive Career Success." *Personnel Psychology* 48, no. 3: 485–519.

Sartain, L. 2003. *HR from the Heart.* New York: AMACOM.

Schein, EH. 1990. *Career Anchors: Discovering Your Real Values.* San Diego: Pfeiffer.

Siebert, SE, JA Crant, and ML Kraimer. 1999. "Proactive Personality and Career Success." *Journal of Applied Psychology* 84, no. 3: 416–427.

———. 2001. "What Do Proactive People Do? A Longitudinal Model Linking Proactive Personality and Career Success." *Personnel Psychology* 54, no. 4: 845–874.

Ulrich, D. 1999. "Advance from Activities to Results." *HR Focus* 76, no. 4: 1–4.

5

Actions to Take: Self-Knowledge

Consider these two scenarios: In the first, you are talking with someone about a topic and they light up. The words come out faster, there is a twinkle in their eye, and you can't help but be drawn into their excitement. The topic could be aviation, fashion, or the new web-based learning system in their company. All you know is that person has some kind of passion about that subject (in fact—sometimes you can't even get them to stop talking about it!), and they want to share their excitement with you.

In the second scenario, you meet a lawyer who left a successful career as a litigator with lots of money and recognition. She talks of moving into such a deep depression that she had contemplated suicide. It was only after stepping out of the path of this downward career spiral and getting help that she realized she was never meant to be a lawyer. She entered law originally because friends and family had told her, "You write and speak well and can argue."

Why Self-Assessment?

How can work generate such interest and, on the other hand, such disillusionment? It has, in our opinion, a great deal to do with the fit. How well do you match who you are with the work you are doing and where you are doing it? By understanding yourself and discovering work that plays to your experience, skills, traits, values, and emotional intelligence, you increase your chances of becoming the person in scenario one—a person who is energized by and connected with the work he or she does. This chapter will provide some ideas for ways to get there.

Why else is it important for you to know yourself? In addition to making appropriate career choices, knowing who you are helps you to stay rooted in the many twists and turns of your job. When called upon to make decisions, to deal with ambiguity, and to show empathy for your clients, you can be more effective when you know your strengths and weaknesses. This knowledge helps you to be more objective, detach when you have to, and show appropriate concern when called for. Understanding your limitations also allows you to ask for help when you need it and not shortchange your clients by letting your need to be known as the expert impede your effectiveness. Self-awareness also helps you realize the value you bring to the team and gives you the confidence to ask for the challenging assignments and pay you deserve.

Several years ago we were moderating a series of leadership development seminars at a Fortune 10 company. Senior executives were asked about the greatest mistake they had made, a question we asked our interviewees for this book (see Appendix C). One by one they told of embarrassing mistakes they had thought were career ending at the time. In one such class, the Senior Vice President of Finance told of introducing the current CEO to a group of investors and butchering the pronunciation of his name. He hesitated for a few seconds after talking about this situation and broke out in laughter. The rest of the class joined in with him, and the decibel level increased as they allowed themselves to relax. Being able to laugh at himself made this usually serious man more human. He was also modeling the behavior he wanted these high potential managers to emulate. The ability to "lighten up" and not take yourself too seriously is also at the root of honest self-appraisal.

Should you take your job seriously? Yes. Should you take your organization seriously? Yes. Should you take your HR career seriously? Yes. Then how much should you take yourself seriously? As little as possible.

Your organization and clients also reap tremendous benefits when you display solid knowledge of yourself. As we know now from the research done on high-performing organizations, leadership is a characteristic that occurs in all levels of employees. Companies thrive when they cultivate leadership through the system (Goleman, Boyatzis, and McKee 2002, 36). Former GE CEO Jack Welch, a renowned and respected business leader, required his managers to engage in ongoing assessment. Many organizations have integrated multi rater feedback systems into their performance and development processes. They encourage people to use the feedback they get to develop themselves in specific areas and support that development with training and coaching. The investment of millions of dollars in the executive coaching industry is also evidence that organizations see a correlation between self-assessment and improved performance. Coaches work on helping clients to eliminate blind spots, and clients use this awareness to make changes in how they lead.

Recent work on emotional intelligence reinforces the importance of self-awareness when taking on the leadership roles required of HR professionals today. In their book *Primal Leadership*, Goleman, Boyatzis, and McKee (2002) state, "Simply put, self-awareness means having a deep understanding of one's emotions, as well as one's strengths and limitations and one's values and motives. . . . People with strong self-awareness are realistic—neither overly self-critical nor naively hopeful. Rather, they are honest about themselves with others, even to the point of being able to laugh at their own foibles."

The authors go on to say, "Self-aware leaders also understand their values, goals and dreams. They know where they are headed and why. Because the decisions of self-aware people mesh with their values they often find their work energizing. All of these traits enable them to act with conviction and authenticity . . ." (2002, 40).

Because you are a helping professional in the business of supporting people, what you don't know about yourself can both affect yourself and those you are attempting to help. Self-awareness opens the door to a new, honest self-perspective. By understanding your potential biases and playing on your skills and strengths, you are better able to prepare for the complex situations you face each day. By being open to ongoing self-assessment, you minimize your blind spots and greatly increase your effectiveness.

What Is Involved in Self-Assessment?

In the rest of this chapter, we will provide ideas and strategies for pursuing self-assessment. Each section will focus on another aspect of the process. We will examine aspects of the self-assessment journey through the use of examples, tools, and focused questions you can ask yourself at each juncture. We will focus mainly on six aspects of self-assessment that we think are critical signposts. They are (1) experience, (2) skills, (3) traits, (4) values, (5) likes and dislikes, and (6) emotional intelligence. Other components of self-assessment also can be explored, and we provide references for them in the book and on our website (www.myhrsuccess.com).

As a young child, our older daughter used to squeeze herself and say, "I can't believe I am me!" In her youthful innocence, she was expressing the excitement of being alive. As you consider the components of self-awareness, we hope you will turn the mirror toward yourself, experience this same sense of uniqueness, and most of all, learn from it.

Experience—The Great Teacher

The past is one predictor of the future. You are made up of your life experiences, and you are greatly influenced by those experiences. You can learn from them if you take the time to do some honest reflection upon them. Choosing HR as a career was a conscious choice by some of our interview respondents, and for others it was pure serendipity. Somewhere along the way, all of them realized that they enjoyed helping people, solving problems, and seeing results. It was only after they were exposed to different work and life experiences that they refined their focus and discovered the right fit.

Dianne Smith was a university librarian who knew she wanted to advance. When a Personnel Officer position came open, a mentor encouraged her to apply. She said that as the oldest of five children she was used to taking on extra responsibility. "I had taken on additional duties (in my librarian role) such as creating a training plan and planning student activities and found that I liked those kinds of projects." Human resources was a natural segue for her. Dianne returned to school and earned a master's degree in Human Resource Development. Since then, she has moved on to a larger HR role in another university and seems to have found her niche.

In listening to our interviewees reflect on their careers, we were struck by how important learning has been in their lives. A majority of respondents told us that the stimulating nature of Human Resources—that is, the opportunity to acquire new skills—was a key reason they stayed in this challenging field. Research also shows us that learning is a key work motivator (Buckingham 2001). People experience more work satisfaction when they are learning.

Kay Yoest, Vice President of Human Resources at Munich American Reinsurance Company, reflected on her career as a series of steps, each one preparing her for the next move. "I was pretty deliberate in my moves," she said. "All my jobs were built for the one above." She even took lateral moves when she felt that she could learn new skills and strategies, an approach we strongly recommend. Volunteering for diverse projects in compensation, affirmative action, and training also helped her to continually ramp up her expertise.

In a period of two years, Kay moved from the excitement of building up a high-tech company to the low of dismantling an entire organization. She was able to parlay this strategic business experience from her 20 years as an HR generalist into her current role. Kay hit the ground running and has already successfully integrated multiple benefits systems. She is proud of the fact that she has become the "go-to person" in her organization and HR community and attributes this success to her willingness to take charge of her own ongoing learning.

Kimberly Douglas, President of Firefly Facilitation and former president of SHRMAtlanta, felt that some of her greatest insights came from time spent in the field. She provided us with vivid verbal snapshots of running meetings for housekeeping staff in crowded hotel bedroom suites, wearing her fast-food company uniform and going on "runs" with delivery truck drivers. These pivotal learning experiences greatly influenced her. "It helped me not to be an ivory tower person and understand their (my clients') issues. I also gained credibility and confidence."

As in the case of the executive described earlier, making mistakes is a major part of the learning odyssey. When we asked our interviewees about their biggest mistake, the answers were all over the map. Focusing on the right goals, underestimating people's resistance, and getting sucked up in politics were just a few they mentioned. They also followed up with telling us what they had learned from their experiences—that is, the power of making mistakes. You don't learn from the easy times; the chance to grow comes from the post-game replay. "What can I do differently the next time?", they all asked themselves.

We were working for a consulting firm that required HR consultants to sell a certain amount of business. Closing a deal with a client meant that the consultant would receive a percentage of the sale. After several successful sales, we learned that the amount due us had been calculated in favor of the regional sales manager who sliced a hefty amount off the top. Confronting the sales manager didn't resolve the situation, and eventually the disagreement led to a breakdown in the relationship with this person. What do you think we learned from this experience? You are right if you said, (1) Watch your back or someone may stab you, and (2) Clarify specific expectations up front and in writing—especially when it comes to money. A third important lesson, in retrospect, was the realization that we weren't motivated primarily by money. Thus, a seemingly unfortunate event turned out to be a very helpful one because it affirmed that the sales profession was not where we wanted to go. Now let's look at how, in addition to building on experience, it is also important to examine what skills and strengths you have to offer.

Skills—What Do You Bring to the Table?

When Marketing professionals figure out how to best position a product, they search for the unique, appealing features and benefits it offers. Diet cola may taste

OK and be sold at a decent price, all features of the product. The real benefit to consumers, however, is that it has no calories. These marketers have to do their research to determine the unique selling point or USP. In similar fashion, the self-assessment process mirrors marketing a product. You need to do research to understand your skills and assets and the way your USPs can serve to benefit different types of organizations.

Skills are basically those things you do well. Transferable skills are those talents that are portable. If you are a good problem solver, you can take that skill and transfer it to any one of thousands of work environments. The same is true with decision-making, organizational, or communication skills. You get the picture. There are numerous inventories of transferable skills. One interactive, free resource we located is www.careergames.com. You can find a complete inventory of transferable skills there. Others are available on line by doing a little research.

As an HR professional, you need to focus on the specific skills that are called on in your field. We have reviewed the literature and have drawn from our interviews to identify the major categories of skills necessary for success as an HR practitioner today. We have titled them (1) HR Skills, (2) Business Skills, (3) Interpersonal Skills, and (4) Analytical Skills (see the list in Figure 5.1).

HR Skills	Business Skills	Interpersonal Skills	Analytical Skills
HR Legislation	Business Literacy	Consulting	Problem Solving
Recruitment and Staffing	Financial Acumen	Persuading and Influencing	Process Improvement
Compensation	Marketing/Sales	Active Listening	Systems Thinking
Benefits	Measurement	Empathizing	Visionary and Strategic Analysis
Employee Relations	Global Literacy	Negotiating	Applying Technical Solutions
Organizational Development	Managing Change	Coaching/Feedback	
Training Technology	Project Management		
Performance Management	Team Leadership		
	Time Management		

Figure 5.1 Skills needed for today's HR practitioner.

At any one time, your slate of needed HR competencies will vary. Circumstances such as the role and organization you are in will dictate which skills are most in demand. We also ask you to look at this list from an even broader perspective. Also question what you are doing to enhance your expertise in all of these areas. Obviously, the more skills you have under your belt, the more resilient and marketable you will be. In Appendix A, the HR Skills Assessment walks you through a step-by-step process to define your strongest and weakest skills.

After you assess your skills, either by completing the assessment in Appendix A or making a quick assessment of your areas of strengths and weaknesses on this skill listing, you should have a better sense of the areas to which you need to devote some effort. Consider how important these skills are in achieving your current and future goals. These are the critical few you should shine your searchlight on. Focus on the relevant.

Traits—How Do You Approach the World?

In addition to skills, personality characteristics (or traits) are what help you perform at your peak in Human Resources. Richard Bolles, author of *What Color Is Your Parachute?* (2004), describes traits as the style in which you perform your transferable skills. If you are strong at problem solving, you might demonstrate that skill using a linear, logical outline. On the other hand, you could be a problem solver who uses colorful sticky notes and storyboarding to create a visual picture for yourself. Though you are demonstrating the same skill, you have different ways of getting there. Words such as "structured", "organized", and "focused" might be associated with the first individual we described. On the other hand, "spontaneous"and "creative" could be associated with the second individual.

Understanding your style is helpful in knowing where you fit in and where you can be yourself. Try this exercise: Write your name with your dominant hand. Now try writing it with your other hand. What is the difference in the way you felt between the two? Typically, using the dominant hand will feel easy, quick, and natural. Using your other hand will feel awkward and deliberate. When you are working in an environment or doing a job that draws upon your preferred style, you will feel comfortable and in your element. It is when you are always compensating with your unnatural style that you feel stress, tension, and a general feeling of unease.

Fit played a major role in the stories of many of our interviewees. Several former classroom teachers we interviewed felt that they wanted to have an impact beyond the classroom. The current owner of a successful consulting firm left an auditing job with a large accounting firm because he "was miserable." Some psychology majors were drawn to the more results-oriented world of corporate HR. Usually, you can make things work for a while. You can find enough tasks to interest you, or you connect with people from whom you can learn. But ultimately, you are unhappier the more time goes by unless you initiate a change in the job or work environment.

The other tremendous benefit in understanding your personality preferences is using this knowledge as a framework for understanding and working with others. You can apply this information to communicate in a way that others will understand you. Furthermore, becoming more effective in managing your work relationships is directly connected to job satisfaction (Deer 1986).

You can take a number of assessments to determine your key personality type. The more popular ones are the Meyers Briggs Type Indicator (the MBTI), (http://www.cpp.com/), the DISC (http://www.inscapepublishing.com/home), the Birkman (http://www.birkman.com/), and the Hermann Brain Dominance Instrument (http://www.hbdi.com/). It is required that you have a person certified in these instruments to administer and interpret them for you. There are also a number of free instruments you can access on the internet by doing searches. To uncover the key themes of their work style, individuals and organizations use all of these assessments.

According to Tieger and Tieger who have written extensively on personality type and careers (1995), personality type is based on four aspects of human personality: how you interact with the world, what kinds of information you naturally notice, how you make decisions, and whether you prefer to live in a more structured way or in a more spontaneous way. Understanding how you fit into these dimensions becomes very useful as you assess the work you are doing and in making career choices (http://www.inscapepublishing.com/home.asp).

Traits for HR Success

Figure 5.2 lists the traits we consider among the "Top 10 Lineup." They were mentioned the most by our interviewees and are repeatedly stressed in the literature as critical components of the HR professional's toolkit. Consider what traits you think are important to develop and leverage the ones you are already strong in.

| Comfortable with Ambiguity |
| Comfortable with Risk Taking |
| Innovative |
| Flexible |
| Has Integrity |
| Authentic |
| Perseveres |
| Big Picture Thinker |
| Empathetic |
| Enthusiastic |

Figure 5.2 "Top 10" traits for HR success.

In addition to skills and trait assessment, understanding and clarifying your values are also key components of self-assessment. Let's look at the impact of career values in this process.

Values—What Would You Fight For?

We once left a job after deciding that the required lifestyle of the firm (frequent travel and long hours) did not match up with our needs as parents of young children. Subsequently, we found an internal position in an organization. Although this position was not as intense and challenging as the previous job we had left, it allowed us to "be who we were" and better suited our needs at the time. Values are the drivers that determine how you achieve satisfaction at work and at home. Living by your strong beliefs or values allows you to maximize your performance, job satisfaction, and emotional investment in your work. Understanding what your values are is immensely useful in making wise choices about the career steps that you make.

It is important to realize that your values and needs change over time. Although advancement and recognition may have been very important to you at one time, now you may be more interested in a dynamic learning opportunity, for example. Trade-offs are also a part of the values discussion. Having it all is just not possible. So although that lateral move we just described enabled us to spend more time with family, we probably missed out on some interesting travel experiences.

In addition to lifestyle and family, what are some other examples of work-related values? Opportunities to help others, advancement opportunities, intellectual stimulation, collaboration with others, structure, and predictability are all different work motivators. We often ask clients to rank their values from a selected list and choose the top five. That task is often difficult and challenging because people tend to want it all. But if you get a clearer idea about what is most important to you in your life right now, then you will be much more goal directed and focused in making career choices.

Not surprisingly, work/life balance came up high on the radar screen of most of our interviewees. This is a direct symptom of the action-packed lifestyles people lead. We believe that it is important to understand how you can effectively align your espoused and enacted values—that is, to walk your own talk.

Try a brief exercise to illustrate this point. Draw two circles. Now divide the first circle like a pie with portions representing how, if given the opportunity, you would like to apportion the time in your week. See Figure 5.3 for a sample pie chart reflecting these divisions. Categories might include work, family, health and wellness, etc.

In the second circle, divide the pie. This time, ask yourself how much time you are *actually* spending in each section each week. Is there a difference between the two? Where are the gaps? Are you comfortable with the trade-offs you are making? Why? Over which areas do you have more control than others? This visual representation can help you to see quickly where you may want to recalibrate. If the family, for instance, is getting shortchanged, can you look at adjusting your schedule to better meet your family needs? Have you considered telecommuting some days or learning to get better at saying "no" when you are overloaded? Have you used all your vacation time this year? Perhaps some of the chores around the house

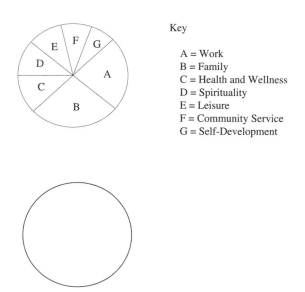

Key

A = Work
B = Family
C = Health and Wellness
D = Spirituality
E = Leisure
F = Community Service
G = Self-Development

Figure 5.3 Work/life balance exercise.

can be delegated or renegotiated? Some slight adjustments can make an impact on closing the gap between the two pies.

You also can interpret the pie exercise by asking yourself, "What is my desired, or ideal vision of the way I would be living this value? Now, what is the reality?" Keep in mind that a value is not truly a value unless you are living it. See Appendix A for a values inventory to help you gain even more clarity.

Likes and Dislikes—Knowing What Excites (and Deflates) You

Tuning your dial into your critical likes and dislikes is also essential in getting clear signals about what work activities to focus on. What skills you enjoy using, the type of work that "floats your boat," and the climate you perform it in all contribute to career satisfaction. These areas relate to the experiences, skills, and traits discussed earlier in this chapter. Each person has his or her own unique imprint of likes and dislikes, and the clues are often found in your life outside work.

Case in point: We recently took a break from writing to travel in Europe. One of us relaxed after a full day of sightseeing by poring over maps to chart the next day's ventures. The other was equally as absorbed in reading and talking about the history and people of each region. The map-reader thrived on using his problem solving, logic, and special abilities to plan the best route possible. Studying social and cultural forces energized the historian. If asked to switch roles, our focus and energy would not have been there. As with the left and right hand exercise earlier, it just wouldn't be natural for the historian to study maps and for the map reader to study history.

When speaking with HR professionals for this book, we allotted a set amount of time for each interview. Inevitably, the discussions ran overtime as the interviewees expressed themselves with zest and excitement. As we mentioned in the beginning of this chapter, this is what happens when you find people who work in "the zone." They care deeply about what they do. This outcome also seems to occur when you like or enjoy what you are doing.

So what did our HR sample say they liked most about the world they inhabit each day? Many of them used words such as "passion" and "calling" when discussing their careers. They relish the endless variety and the fact that they are never bored. A majority spoke of the ability to make a significant impact on others and organizations. Related to this was the opportunity to solve problems. Continuous learning and the ability to grow and stretch were also high on the list. One interviewee stated with satisfaction, "I grew well beyond where I thought I could."

At the same time, recognizing your dislikes is also important. Parts of your work won't be enjoyable. Some aspects of any job are required and are not highly enjoyable, such as taking out the garbage or doing the laundry. External HR consultants have all the joys and agonies of owning a business. For instance, managing a business—even if it is only "Me, Inc."—involves accounting, marketing, plus many operations and tasks that are not directly related to performing Human Resource consulting. If you work in this role, you need to accept these other business-related tasks and perform them competently (or delegate them) to be able to do the work you may really want to be engaged in—HR consulting.

You can gain clarity into your likes and dislikes in a number of ways. Go into a bookstore with no plan in mind. Where do you find yourself browsing? Is it the self-help, cooking, or biography section? Where you roam provides some important clues as to where your key interests are. And know that just because you wander over to art books doesn't mean you are destined to become an artist. A good guess might be that you have a creative streak within you. Self-expression is probably important to you. Or perhaps you appreciate aesthetics and your surroundings are critical. You need to find a way to satisfy that interest through work or leisure.

You can perform the next exercise with a partner who is interested in self-assessment. We run this exercise in groups and are always amazed at how much rich information emerges. Ask each other the following questions and take time to listen to the answers. You can paraphrase and ask open-ended questions to encourage deeper exploration.

1. What do you enjoy most about your work?
2. What does that do for you? What do you get from that?
3. What do you like least about your work? Why?
4. Is there anything I can do to support you in this?

Another way of assessing yourself has gained increasing popularity in recent years. Let's look at the concept of emotional intelligence and the ways you can use this idea to deepen your understanding of the ways you manage your relationships and yourself.

Emotional Intelligence

Emotional intelligence (EI), a concept popularized by Daniel Goleman (Goleman, Boyatzis, and McKee 2002), refers to the idea that the measure of your success depends not just on your intellectual ability but the way in which you manage yourself and your relationships. Richard Boyatzis, another pioneer in the field, writes that emotional intelligence arose from the realization that many more competencies than just cognitive ones distinguish outstanding and effective performers. He drew his research from a cross section of occupations and roles around the globe (2004).

To us, this notion is a powerful one. EI is that *je ne sais quoi* that emerges in those leaders you come across. Those people who know just how to read a situation and communicate and build trust with those around them have high levels of EI. At the same time, everyone has known people who have a serious lack of EI! Brilliant though they may be, they either don't control their emotions or fail in their ability to connect with others and thus are not successful at many of their initiatives. If you look at the EI framework as a way to enhance your self-knowledge, it will help to know which qualities to work on. In the next section, we will provide an overview of EI, illustrate how some of these principles can be applied to typical HR situations, and describe how they pertain to success. We will also suggest some "quick actions" to take to immediately enhance your EI. As in the other sections in this chapter, see the Emotional Intelligence Assessment in Appendix A for a more in-depth exercise on emotional intelligence.

Emotional Intelligence Categories

In *Primal Leadership*, Goleman, Boyatzis, and McKee (2002) identify four emotional intelligence components: (1) self-awareness, (2) self-management, (3) social awareness, and (4) relationship management (see Figure 5.4). We consider all of these elements essential for any HR professional's success.

Self-Awareness

The self-awareness component of emotional intelligence involves having emotional self-awareness, taking an accurate self-assessment, and having self-confidence. Being able to read your emotions and recognize their impact on you as well as using an intuitive sense to guide decisions is also essential. Let's look at some examples.

When we were leading a recent three-day management seminar, a class participant who refused to participate in any class exercises threw us off balance. We found ourselves increasingly irritated at her behavior and were concerned that she would have a negative impact on the group. At a break, we approached her to find

Emotional Intelligence Domains and Associated Competencies

PERSONAL COMPETENCE: These capabilities determine how we manage ourselves.

SELF-AWARENESS

- Emotional self-awareness: Reading one's own emotions and recognizing their impact; using "gut sense" to guide decisions
- Accurate self-assessment: Knowing one's strengths and limits
- Self-confidence: A sound sense of one's self-worth and capabilities

SELF-MANAGEMENT

- Emotional self-control: Keeping disruptive emotions and impulses under control
- Transparency: Displaying honesty and integrity; trustworthiness
- Adaptability: Flexibility in adapting to changing situations or overcoming obstacles
- Achievement: The drive to improve performance to meet inner standards of excellence
- Initiative: Readiness to act and seize opportunities
- Optimism: Seeing the upside in events

SOCIAL COMPETENCE: These capabilities determine how we manage relationships.

SOCIAL AWARENESS

- Empathy: Sensing others' emotions, understanding their perspective, and taking active interest in their concerns
- Organizational awareness: Reading the currents, decision networks, and politics at the organizational level
- Service: Recognizing and meeting follower, client, or customer needs

RELATIONSHIP MANAGEMENT

- Inspirational leadership: Guiding and motivating with a compelling vision
- Influence: Wielding a range of tactics for persuasion
- Developing others: Bolstering others' abilities through feedback and guidance
- Change catalyst: Initiating, managing, and leading in a new direction
- Conflict management: Resolving disagreements
- Teamwork and collaboration: Cooperation and team building

Reprinted by permission of Harvard Business School Press. From Primal Leadership *by Daniel Goleman, Richard Boyatzis, and Annie McKee. Boston, MA, p. 39. Copyright © 2002 by Daniel Goleman; all rights reserved.*

Figure 5.4 Emotional intelligence domains and associated competencies.

out how we might assist in improving her learning experience. In that discussion, we learned that she had recently lost her younger brother to cancer. Our feelings of frustration changed to those of empathy, and we were able to demonstrate patience and allow her to engage in the class on her own time frame and in her own way. Being able to understand and filter our own personal reactions in this situation prevented us from wasting energy on trying to "rope her in." She eventually did become a part of the interaction. Having self-awareness enabled us to practice acceptance and tolerance, which was of great benefit in this situation.

In another scenario, one of our interviewees, who was a manager of training and OD, was honest in his appraisal of his developmental areas. As a recent hire, he admitted openly that he still was not up to speed on the business issues facing his company and planned to take a few key individuals to lunch to learn about recent critical changes in the organization. Greg Day, owner of an HR consulting firm, worked for the Monsanto Corporation as a production worker for more than 11 years. He decided that he was going to move out of that role after becoming introduced to Human Resources by a mentor in the company. Greg carefully assessed his interests and goals and mapped out a structured career plan with timelines and goals. He then relocated to a university that offered a master's degree in Human Resource Development so that he could break into the field.

Linda Kammire Tiffin, Ph.D., a psychologist and principal of her own firm, learned to pay attention to the signs of burnout. Early in her career, she says that she stayed on longer than she should have in one position. After that time, she learned to listen to herself and take action when she was feeling overwhelmed by work.

What about self-confidence? Carol Dubnicki, who is a Vice President of Human Resources with Shell Oil's Exploration and Production business in the Netherlands, exhibited a high degree of self-confidence, one of the hallmarks of self-awareness when she stated, "I am as smart as almost anyone I deal with. I have the conceptual ability and the quality of thinking that is necessary. I also have to be practical and get results." Carol says that her strong sense of self-worth was the reason she was able to successfully turn around highly resistant departments. She also believes that by being true to herself and not being "a yes person," she "is able to help people be more creative."

Self-Awareness Quick Action: 1) Write down three developmental goals for this year. 2) In what situations at work do you want to practice taking a breather before reacting? 3) What do you want to improve in yourself? 4) Where can you take initiative on the job or on your own? 5) What can you do to improve your self-confidence?

Self-Management

The next key dimension of EI, self-management, includes emotional self-control, transparency, adaptability, achievement, initiative, and optimism. Keeping your emotions in check does not mean you repress them but that you respond thoughtfully instead of reacting impulsively. Often clients or other employees may frustrate you, but you learn to think through your responses to maintain the relationship.

One senior HR executive demonstrated how she used self-management to handle an uncomfortable situation at a business dinner. The CEO of her company had too much to drink and was using some off-color humor in his stories. The HR executive noticed several people around the table, in addition to herself, looking uncomfortable. She let the situation pass and the next day paid a visit to the CEO. She gave him specific feedback on the impact she thought his behavior had on the group and suggested that this wasn't the kind of behavior she thought he wanted to model for his organization. What he chose to do with the feedback was up to him. She maintained her dignity by choosing the proper setting to share the seriousness of her concern with him.

Taking initiative was mentioned several times through our interviews. We have been hearing for years the maxim that everyone is in charge of his or her own career. In addition, this quality is also highly valued by management in today's fast-paced and competitive environment. New ideas and innovative approaches to getting things done are essential today. Yet how many people step out of their comfort zones to make an effort to do this? It often becomes easier to sit back and wait to be asked to do a project or make a move. Unfortunately and increasingly, this move will push you out the door as internal HR positions shrink in number.

A director of leadership programs at an international communications company had a pivotal experience in this regard. For more than eight years, she had performed well and was promoted to positions of increasing responsibility. "It just happened for me . . . ," she said. A job that was not within her specialty became available, but she thought she could do it and decided to apply for the position. Explicit in her application as to why her skills and expertise transferred, she was successful in landing the opportunity and several more after that. She firmly believes that her initiative has paid off handsomely in great career opportunities.

Self-Management Quick Action: Take "five." Write down all the emotions you are feeling before you respond to that angry outburst.

Social Awareness

Social awareness, the third major element of EI, refers to having empathy, demonstrating organizational awareness, and providing service. Empathy is the glue that helps people to respond to you. Chris Lee, Director of Human Resources at Bates College, believes that his ability to provide support, direction, and advice to other people is the key success factor in his career. He sees his role as "nurturing a community of people" and "being human and productive as an organization."

High performer Meredith Hodges, who started out in economic development at the Georgia Power Company, demonstrated being aware of her organization. After receiving a master's degree in Human Resource Development, she moved into various HR roles at her company. As a person who has strong organizational savvy, she knew that to increase her credibility with employees and managers, she needed to "walk the talk." Meredith worked with her boss to obtain an operations job. While there, she gained new perspectives on the business and utilized her HR background to achieve results as a line manager. She was recently promoted to Manager of Key Accounts for Southern Company Gas. Meredith knows that when she returns to Human Resources, her customers will perceive her through new eyes.

Keeping the relationship on the "right track"(Goleman, Boyatzis, and McKee 2002) and providing excellent customer service are threads that ran through all our interviews. In our experience, these actions are both critical to the HR role. At the beginning of your involvement with your clients and throughout your career, you need to build bridges by assessing who your stakeholders are, understanding their goals, and determining how you can best help them to meet their goals. A part of service also involves making yourself available as needed.

Dave Potts, a Manager of Training and Development, sees himself as a key resource for leadership development in his organization. Art Blake, a former internal Organizational Effectiveness consultant, put some parameters around this helping role. He saw himself earning trust with his clients by "challenging them compassionately, by being authentic and . . . by not hustling them."

Social Awareness Quick Action: 1) Put time on your calendar each week to meet informally with other departments. Make an effort to listen and show an interest in people across the organization. 2) Before your next client meeting, pretend you are them and write down the issue you are discussing from their view.

Relationship Management

The last key component of EI, relationship management, involves such elements as providing inspirational leadership, using influence, developing others, being a change catalyst, managing conflict, and facilitating teamwork and collaboration. You need to think of yourself as a leader using these skills if you are to impact people as strategic business partners. Following are a few selected examples from this list; others will be described in later chapters.

John Courtney, Learning Technologies Manager at Intercontinental Hotels Group, echoed the sentiment of many of our interviewees when he said, "It is not about the power . . . all you can do is influence." Coaching managers, employees, and team members has also become a critical part of the equation. Meredith Hodges spoke with pride of the opportunity to apply her coaching skills to turn around a nonperforming team.

Most HR professionals also describe coaching as an important part of their role. This task involves coaching individuals at all levels of the organization. If these individuals can establish themselves as people to be trusted with valuable insights, then they have unlimited opportunities to help in this way.

Senior management increasingly relies on HR leaders to provide coaching. As a person moves up in an organization, the feedback received from peers and direct reports decrease. The HR professional is often the only person who is able to provide honest feedback to those at the top.

All relationships involve conflict at some level. Resolving those conflicts is a significant part of your role as you find yourself negotiating the needs of different groups. Whether you are helping to resolve disputes between employees and managers or facilitating team interactions, you are often called on to step into the challenging role of mediator.

Accepting conflict as a normal, necessary, and even beneficial life process leads to success in this area. Also, being willing to confront conflict and not shy away from it builds your confidence and competence in handling it. After successfully handling your own conflict situations, you are more equipped to assist others in negotiating successful outcomes.

Carol Dubnicki, the Shell Oil executive mentioned earlier, spent the first part of her career with a large consulting firm where she learned to deal with all kinds of conflict situations. She believes that she became comfortable in dealing with senior executives by learning to manage conflict in this early phase of her career.

You can also increase your comfort level in conflict management by developing your communication and negotiation skills. Taking classes, observing successful role models, and practicing in low-risk situations can help you fine-tune this highly utilized skill.

Throughout this book, we speak of the need to build partnerships. In Human Resources, you accomplish your work through others, so the stronger the connections, the more effective you are. Seeking out others in your field, industry, and community is important to getting your work done well. We believe your focus should be on learning what resources people have and how you can support them in accomplishing their goals.

Tom Darrow, the incoming president of SHRMAtlanta, is a networker extraordinaire. Recently, a fellow member of our group lost her house in a fire. Not surprisingly, Tom immediately sent an email out to hundreds of people asking for small donations. Knowing Tom, he did this out of a spirit of service. What this service philosophy has also done is position him as a person who people want to help in return. When HR professionals have a recruiting need, Tom is often the first person to whom they turn.

Relationship Management Quick Action: 1) Commit to scheduling one networking meeting per week. 2) Get involved in a nonprofit organization by volunteering for a committee in which you have an interest. 3) Sign up for a conflict management class. 4) Take the Thomas-Kilman Conflict Assessment (http://www.cpp.com).

More Strategies for Gaining Self-Knowledge

As an HR professional, you should commit to completing one of the following strategies for gaining self-knowledge this month. See Appendix A and www.myhrsuccess.com for more follow-up actions to increase your emotional intelligence and gain self-knowledge.

Keep a Journal

Buy a notebook that you title your "Career Journal." Write in it as often as you can. Let your journal be a sounding board. There is something helpful about the act of expressing your thoughts in the quiet moments you create for yourself. Just let your hand flow with your thoughts and feelings. Don't judge what emerges.

Use your writing as a way to uncover some of the feelings behind your actions. Having trouble with a situation at work? Write about that. You will find that, frequently, writing allows you to release some of the pent-up feelings you have. It also helps you to look at challenges from a new perspective. Have you ever taken a break from a meeting in which tensions are high? Did you gain more calm and clarity by doing that? You will find the same phenomenon can occur when writing. It allows you to see the same situation through a different pair of lenses.

Find a Coach (Or More Than One)

Coaches can serve as personal cheerleaders, honest friends, and guides. They can provide objective feedback about situations and can help you learn from experiences and mistakes. They also can help you target specific goals and hold you accountable for achieving them. Although coaches can be paid professionals from inside or outside your organization, they also can come from the ranks of trusted colleagues. We have known peer coaching to be extremely effective. Group peer coaching is another option. Using this approach, like-minded peers who want to move forward with their development schedule regular sessions to enhance their learning.

Seek Out Mentors

Mentors are similar to coaches. They are people who have been in your shoes and can offer advice, support, and the savvy gained from experience. They also have something you want: skill, knowledge, or even a personal trait. Look inside and outside your organization for people you admire. Seek out those people and be prepared with specific learning outcomes that you are committed to achieve. What do you want to learn from them? Mentors themselves gain a great deal by being able to share their insights and wisdom, so don't be shy about asking.

Record Your Actions on DVD

When you are experiencing new or challenging work situations, imagine that you are being recorded. What is the camera seeing? How are you acting and sounding on camera? Take some time afterward to assess your performance. What did you do well? What could have been done better? What is the key learning you will focus on the next time you are faced with this type of situation? These are excellent learning situations to record in your journal. By engaging actively in this "self-coaching," you will gain new perspectives and continue to raise the bar on your own development.

Target Gaps in Your Experience

Think about your future moves. Decide what gaps you have in your work history. Maybe you need some direct management experience or to increase your exposure to compensation and benefits. Perhaps you need to dive into some small consulting projects. The next step is figuring out where you can get that experience either inside or outside your work situation. Sometimes filling these gaps internally is difficult. Consider volunteer experiences or training on your own. Coaches and mentors can also suggest experts to network with as well. In Chapter 8, we will offer more detailed suggestions for closing these gaps in your career.

Concluding Remarks

In this chapter, we discussed self-knowledge and the reason it is key to succeeding in your HR role. We laid out the roadmap for gathering information about yourself, including experience, skills, traits, values, likes and dislikes, and emotional intelligence.

The chapter also provided tangible action steps for gaining this critical understanding.

References

Bolles, R. *What Color Is Your Parachute?* 2004. Berkeley, CA: Ten Speed Press.

Boyatzis, R. 2004. Personal correspondence.

Buckingham, M and D Clifton. 2001. *Now Discover Your Strengths.* New York: Free Press.

Deer, CB. 1986. "Five Definitions of Career Success: Implications for Relationships." *International Review of Applied Psychology* 35, no. 3: 415–435.

Goleman, D, R Boyatzis, and A McKee. 2002. *Primal Leadership.* Boston: Harvard Business School Press.

http://www.birkman.com/ (The Birkman Method)

http://www.capt.org/ (The Meyers Briggs Type Indicator)

http://www.cpp.com/ (The Thomas-Kilman Conflict Mode Instrument)

http://www.hbdi.com/ (Hermann Brain Dominance Instrument)

http://www.inscapepublishing.com/home.asp (The DISC)

Porot, D, and F Haynes. Career Games Website, http://careergames.com/

Tieger, P, and B Tieger. 1995. *Do What You Are.* Boston: Little, Brown & Company.

6

Actions to Take: Learning about the Field

This chapter contains steps, tools, and guidelines for becoming more knowledgeable about various aspects of the HR profession and the trends that impact it. Why is continual learning about your field and the trends that affect it important? First, as one of our interviewees told us, a hallmark of any profession is that its members engage in ongoing learning to stay at the forefront of developments and trends. Second, you are increasing your marketability and value to organizations. And as we noted in Chapter 2, HR is a dynamic, growing field that takes place in ever-changing organizational venues. To not try to keep up with all this by taking an "I know all I need to know about HR" stance spells trouble for your career, even if you have been an HR professional for several decades.

In this chapter, we will be focusing on the two major elements of field knowledge in the HR Career Success Model: (1) knowledge about the field and (2) knowledge of issues and trends in HR. Knowledge of organizations will be covered in Chapter 7.

A few caveats are in order before we begin. First, the steps, tools, and guidelines in this chapter pertain to the process of gaining knowledge of the field. They do not provide specific HR content area knowledge. Thus, you will learn the most effective ways to acquire knowledge about different HR specialties as well as guidance on how to choose which methods may work best for you. But we will not provide detailed content knowledge on, for example, the latest trends in EEO compliance, executive stock plans, or behavioral interviewing techniques. Abundant resources on HR content knowledge are available elsewhere.

Second, as you go through this chapter, keep in mind a major assumption of the Success Model: It is knowledge however acquired. The key is having the knowledge and not how you obtain it. Thus, it is important to know yourself well enough (see Chapter 5) to know what areas of HR you need to brush up on and want to know more about at a given point in your career and then apply the principles in this chapter to learn about those areas.

Learning about the Functional Areas of HR

As you saw earlier, not only is HR a growing and dynamic field, but it also is a very broad and deep one as well. When someone asks the typical social chit-chat conversation starter "What do you do?" and we say "HR," sometimes we hear responses such as "Oh, so you teach people how to hire people?" or "Interesting. So you consult with companies on how to make employees happy?" We find these questions somewhat amusing in that they are based on what we think is an extremely narrow (or narrow-minded) and simplistic view of the field. HR is, of course, considerably more than most people apparently think. There is much that you can and should learn in HR, regardless of your place on the specialist-generalist continuum and where you aspire to be on it. Because the amount of information and the number of ideas and tools pertinent to HR continuously expand, finding the critical information, knowledge, and tools you need to succeed can be a real challenge. This chapter will help you wade through the maze of knowledge and leverage it to your advantage.

One way to sift through the morass is to distinguish the major functional elements of HR. Different ways of capturing these elements have been created by various individuals and professional associations. We summarize three of them here, just to demonstrate the considerable breadth and variety of functions under the HR umbrella and to assist you in identifying what area or areas you need to learn more about.

A brochure for a recent conference sponsored by the Society for Human Resource Management (SHRM) organized programs and presentations in six categories: (1) Business and Strategy, (2) Employee Relations, (3) Skills Development, (4) Employment, (5) HR and the Law, and (6) Compensation and Benefits. Of course, there are many subfunctions within each one. Take category 6 as an example. Nonexempt salary administration, executive incentive plans, health care benefits, tuition reimbursement, job evaluation, the Fair Labor Standards Act, and a host of other knowledge areas exist within the broad category of compensation and benefits. And within any one of these knowledge areas, there is much to know.

One of the online resources for HR professionals that has emerged recently is HR.com. This weekly electronic newsletter contains brief articles, essays, and interviews with well-known HR and workplace experts, and new developments of interest to HR professionals. The latter part of each newsletter is devoted to issues and trends pertaining to specific HR functions, which HR.com terms "HR communities." The editors have identified seven of them: (1) Compensation and Benefits, (2) Labor Relations, (3) Legal, (4) Organization Development, (5) Staffing, (6) HR Information Systems, and (7) Training. Obviously, a great deal of overlap exists between HR.com's seven pieces and SHRM's six. HR.com also contains resources specifically targeted to senior HR executives.

A third way to view the major elements or functions of HR was formulated by McLagan (1989) as part of a competency study commissioned by the American Society for Training and Development. Although this study focused on the developmental aspects of the field, McLagan's study viewed the entire HR field and the way developmental and nondevelopmental functions interacted with one another. Her model distinguished 11 functional HR categories: (1) HR Research and Information, (2) Union/Labor Relations, (3) Employee Assistance Programs, (4) Compensation and Benefits, (5) Selection/Staffing, (6) Performance Management, (7) HR Planning, (8) Organization and Job Design, (9) Career Development, (10) Organization Development, and (11) Training and Development.

We are not advocating you use one of these ways of dividing the HR pie to the exclusion of the other two or even other frameworks that have been created. We are advocating you choose some method to break down the broad and varied field of HR into manageable pieces. In this way you can then make informed choices about the learning and development goals you set. This approach should assist you in avoiding being overwhelmed with the sheer amount of knowledge that is "out there" or not knowing where to start. Do not become enslaved to information overload. You simply need to start somewhere!

Learning about Issues and Trends in HR

What about trends that impact HR? What about the trends within HR that impact it and ultimately your customers? What about the myriad issues in the workplace that HR professionals need to be aware of, if not possess expertise in, or at least are expected to be the expert? What about the near constant shifting of trends, emphases, and issues within the HR profession? How should you go about trying to keep abreast with but a few of these, much less most of them?

Just as the sheer amount of information about HR functions can seem overwhelming to tackle, keeping up with the issues and trends of the profession can likewise seem like trying to nail gelatin to a telephone pole. Yes, there is certainly much to be learned on the issues and trend front. In fact, the information can seem so overwhelming that you could spend all your time just trying to keep your head above water, much less "always staying current."

We suggest that, as with learning about HR functional knowledge, you start somewhere. Just start! And continue learning as much as you can, as often as you can, about various HR and HR-relevant issues and trends. We recognize HR professionals cannot, and should not, be students all the time. Having that luxury would be wonderful, but clients expect you to deliver, and rightly so. You simply cannot forget about your customers nor dump their needs onto your "low priority" stack. At the same time, remember that ongoing learning is the hallmark of being a professional, especially an HR professional. Later in this chapter we will outline various ways you can learn about the field. Suffice it to say for now that you simply must find the time, and often make the time, to do this. Enhancing your value to organizations demands nothing less.

The questions we asked our interviewees that elicited the most varied responses had to do with keeping up with HR trends and issues. We asked two specific questions here: (1) What are the current key issues and trends in the field that you need to attend to? and (2) How do you keep up with them? Although there was some overlap in their responses to both the what and the how, by and large all the interviewees we spoke with tried to stay abreast on those issues and trends that they thought were important at the time. So if you are feeling overwhelmed with the prospect about keeping up, take some solace in knowing that the highly successful HR professionals we interviewed focus on the issues and trends they choose to learn more about. They do not try to "do it all." The "whats" ranged from health and retirement benefits, technology, legal issues, retention, and outsourcing to coaching, mentoring, employee involvement, leadership development, and measurement of HR's efforts. Similarly, the "hows" ran the gamut from reading, attending seminars, and learning from peers to consuming professional association products and services, furthering formal education, and completing certificate programs. Remember that all these people have achieved significant success in HR. However, when it comes to the aspects of HR and the issues important to HR that they try to stay abreast of, they are much more different than alike. And we suspect if we asked these same people (or even a different sample of successful HR practitioners) the same questions about their learning strategies and the content of their learning priorities a year from now, their responses would probably change. That is, they either would be trying to keep up with different aspects of the field, different issues and trends affecting the field, or they would use different methods to try to keep up. The key element is to be teachable and then commit to the learning process.

Another way to look at this situation is through the customers' lens. How much faith would you place in your physician if she graduated from medical school years ago and you got the sense she devoted little effort since then to stay abreast of her branch of medicine? How confident would you be that your accountant is minimizing your tax liability if he told you he didn't have time to stay abreast of changes in the tax codes? Now turn the tables around. How confident would your customers be in your ability to help them if they knew, or had suspicions, that you have allowed your learning about HR trends or practices to fall by the wayside the last several years?

Let's now take a deeper look at the various ways you can increase your field knowledge. One vehicle to help you decide among the many options at your disposal is to group learning methods into two broad categories: (1) structured approaches and (2) unstructured approaches.

Structured Learning Approaches

First, let's discuss structured learning approaches. By "structured," we mean a well-defined, organized arrangement is already in place. There is little, if any, requirement on your part to design what you will learn and how you will learn it (though it probably helps to be organized yourself when you embark on any of the structured approaches described next).

Professional Association Conferences and Seminars

We highly recommend that if you are not a member of an HR professional association, you become one. The key mission of such associations is to assist members in learning and growing professionally, and through that process, they contribute to the effectiveness of the profession they represent. There are many HR and HR-related professional associations from which to choose. Most have student chapters as well as local and national membership levels. Membership benefits typically include monthly newsletters; online resources such as easily accessible databases that contain the latest research and best practices; and discounts on books, magazines, journals, and seminars. These associations usually hold monthly meetings (at least at the local level) and annual national (and in some cases international) conferences that provide excellent networking opportunities. They also serve as vehicles to learn more about the profession and discuss and debate "hot issues" with your colleagues. Professional associations also host or sponsor seminars on a regular basis. These seminars typically emphasize a particular topic or issue of interest to a sizeable chunk of the groups' membership. Current examples include (and are certainly not limited to) such trends as outsourcing HR functions, measuring your impact, and containing health care benefits costs. Two of the oldest and largest HR professional associations are the Society for Human Resource Management (SHRM) and the American Society for Training and Development (ASTD). Other "sister" associations that have been in existence for quite some time and draw HR professionals as members include (and are not limited to) the Society for Industrial and Organizational Psychology (SIOP), the American Compensation Association (ACA), the International Society for Performance and Instruction (ISPI), the OD Network, the International Personnel Management Association (IPMA), the Human Resource Planning Society (HRPS), and the International Association for Human Resource Information Management (IHRIM). A listing of HR and HR-related professional associations appears in Appendix B.

We suggest you first obtain information on an association from its web site or call and ask that print materials be sent to you. After reviewing these materials, try to attend a local chapter meeting if one is available. Doing this should give you at least a rudimentary sense of what the association is about, the kinds of members it draws, and the nature and scope of services it provides. This kind of information should help you make an informed decision about whether to become a member. Many of these associations will send you a sampling of their publications (that is, magazines and journals) free or for a nominal charge. These publications should also help you see whether the association is a good fit for you. After you become a new member of an association, we strongly encourage you to volunteer serving on a committee right away. This experience will help you gain exposure in the association and accelerate your progress on the learning curve. We have both done this and have found the extra time involved well worth the investment. By serving on committees, we cleared a path to the associations' key players and linked up with more members more swiftly than we otherwise could have. We found this approach particularly helpful when we moved to a new area and did not know many people there. That situation quickly changed as a result of our committee service.

Certificate Programs

Many HR professional associations offer certificate programs to their members. These programs often entail classroom-based learning approaches, e-learning, or both, and require passing an exam or other form of assessment. Certificate programs vary in length, cost, and the time commitment necessary, so be sure to read the fine print and ask many questions before signing up. We also recommend you speak with several "graduates" of these programs to help you assess whether proceeding is worth your time, money, and effort. We suggest you be wary if the sponsor of a certificate program does not provide you any names of graduates to contact. Perhaps some of the better known and more long-standing certificate programs in HR are those offered by SHRM. Although HR has not reached the stage at which particular college degrees, state licenses, and professional association-sanctioned certifications are required to practice it, HR certificate programs recognize there is a need for some HR professionals to acquire specialized bodies of knowledge at various points in their careers and to be recognized for possessing such knowledge.

So how helpful and necessary is it to have one or more of these certifications? Although we do not hold the opinion that having one or more certificates (issued by SHRM or other bodies) is absolutely essential to career progression and success, we also think that, by and large, they cannot hurt you. After all, certification programs are supposed to teach you knowledge of the field. Some of our interviewees are certified to administer and interpret certain products (for example, assessment instruments wherein the publisher certifies people to use them or particular training programs wherein the creators of the programs certify people to deliver them). When asked what benefit is gained from having certificates, aside from being able, legally and ethically, to use instruments or deliver training, Chris Lee, Director of HR at Bates College in Maine, who possesses SHRM certification as well as other certificates, said they can help if you do not have any formal education in the HR field. There may indeed come a time when having certain degrees, certificates, and such is required to practice HR, or at least having those things is highly preferable. We are not sure HR has reached that stage of maturity as a profession. But we think it likely will. Thus, in addition to Chris's point about the benefits of certification for people without formal education in HR, we suggest people get certified to increase their options. Some organizations prefer that job candidates and external consultants possess a certificate such as those issued by SHRM; a few that we know require them. Because HR is well on the path of increasing professionalization, we think it is likely that being certified in some aspect of HR will become more the norm rather than the exception. Older, more established professions such as law, medicine, engineering, and accounting experienced the certification trend when they were at the stage of maturity where HR is now. So why not be prepared for the future now?

Training Programs

A third structured approach to learning about the field is through seminars, work-shops, and classes in both HR functional areas and issues and trends in the field. Chances are if you are a member of a professional association, you receive notices about these events all the time (we will leave it to you to judge whether they qualify as junk mail or e-mail spam). These programs can range from a half-day to several weeks in duration and are offered by colleges and universities (usually through their continuing or adult education program), private firms (such as the American Management Association, consulting firms, training companies, etc.), and through professional associations (for example, SHRM's self-study and online course offerings). As with certificate programs, we suggest you try to contact several graduates of these training programs rather than rely solely on the mar-keting materials describing the programs. In many instances, volume discounts are available if several people in your organization wish to enroll in one of these programs at the same time. Sometimes the vendor will bring the program to your organization if sufficient numbers of people there want to take the course. This can save your organization money on travel and living expenses.

College and University Degrees

The increasing professionalization of HR is reflected in the growing number of institutions of higher education that offer bachelor's and master's degrees in human resources and related fields. We are also witnessing an increasing number of jobs, including those at entry level, that have a bachelor's degree as a minimum requirement and a master's degree as a preferable credential. Some undergradu-ate programs offer specializations in HR (typically 4–6 courses in HR), while a growing number offer a complete major in HR (typically 8–12 courses). Master's programs go by various names, and the curricula of these programs can vary con-siderably. For example, many programs in human resource management are often housed in business schools, whereas others are housed in public administration. An increasing number of master's programs in human resource development, organization development, I/O psychology, organizational behavior, and organi-zational leadership and change are housed either in business schools or elsewhere. As with undergraduate degree programs, some master's programs offer either a specialization in HR or more intensive study of the field. Internships and other field-based experiences are common elements in HR degree programs so that students with little or no practical experience in the field can acquire some as part of their studies.

Many HR programs attract the so-called nontraditional student, meaning those over the age of 22 who work full-time. If you are one of those people who cringe at the thought of sitting in a classroom all day with people who are half your age, you can relax. The nontraditional college student, at both the undergraduate and graduate levels, is increasingly the norm in the United States, Europe, Australia, Africa, and Asia.

It is worth noting that several of our interviewees told us that one of the most important and helpful development strategies they have used in their career was going back to school. They said that school forced them to do a number of things that they otherwise would not have done, such as think more critically, view the field more broadly, improve their verbal and written communication skills, and challenge their own assumptions. Further, being in a degree program expanded their professional networks and opened up new opportunities job-wise.

Unstructured Learning Approaches

One of the potential disadvantages of all the structured learning approaches we have described is that you are somewhat at the mercy of what a school, professional association, training vendor, or consulting firm offers. With an unstructured approach, what you learn and when you learn are essentially up to you. Of course, this can often mean you need to provide your own structure to make it work, and that can feel like more work for some people.

Think about your preferred learning style. Do you feel restricted when participating in a structured learning situation? Or do you tend to be ill at ease, frustrated, or "lost" without such structure? Are you comfortable when an organized learning activity is imposed upon you, or do you tend to learn more when you can decide what, when, and how to learn? Being aware of the ways you tend to learn best can provide helpful clues to choosing between structured and more autonomous approaches to learning about the HR field.

There are primarily three unstructured methods to gaining field knowledge. We will discuss each of them briefly.

Learn by Doing

Conventional wisdom suggests that experience is always the best teacher. We would simply add that it is if you bother to reflect on your experiences. As we noted in the preceding chapter, experience is a key component of self-knowledge. It can also serve to expand your field knowledge. Taking a new HR job that involves an area of the field you have had little or no experience with, volunteering for a project that requires you to acquire new HR knowledge to perform the work successfully, or conducting some research for a client on "best practices" can all result in your gaining HR field knowledge. Even performing tasks with a new angle, or working with a new customer, can result in meaningful new learning about the field.

Self-Study

Many, if not all, successful HR professionals, including all of our interviewees, carve out some time on a regular basis for learning about the field despite their busy schedules. This self-study can take the form of reading magazines and journals to which they subscribe; receiving online newsletters and briefings from an abundance of services (such as HR.com and NetAssets [www.hrms.net]); and, in effect, creating their own course in a particular HR function, issue, or trend. A critical element in self-study is self-discipline. That is, you make the time and take the time, on a regular and consistent basis, to read, study, contemplate, and discuss your learning with others. Remember to keep in mind your learning style preferences. If you tend to learn more effectively when structure is imposed upon you compared to when you have to create and execute your own structure, a "create my own course" approach will, in all likelihood, not come as easily to you.

Mentoring

We will cover mentoring as a development strategy in more detail in Chapter 9. For our purposes here, consider having one or more mentors who are willing and able to assist you in the area of field knowledge acquisition. Perhaps a more senior person in HR, either inside or outside your organization, can serve in this capacity. Peers can also serve as field knowledge mentors to each other when they have field knowledge bases that differ from one another. In this way, you can have a field knowledge mentor as well as be a field knowledge mentor to that person. We have known many such reciprocal arrangements to work quite well for both parties.

Additional Guides, Steps, and Tips for Gaining Field Knowledge

Do you embark on one or more of the structured approaches or less structured ones? How do you choose among all these options? How will you know you're making a worthwhile investment by going back to school, taking a seminar, or joining a professional association? Will that certificate really help you advance in your career? These and similar questions can be daunting. Unfortunately, there are few hard and fast rules. Here, we will provide some guidelines, steps, and tools to help you make informed choices among the many options for gaining HR field knowledge.

Making Informed Choices

Recently, one of our graduate students approached us asking what she should do to increase her knowledge in an area of HR that fell outside her degree program curriculum. As the conversation unfolded, it became apparent that she was confronted with an array of choices. For example, she asked which seminar offered by whom should she consider? How will she know it's "a good program"? Which professional association, or more than one, should she join now? How can she evaluate the quality of an online learning opportunity before signing on the dotted line? One of the things we asked her to consider was exactly what we asked you to consider a few pages ago—her preferred learning style. Did she learn best on her own at her own pace? Did having others with her, in a classroom setting, for example, provide for a richer and more valuable learning experience? What about her self-discipline? Did she learn better by reading or by performing more hands-on activities? Identifying preferred learning styles and modes helped this student to clarify what she wanted in terms of approaches as well as eliminate some options that did not play to her preferences.

As far as the issue of prequalifying various choices before making a commitment, signing on the dotted line, and issuing a credit card, like life itself, there is no foolproof way to guarantee that what you get is what you bargained for or expected. However, as we noted earlier, you need to do your homework before making a choice. If you are considering a degree or certificate program, by all means your homework should involve much more than simply digesting marketing and promotional materials. Talk to people who are currently in these programs as well as graduates. Perhaps the school you are considering will allow you to sit in on some classes to see what they are really like. The same goes for training classes, seminars, and professional association offerings. Ask those who are hosting these events to sit in for an hour or so to get a sense of their value. When contemplating joining a professional association, ask for free copies of some of its publications. Attend at least one of its monthly meetings. Talk to members and ask them what they see as the benefits. Press them to be specific. Some schools, vendors, firms, and associations may balk at your asking them for sneak previews, free materials, or other ways for you to engage in the prequalification process. At least you have asked. The worst they can say is "no," which is no worse than if you hadn't asked in the first place.

Is School for Me?

For some people, the thought of school brings back harsh and unpleasant memories, and thus the mere idea of returning to school for a degree engenders less than pleasant emotions. We have known thousands of people who have returned to school and excelled after being away from it for decades. Many of these people had negative memories of their formal education experiences and approached the idea of returning to a classroom with some trepidation and concern. So never say never. What you experienced in high school does not automatically mean that is what awaits you as an undergraduate or graduate student. In fact, many of our interviewees told us that if they could turn back the clock and do something differently, they would have gone back to school for a graduate degree sooner than they did. In looking back to earlier times in their career they had thought that going back to school would consume too much time to the detriment of their career progression. Some said they were tired of school and just wanted to work and have free nights and weekends. It is indeed never too late to return to school (we have both had students well into their 60s), so we encourage you to try to keep an open mind about this idea. Some of our interviewees achieved considerable success by returning to school at the middle and latter stages of their careers. Others had gone back to school earlier and felt this positioned them for future success. *When* you return to school may be less important to your success than your being clear on *why* you want to return to school. And when you decide to return to school and are clear about your motivations, you will be more likely to gain the benefits you sought in the first place after you are enrolled.

Among the thousands of people we have taught, at least 95 percent of those who know why they are in school tend to perform better than those who aren't sure why they are in school or have some vague reason (for example, "to improve myself" or "get a better job") for being there. When you know specific reasons why you have gone back to school, you will accrue more benefits from your investment. Based on our experiences these students who have crossed our paths, we believe you will get more out of classes, be a more enthusiastic learner, and be a more active and engaged participant in the learning process when you know why you are in school and have realistic expectations of what the degree can and can't do for you. We have found there are basically two kinds of students who attend school: learners and box checkers or ticket punchers. The former seek an education, and the latter seek a diploma. To be a learner, think long and hard about what you hope to gain from school and the degree it offers. Then test your hopes to verify or refute the validity of those hopes. Yes, homework starts (or it should start) before you even apply to school.

Let's say you are seriously, or somewhat seriously, thinking about getting that degree. What should you find out before taking the plunge, in addition to the length of a program, its costs, how you are going to pay for those costs, how many students are admitted per year, and the criteria for admissions decisions? As with seminars and training programs, we suggest you interview several current students and alumni about their experiences in the program—the good, the not so good, and the downright ugly. If you are not allowed to speak with current and former students, we suggest you be wary of the program. What are the program's graduation rates, and what kinds of jobs are obtained after graduation? Ask to see hard data, not simply verbal testimonials from administrators or professors. Faculty/student ratios can be an important factor to consider as well as the background of the faculty and their teaching styles. Are classes typically traditional lecture format, team projects, group discussion, or hands-on activities? Find out what practical experience faculty have in HR and how they use this experience in the classroom. Ask how much time you should expect to spend each week with classes, homework, and studying. Get a sense of the backgrounds of students in the program, both in terms of their previous work experience, the reasons they are in the program, and their career goals and aspirations after obtaining the degree. How well do you fit these profiles? Would you be comfortable being in school with these sorts of people? In sum, we strongly advocate you do your homework before rather than after starting a program.

Tips for Self-Study

One thing we can say with complete confidence and certainty is there is no shortage of reading material on any subject, and this most assuredly includes material devoted to HR field knowledge. The range and sheer number of books; magazine articles; research studies; academic and practitioner journals; and online resources about HR functions, issues, and trends are staggering. How you choose the right material often boils down to trying out particular publications, be they print or electronic. You may tire of certain materials or feel they no longer serve a useful purpose. In that case, dump them and try some new ones. If you want to learn about a particular HR function and have virtually no knowledge about that function, we recommend you read a textbook or at least skim it. Although some claim that textbooks on various HR functions can be outdated by the time they reach readers, we think they offer a useful start when you need to learn the fundamentals about an HR function, be it compensation, EEO compliance, or labor relations. A textbook can provide a useful overview of the knowledge bases of the HR function or functions it covers. Note the references in such books for further study.

Some HR professionals find it helpful to form study groups as an adjunct to self-study. These groups can provide you with an incentive to stay on task as well as additional learning opportunities through discussions of readings with other people. Preparation for certification exams can also be an excellent way to structure this kind of learning.

Joining Professional Associations

As we noted earlier, if you are not a member of at least one professional association that is about HR or at least related to HR, join one now. Perhaps more than any other single resource, professional associations can be extremely helpful in your quest to stay abreast of issues, trends, and other important developments in the field. They also provide outstanding networking opportunities for members. Indeed, many of our interviewees told us that one of the keys to their success was joining a professional association early in their HR career and becoming actively involved in the local chapter, the national level, or both. Being actively involved means more than showing up to a monthly dinner meeting, the annual conference, and reading the association's flagship publication. Volunteer on task forces. Chair a committee. Get involved in a special interest group. These sorts of "extra efforts" can pay handsome dividends, not only in the knowledge you will acquire but also through the people you meet.

Before attending a conference or association meeting, be clear about what your purpose is. Is it to meet certain people? Gain some specific information or knowledge? As we proposed with the possibility of returning to school, when you are clear on your motives before attending an association's conference, becoming a member of one of its committees, or agreeing to serve as a participant on a special task force, you will get more out of your investment down the road.

You may find, as others have, that the utility of a particular association wears thin after some time. This may occur because the direction of your HR career has shifted, the membership profile of the association no longer fills your needs, the costs for attending conferences becomes prohibitive, or for a host of other reasons. By all means, do not stay with one association throughout your career if it is not meeting your current needs or helping to fulfill your future aspirations. Join another one. Or two or three other ones.

Concluding Remarks

We question any professionals who come across, however subtly, as knowing just about all they need to know about HR as a field. Yes, anyone, even if that person has been in the field for 40 years. You have probably heard the term "lifelong learning," and it certainly is applicable when it comes to acquiring and expanding your knowledge of the HR field. One of the reasons HR is such a dynamic field is that new knowledge, practices, issues, trends, and strategies are constantly being created. HR is anything but a static field, which makes it quite an exciting one. This underscores the necessity of being a perpetual student. Even if you have gone to school and compiled many degrees in HR, up to and including a Ph.D., the process of gaining HR field knowledge is one from which you should never graduate. Nor should you try.

Indeed, a common thread we heard from our interviewees concerning key success factors in both their own career and what they suggest to others in the field, be they just starting out in HR or senior-level HR executives, is to remain teachable about HR field knowledge throughout their careers. It takes a certain form of humility to be teachable. To rest on your laurels and believe in your heart of hearts that your level of knowledge is such that there is little, if any, need for you to continue learning about the HR field has, at least to us, an arrogant ring to it.

Yes, you will likely have much more HR field knowledge than any of your customers will ever want or need to possess. At the same time, there is always more to learn about the field. Even the brightest, most intellectually gifted cannot learn much if you take the stance of not being teachable or not needing to engage in continuous learning about your craft. A recent study of HR careers (Wiscombe 2001) found that the smartest thing HR professionals said they ever did in their careers was to engage in continuous learning and development. Conversely, we would say the most unwise thing you can do is refuse to commit to lifelong learning or not follow through on such a commitment.

References

McLagan, PA. 1989. "Models for HRD Practice." *Training and Development Journal* 49, no. 9: 49–59.

Wiscombe, J. 2001. "Your Wonderful/Terrible HR Life." *Workforce* 80, no. 6: 32–37.

7

Actions to Take: Learning about the Organization

As you saw in the preceding chapter, gaining knowledge of HR functions, issues, and trends in a continuous fashion is necessary for success. That knowledge alone is also insufficient for success. HR takes place in organizations, not in a vacuum or in some secret hiding place. Thus, having knowledge about how organizations function, at their best and worst, is a key component of success throughout your HR career. You may be one of the planet's renowned authorities on labor law, HR information systems, or 360-degree feedback mechanisms, but if your knowledge of the way organizations work is limited, your vast reservoir of other kinds of knowledge will have very limited applicability.

You might be wondering, "But what if I am recognized throughout my organization for my expertise in X (where X could be any of a number of HR issues, trends, or functions)? What if people are constantly seeking my expertise on X? What's wrong with that?"

There is nothing inherently "wrong" with being an expert, and certainly nothing is wrong with being recognized as such throughout an organization. If people come to you for help on X, that's fine. If those people are satisfied with the assistance you provide them on X, that's fine, too. If those same people refer to you others who are having issues on X, that's also fine. There are, however, some potential downsides or risks to shaping your HR role exclusively around being the HR guru without incorporating knowledge of organizations. Let's look at some of these possible risks.

Being a deep and narrow specialist with little, if any, organizational knowledge is akin to being an advisor hired by a motion picture production company. Suppose the advisor is one of the world's renowned authorities of cardiovascular medicine and the company has engaged her to assist screenwriters who create films that involve cardiovascular disease in some way. Becoming a world-renowned authority in this area has required the advisor to possess huge amounts of knowledge about cardiovascular disease—perhaps more knowledge than any other single individual on earth. The production company wants to tap this knowledge to create realistic scenes in some films that depict heart problems and heart surgery.

Of course, the company needs to tap large amounts of knowledge in several other functions to be able to operate, including but not limited to writing, acting, special effects, costume design, and set construction. The company also needs what the deep and narrow expert brings, but it cannot operate effectively using only her knowledge.

The cardiovascular advisor is product- and not market-driven. Her product (cardiovascular knowledge) may be at the leading edge in the minds of other cardiovascular specialists; however, in the minds of those on the movie set, the advisor's leading-edge product may have little meaning or importance.

Conditions on the set can often change. They're affected by a number of factors (such as an actor and director disagreeing on how to shoot a scene, unanticipated but necessary alterations to the script, or unplanned budget overruns) that may not seem to directly impact the advisor. Likewise, markets change constantly and affect and are affected by any number of factors. Perhaps films about medicine have flooded the market, and the producers have decided this is the last film involving medicine they will fund for a while. Or the advisor's recommendation to change the props in an emergency room scene "to make them more realistic and believable" is ignored by the producers because those changes are too expensive and will throw the schedule out of whack. When you are product-driven, you are likely blind to these factors and ultimately unaware of what is going on in the marketplace. Thus, the advisor's product may look and sound top drawer on its own, but its utility in the marketplace may be short-lived, especially in markets that undergo rapid and unpredictable change (and which markets these days enjoy long-term stability and predictability?).

You can offer a high-quality product, and customers may find it (and you) helpful. At the same time, if those customers sense you know little, if anything, about their business, the context in which their business is conducted, and the factors that affect their business, at best they will seek you out for only those issues and problems for which your product is designed. Thus, the market you have carved out for yourself is very, very limited. The world-renowned cardiovascular expert found this out when the film company changed its mind and stopped making movies that contained scenes about cardiovascular disease.

You likely know the phrase "perception is reality." HR's customers can sometimes hold the perception that you are an "HR silo" (that is, a deep and narrow specialist) and the negative connotation that accompanies this perception. How many times have you heard individual HR professionals or the function as a whole referenced by comments such as "Yeah, HR knows a lot about that HR stuff, but they're clueless when it comes to understanding our business and the realities of our organization"? Perceptions like these may indeed be inaccurate or distorted. Or just plain wrong. But if they exist, they are true to the people who own them. They may be unspoken. In our experience, such comments about HR are more openly critical.

More likely than not, if your organizational knowledge is minimal, even when your HR knowledge is vast, your credibility with customers is tenuous. And if your credibility with customers is tenuous, guess what's next? Your job is probably in very serious jeopardy. Dave Ulrich notes this dynamic (see Meisinger 2003; and Vosburgh 2003) and suggests that credibility is your most important competency. One way you put your credibility at serious risk is by being seen solely as "an HR expert."

When you are enslaved (or more accurately, enslave yourself) to "the HR silo," you tend to see all issues, problems, and situations from the silo's frame of reference rather than the broader point of view that has meaning and relevance to your customers. This is often referred to as "the hammer in search of a nail" syndrome. You may be the best darn hammer the world has ever seen. But if you do not have and incorporate knowledge of the environment in which hammers operate, all that remains is the knowledge you apply to nails. Most environments are more complex and thus contain much more than just nails. And even when you find a nail, or it finds you, you may discover that the nail needs something in addition to or instead of a hammer.

This chapter offers ideas, tools, and guides for learning about organizations that are, by necessity, generic. It is beyond the scope of this book for us to provide precise suggestions and advice on how to acquire unique organizational knowledge. Our generic guides, tools, and ideas apply to virtually any organization. They may require some tweaking and sculpting to learn more about a particular organization and its particular circumstances at a particular time. At the same time, this chapter will help you acquire organizational knowledge that you can use throughout your HR career.

Our Assumptions about Organizations

Before we present the actions you can take to enhance your learning about organizations in which the HR craft is practiced, let's look at some basic assumptions about organizations. We have amassed these assumptions during our 60+ years working in, consulting for, studying, and observing hundreds of organizations of every conceivable type. As you might imagine, we have learned quite a bit and are still learning about organizations. Here are our five assumptions:

1. **Rationality.** Organizations are not totally rational, though they can appear that way. Procedure manuals, organization charts, job descriptions, office and factory layouts, and building designs can give the appearance of a highly rational machine that hums along day after day, week after week, and year after year at peak efficiency. Memos, executive briefings, and other forms of communication can feed the belief that all decisions in the organization are born through a highly rational, by-the-numbers process. Consider that people inhabit organizations. Although our species is more rational (as our species defines that term) than other mammals, are we totally rational? Think about a time you lost your temper over something that you later discovered was pretty insignificant. Or perhaps there was an instance when you analyzed a situation "logically," carefully, and thoroughly weighed all the relevant pros and cons; consulted others about your reasoning; and then made a decision. Subsequently, you became aware of a "blind spot" that you overlooked but should have incorporated into your decision-making process. Being less than 100 percent rational is what makes you human and often makes human resources so interesting and organizations so fascinating.

2. **Irrationality.** Organizations are not totally irrational, though they often can appear that way. Have you ever said to yourself, a work colleague, a friend, or a family member, "That place (where you work or a client organization) is *crazy*!!" Or, after hearing of a decision by a member of management, have you thought, "They're nuts"? Chances are you are somewhat right. Everyone does things that most reasonable people would term "crazy" or "nuts." For sure, everyone thinks things from time to time that can rightly be placed in the category of "nuts" or "crazy" or "insane." Or at least "odd." This is part of the human condition. At the same time, chances are most people who work in organizations are not truly "insane" in the clinical and legal senses of the term. Yes, most mere mortals have their moments, but on balance, they're at least somewhat in touch with what is going on around them. Thus, organizations (and the people they employ) can seem to be insane periodically; they can also drive you a little insane. But somehow things get done, the organization works in spite of itself, and organizational life goes on.

3. **Family.** Organizations function like families. You might be saying in a sarcastic tone, "Oh yeah, right. We sure are one big happy family around this place." We don't mean family in that sense. Nor do we mean family as in "one, big, happy, unconditional love fest" (said in a nonsarcastic tone). Most families we know are fascinating entities interwoven with joy, heartache, humor, caring, injustice, fun, misery, fulfillment, frustration, gratitude, energy-enhancing and energy-draining interchanges, and a host of other social dynamics. So are organizations. And if you think about it, aren't families organizations, too? They don't go to the lengths some organizations do in terms of formalized systems (can you imagine your family having a "new member orientation" or "annual performance reviews"?). But they are organizations nonetheless. It's quite likely that your own family of origin (parents, siblings, and/or others you grew up with) was the first organization of which you were a member. And after a while, you likely learned the rules, the cultural norms, those who had power and those who didn't, and the like. Suffice it to say that, like families, organizations are venues in which the peaks and valleys, the good and not so good, and the inspirational and disappointing aspects of the human condition are played out daily.

4. **Systems.** Organizations are systems. What does that mean? Some commonplace examples should help. Bodies are composed of many organs, bones, tissues, joints, nerves, fluids, and other matter. Somehow all the elements come together into a miraculous functioning whole. What about cars? All the parts—from the hoses, belts, fluids, and tires to the engine, fuel, steering column, exhaust system, and brakes function together and make a car operable.

   A fundamental characteristic of a system is that it is greater than the sum of its parts. A conglomeration of body or car parts works only by being in sync with the other parts. A liver by itself is pretty useless. So is a fuel injector. But when all these parts, often numbering in the thousands or millions, are all connected in some fashion, the result is an impressive system that works!

   Organizations are systems, too. They are composed of thousands of "parts," some of which are tangible and others which are hidden. There are various subsystems in organizations (for example, the budget system, the accounting system, the sales system, the customer service system, the human system, the technical system, ad infinitum). Somehow, each of these subsystems is formed, refined, and launched, and eventually each of them joins up with other subsystems. This "joining up" process creates the whole system and makes it work. When the parts don't work together, trouble brews—a prime instance being when the HR system is not joined or aligned with other parts of the organization but in effect is operating in isolation. An example is an organization that needs to attract and retain team players, and its compensation system fosters competition between individuals.

5. **Fluidity.** Organizations are living systems. A living system changes constantly whether you notice it or not. You may have had the experience of seeing a friend you had not seen in quite some time and were quite shocked to see how much that person had aged (you twenty- and thirtysomethings, be forewarned—this is something you can expect down the road!). You might have another friend you see quite frequently, and that person may have aged even more than your other friend. But because you see the second person all the time, you don't notice how the aging process marches on (relentlessly, we're afraid). Cars age, too, though if you drive one every day, chances are you cannot and thus do not notice how the car is aging because the changes that transpire in a day are miniscule (until that day when the transmission stops working, the battery dies, or the engine overheats). Aging is just one way change plays out in a system. Sometimes entire new subsystems (be it an artificial heart or new tires) replace previously existing ones, and other subsystems have to adjust. Organizations are living systems, too (at least while they are in existence). Like a car or a human body, they also undergo change constantly, even when such changes aren't visible or noticeable to you. And during the change process, which is more or less constant, adjustments by subsystems are taking place to enable the entire system to keep running—in effect to remain alive. Like the human body, and to some degree automobiles, organizations have a survival instinct. And like human bodies and cars, they eventually die.

As we review the many ways to acquire knowledge about an organization, keep in mind these traits or qualities that organizations have. They are complex systems that are alive, a little crazy while also rational, and they possess many of the qualities that most families have. Being aware of these issues will help you gain as much organizational knowledge as you can.

Let's first look at what we advise you to learn about an organization based on our Success Model. We will then provide ideas and strategies—the hows—that will help you acquire organizational knowledge.

The Success Model Factors

Our Success Model suggests six major elements of an organization you need to know about to achieve career success in HR. Now let's look at each of them separately.

The Way the Organization Goes about Its Business

As the term relates to our Success Model, when we say "business," we mean the core purpose, primary mission, or the raison d'etre of the organization, whether it is in fact technically a business. Thus, we use the term "business" in a generic sense. Government organizations have a business, as do nonprofits. Of course, organizations that exist to make a profit are businesses, too.

For decades, we have been hearing how much "HR needs to know the business." What is puzzling, and somewhat disturbing, is that we keep hearing this call, and it seems to be stated more emphatically and vociferously than ever—both from within and outside the HR ranks. Indeed, practically every one of the successful HR professionals we interviewed for this book said that, without a doubt, a key success factor for any HR professional now and in the future is to have a general knowledge of business as well as more specific knowledge pertinent to their own organization (the one that employs them or with whom they consult).

Rather than simply reiterate this long-standing call for HR to "know the business," we want to provide some specifics about what this means, what it entails, and what you can and should do about it.

For one, HR professionals need to acquire knowledge of the organization's business that goes beyond what is readily available on an organization's web site, its PR materials, and annual reports. For sure, you need to be up to speed on all the information contained in these documents. But don't stop there. If it is a for-profit organization, how does it make money? How does it minimize costs and optimize revenue? What strategies, processes, and systems are in place to achieve these outcomes? How well are they working? How could they be improved? If it is a government or nonprofit organization, how does it seek to fulfill its core mission (and not lose money in the process)? What strategies, processes, and systems are in place to enable this to happen? For all kinds of organizations, who are its constituents or stakeholders? That is, who is it accountable to (for example, customers, employees, shareholders, donors, funding agencies, citizens, the community)? What are the conflicts these multiple allegiances create, and how does the organization attempt to resolve them?

Another way HR professionals can gain knowledge about "the business of the business" is to find out, observe, and understand the various subsystems that are in place in the organization. This is not just about getting a bunch of organization charts and studying them. What it means is that HR professionals should be well versed in what these subsystems are (for example, management, information, marketing, finance, product development, and customer service systems) and (1) possess at least a basic understanding of the purpose, operations, and key accountabilities of each subsystem; (2) see how all the subsystems fit together (if they indeed do, and if they don't, that in itself is an opportunity for HR professionals); and (3) understand and be able to explain how the HR subsystem (the organization's "people processes") fits, supports, and aligns itself to these other systems. Later in this chapter we will provide suggestions for how HR professionals can learn about these things.

You might be asking at this point, "How will I know when I have enough knowledge about these various subsystems or functions of the organization?" In an ideal world, HR professionals would know everything there is to know and would always have sufficient time to keep learning these (and other) things. One, albeit informal, "acid test" is to ask yourself periodically the following question and then respond to it honestly: "If I were a fly on the wall visiting these different subsystems (for example, a meeting of marketing staff, finance managers, etc.), what would I see and hear?" If your honest response does not contain some specific information that reflects the current challenges, opportunities, problems, and goals of the subsystem, chances are you need to learn more about what is really going on in that function. It is probably a reasonably safe assumption that people in HR are never going to reach the point where they know everything about the organization and can rest on their supposed laurels. If you are going to make assumptions about this, assume you always have to be in an organizational knowledge learning mode.

A few other aspects of "the business of the business" that HR needs to stay abreast of are the overall health of the organization and some of its history. What does the balance sheet look like, and what factors are primarily responsible for the organization's current health status? Does the organization's viability seem to be in jeopardy? If so, why? Are things improving? What is causing this to happen? How does the organization's overall health compare to last quarter? Last year? Five years ago? What are the trends, and what do they mean for the organization (as well as for HR)? How did the organization's current status materialize, and what implication does that have for where it wants to go tomorrow? How will that affect HR in general and you and your career in particular? You should have a solid handle on these questions. Never stop asking them, and you will continue to strengthen your effectiveness.

In addition to your professional identity being linked to Human Resources, add to that title "a professional student of organizations." Consider what good students do. We are not talking about people who memorize textbooks and regurgitate what they memorized on some artificial entity like a test or quiz. Good students ask good questions and lots of them. And they never stop asking questions. Good students know how, where, and when to find the answers, too.

Hopefully, we have sparked your interest in learning at least the fundamentals of your organization and the way it operates. We hope we have sparked your commitment to explore your organization in an ongoing way. Let's now look at the second element in the Organizational Learning portion of our Success Model.

Issues and Trends in the Organization's Business

As you go about acquiring knowledge of the organization's business, its subsystems, and the like, chances are you will pick up some information and knowledge about the issues and trends facing the organization. But don't leave such things to happenstance. Target your learning to those dynamics, events, and predictions both internal and external to the organization that have and will affect it.

This task can seem daunting. Consider that, as you saw in the preceding chapter, there is much knowledge to be acquired pertaining to HR issues and trends. Now we are talking about issues and trends impacting and impacted by the organization as a whole as well as other functions besides HR. Indeed, there is much to learn. For example, what industry trends are affecting revenue growth? How are your constituents affected by recent health care legislation? This list can go on almost endlessly. We encourage you not to be overwhelmed by the insurmountable amount of knowledge "out there." As a student of the organization, you will want to learn all you can, especially those things that fall outside "the HR silo." Otherwise, you will be stuck in that silo, and people can easily forget you are even in there.

You should be asking yourself and others several key questions (yes, those questions again!) to help you ramp up on issues and trends in the organization's business. They include

- What are managers worried about? Why are they worried about such matters? What keeps them up at night or wakes them up at night?
- What are employees (nonmanagers/individual contributors) concerned about? Why? How do these concerns compare to management's concerns?

- What are your competitors', stakeholders', constituents', and community members' key issues? How do these issues affect your organization?
- What are the key challenges your organization faces today? Why are they the key ones? What are you trying to do about them? Are you trying at all? Are you trying hard enough? Do your strategies seem to be working? Why or why not?
- What are the key trends in your industry? What are the hot buttons? Will they be hot a year from now?
- What is going well in the organization? What's working and why is it working? Chances are even the most ineffective, dysfunctional organization does some things well, even if it is filing for bankruptcy. As of this writing, Delta Air Lines seems headed for that fate. Despite this likelihood, Delta continues to do many things well. And if nothing else, looking at and appreciating what the organization is doing well provides some relief from dealing with problems all the time.
- What are likely scenarios for the organization in the short- and long-term future? Be that fly on the wall again. What would you be seeing and hearing perched on that wall three years from now? Although "crystal balling" always has its hazards in terms of turning out to be completely accurate, you should focus on what appears to be most likely, given where the organization has been and is now and the issues and trends that appear to be important today and those likely to emerge three years from now.

For too long, HR has been accused of being reactive and not proactive. By learning all you can about likely, or at least possible, future states of the organization, you are building your capability to anticipate needs of the organization, at least some of which you can help address. As Gary May, a former chief executive and chief learning officer who is currently a professor at Clayton State University, said, "HR needs to skate to where it looks like the hockey puck's gonna be." And the information and knowledge you glean about the organization and the issues and trends it faces can be instrumental in helping you be an anticipatory hockey player.

Culture

Culture is all about those unspoken, unwritten rules or guides to behavior that exist in every organization. It is an extremely powerful force in an organization, whether it has 5 or 500,000 employees. Culture is thus a very important element of organizations that HR needs to know about.

Have you ever been to a country outside your homeland, or even been in a different part of your native country that you had never been to before, and felt ill at ease? Perhaps you could not understand the language of the people who lived there. Or maybe they spoke the same language you do but their accents were so different from what you were accustomed to that they might as well have spoken a different language. Or maybe some of their customs, food, or ways of talking with each other were unfamiliar to you. If you felt ill at ease, or at least out of place, this can be a sign of what is known as "culture shock." You can be shocked, literally, when immersed in a culture that is different from the one to which you have grown accustomed. What you have taken for granted in your own culture, or what you see as "normal" based on deeply held assumptions in your own culture, can be quite different from what is taken for granted and is "normal" in other cultures. In this sense, normalcy is situation-specific and not an absolute and universal truism. How do you react to these sorts of differences that are often profound and quite disconcerting? Do you dig your heels in deeper and try to exert your own culturally based values and norms? Do you criticize or complain, at least to yourself, that this other culture simply does things the wrong ways? Or do you try to understand and appreciate the differences between your own cultural beliefs and practices with this other culture—one that seemed so foreign and strange?

Everyone in an organization is affected by its culture, most especially including HR professionals. Because you work with people throughout an organization, it is imperative that you understand and appreciate the culture of the organization as well as any and all subcultures. Understanding and appreciating the "rules of the game" are prerequisites to (1) helping improve and change the culture, which is often a key challenge HR professionals face, and (2) shaping your HR career in that culture. HR professionals who operate with little knowledge and appreciation for the culture they are in are at great risk. It is highly doubtful that your ideas, proposals, initiatives, and aspirations will have much merit unless you tailor them to the cultural norms of the organization.

Just what is culture? And specifically, what is a work organization's culture? What do you look for in organizations that provide clues to the powerful and often unspoken and unwritten "rules of the game?"

Numerous books, empirical studies, and practitioner-oriented articles have been devoted to the concept of organizational culture. It is considerably beyond the scope of this book to delve into any of these issues in depth. For our purposes, let's use simple and straightforward definitions such as those offered by two noted management and organizational consultants, Edgar Schein and Tom Peters. Schein (1999) views culture as the potent forces in an organization that teach you how to behave and how not to behave. Similarly, Peters (1999) explains that culture is all about the way things are done in the organization.

You likely have had considerable experience dealing with organizational cultures. This holds true even if you are just starting out in your career. Consider the first organization (of sorts) of which you were a member—as a child in your family. Chances are that when you first learned to read, your parents or others who raised you did not give you a policy and procedures manual and then command you to digest it all and act accordingly. On the other hand, chances are you were expected to abide by at least several unwritten "rules" in the household. They may have covered such issues as what chores you were responsible for completing, when they were to be completed, and the standards you were expected to meet in performing those tasks. How you were to act during meals, when guests visited, and in dealings with your siblings were likely other areas that had rules for you to follow or at least general guidelines with which to comply. These rules, guidelines, or norms were probably very powerful in that they affected your behavior—either through your compliance or your disobedience. Underlying these rules, guidelines, or norms were assumptions about right and wrong, rewards and punishments for various actions or lack thereof, and prescriptions for acting "right." If you broke one of the rules, be it intentional or not, and it was a very important rule to those in charge, chances are you understood, or at least were given the opportunity to understand, "the way things are done around here."

For sure, the behavioral expectations across families can be very different and often contradictory. Some families are very strict; others are lax. Some families give kids much freedom and responsibility; others imprison them. Regardless of the specific nature of familial cultural norms, here are some commonplace examples that exist in many families:

- Don't talk while you are eating.
- You cannot talk on the phone until you finish your homework.
- Respect your elders.
- You can be anything you want to be as long as you put your mind to it.
- Work hard and play hard.
- If you don't have anything nice to say, don't say anything at all.
- Don't ever talk to me like that, or you'll be punished.

- We want you to be happy.
- We love you unconditionally. (Maybe this one isn't so commonplace in families; we hope it is anyway.)
- You better appreciate all we do for you.
- Never sell yourself short.
- Treat others like you want to be treated.
- When I want your opinion, I'll ask for it.
- You and your brother (sister) work out your disagreements yourself. Don't get me involved.
- Tell the truth.
- I can't help you if you lie to me.
- You'll never amount to anything.
- Because I said so, that's why.
- I don't care what your friend's parents allow your friend to do. You are not going out on a school night.
- Do as I say not as I do.
- You're the captain of your ship.
- We're proud of you.
- We're very disappointed in you.
- We want to help you.

Can you see how, at least in some ways, families are like work organizations in that both have cultural norms, expectations for behavior (be they clearly articulated and consistently applied or not), rewards and sanctions, and feedback mechanisms? If you think back to when you were a child, what were the unwritten yet powerful norms for the way you were supposed to act? What happened when you complied? When you didn't comply? Were there instances when it was confusing to understand how you were supposed to behave? Were those in charge (parents) inconsistent in their rewards and punishments?

Families are not work organizations. But both share many similarities in terms of having a culture and conveying that culture to its members. So at minimum, know that you've had a wealth of experience dealing with culture in organizations. Thus, your knowledge of organizations is anything but a blank slate.

The thought of trying to understand something as complex as a culture can seem quite daunting. What exactly should you know? Which norms, unwritten or unspoken rules of the game, and guides to behavior should you be aware of as an HR professional? Some might argue that learning about and understanding an organization's culture (and its various subcultures) entails literally hundreds of elements. We think you could spend your entire career being a student of culture. The problem with that is then figuring out how your work would get done.

Here is a place to start. We would like for you to consider the following four elements of organizational culture as being key areas for you to learn about and to continue to learn about in whatever organization you practice the HR craft:

1. **Accepted, tolerated, and unacceptable behaviors.** When you begin working in an organization, be a sponge. Soak up all the cues, hints, and not so subtle indices of what actions are OK and not OK. These behaviors range from when to show up, what to wear, and how to act in meetings. One of us, who is not "a morning person," once worked in an organization that valued getting to work by 7:30 a.m., though the "official start of the day" was 8 a.m. We found that out after coming to work at 8 a.m. and noticing others smirking at us while looking at their watches. We then asked others whether getting to work at 8 a.m. was acceptable, tolerable, or unacceptable and found out that it was in our enlightened self-interest to arrive at 7:30 a.m. despite our preference for starting later. We then figured it was worth catching up on our sleep later by simply changing our sleep schedule.

2. **The way things get done.** How does the organization accomplish what it sets out to do and what it expects its members to do? Does the organization have a bias for action, or is it more deliberate and analytical as it goes about its business? How important are stated deadlines? Can they be renegotiated, and if so, how? To what degree do different departments and functions communicate with and support one another? What forms of communication, between and within departments and functions, are valued over others? How does the organization incentivize people to perform and get things done? These are among the questions you need to ask yourself, and ask others if necessary, to get a handle on how the organization accomplishes tasks so that you can (1) accomplish your own work in a like manner and (2) design interventions, solutions, and other forms of assistance that align with these cultural values. For example, if you are working in a very formal organization that has strict and unyielding "rules of conduct," communication, and ways to accomplish tasks, a proposal to revamp the organization's performance management system needs to incorporate strict and unyielding procedures. The revamped system needs to be designed and proposed in a formal, by-the-books fashion if it is to be considered and eventually adopted.

3. **The way decisions are made.** As a successful HR professional, you need to go beyond merely glancing at an organization chart to determine who makes what decisions. Often, it is the less publicized and more informal system of decision making that reflects how the organization really makes decisions. This does not mean that the laundry worker in a hospital makes more decisions and more important decisions than the CEO. But how does the laundry organization make decisions? Does the top manager in that operation make them all? Does the manager consult with employees in the laundry on any decisions, and if so, how does he or she do that? Which decisions call for a more consultative approach, and which ones are made autocratically? Implicit in this area is that the organization probably employs a multitude of decision-making approaches, and they can vary quite a bit, especially if the organization is large. This point highlights the need for you to learn as much as you can about each and every subculture in your organization.

4. **Image management.** When you have a firm grasp of the culture in which you operate, you can then engage in effective management of your own image. Recall from Chapter 2 that some people have a less than stellar perception of HR as a function. To elevate this image, you need to demonstrate your knowledge of the culture (and subcultures within the larger culture) by acting in ways that align with the culture. We are not suggesting that you sacrifice your individuality or to value style over substance. But far too often, we have seen HR professionals do more damage to themselves by doing a poor job of managing their image. And usually, the root cause of this poor image can be found by looking at how well the HR professional knows the culture and acts on that knowledge. For example, if one of the key values of the culture is decisiveness, act decisively. If the culture values humor every once in a while (or more often), show your humorous side at appropriate times. If the culture is a work hard/play hard kind of place, do both of those things. Mentors can be very helpful in explaining these unwritten codes of conduct needed for success.

Culture can be described in many other ways. In addition to the preceding four elements, Schein (1999) discusses others that are extremely important to know and understand for career success. Four of them are particularly relevant in light of our discussion here. He conceived these elements on a continuum (rather than as a yes/no or either/or dynamic). The four elements are (1) authoritative-involvement, or the degree that decision making is shared among organizational members; (2) team-individual, or the degree that work is done in groups and by individuals; (3) open-closed communication, or the degree to which information is shared and not shared from the top-down and from the bottom-up; and (4) task-relations, or the relative importance of emphasizing tasks to be done and supporting, leading, and motivating people to do those tasks.

Over the years, we have been fortunate to work in, consult with, study, and observe a vast array of organizational cultures and subcultures. Based on these experiences, we list some words that can serve as descriptors of an organization's overall culture. If you had to attach one concise descriptor to your organization, which among the following would most likely be accurate? If none of them capture the essence of your organization, what would be an accurate label?

Hierarchical	Collaborative	Serious
Free-Wheeling	Individualistic	Cost-obsessed
Individualistic	Open	Chaotic
Workaholic	Fun	Hard Working/ Hard Playing
Informal	Competitive	Collaborative
Secretive	Organized	Creative
Impulsive	Deliberate	Analytic

Keep in mind that any organization has suborganizations (for example, divisions, departments, units within departments, etc.) that may or may not have cultures that align with the total organization's "way of doing things." Typically, management creates and sustains the culture. However, employees can have a profound effect on culture as well. When you act like a sponge, don't restrict yourself to only part of the organization to soak in that culture. Thus, don't restrict yourself to be a sponge only around managers.

Regardless of the ways you conceptualize culture, why is learning about it critically important? For one, you can't be effective without knowing "the rules." You will have a very difficult time getting things done if you are constantly hitting your head against "cultural walls." And as we alluded to already, HR initiatives that you design, manage, and oversee must take the organization's culture into account; otherwise, they are likely to die a slow (or quick) death.

Does this mean that HR simply succumbs to the culture? Is success all about being compliant, obedient, and conforming? Absolutely not! For sure, a key role for HR, especially these days, is to push back and question the existing culture. And often, you serve as an agent of culture change, a culture change champion, or at least a culture change facilitator. However, this task is way too huge for any one person to take on. Even CEOs, who are sometimes viewed as creators and champions of the organization's culture, cannot change it by themselves. To serve as a change agent, or at least to challenge or question some cultural norms, you first have to understand as completely as possible what it is you think needs changing. Is it management styles? Overly inflexible policies? Too few policies or ones that are not followed consistently? Is the organization too bureaucratic? Too laissez-faire? Too emotional? Not emotional enough? To engage others in a culture change initiative, you have to understand how the current culture affects them, both positively and negatively. To elicit others' support for change, you need to know what payoffs they get for maintaining the status quo.

As organizations become more global and their members are composed of an ever-increasing diversity of backgrounds, experiences, and values (that is, cultural foundations), it is important that those in HR are culturally literate. Otherwise, you can easily become as lost, shocked, and ineffective as a traveler in a foreign land who does not know nor understand the customs, language, and the "way things are done" there. If you have ever been in that situation, you probably found it took considerable effort and energy to accomplish tasks that are "no brainers" when in your home country, such as finding a rest room, ordering from a menu, reading a road sign, or knowing whether you received correct change in a store.

Power

Although power can be treated as part of culture, we position it here as a separate element of organizational knowledge to learn about. We think it deserves to be treated separately because of its extreme importance to HR career success. Many times when we have seen HR professionals bemoan the lack of respect they think they get or complain that HR itself is not valued, it comes down to an issue of power. Or lack thereof. HR's lack of power can be seen in many ways, such as when a program you designed was not implemented, your budget request was not approved, or your advice was ignored or discounted.

In this context, what exactly do we mean by power? And how can HR have more? How can you, as an HR professional, enhance your power?

Power is influence. It is the ability to have an impact on others. When you have sufficient power, you garner respect. Many people usually think of power as having decision-making authority and responsibility. That is but one form of power.

More than 40 years ago, French and Raven (1959) studied power and then devised a theory of power as it pertained to leadership and interpersonal relations. Later, French and Bell (1990) applied the original theory to organizational development and change, which brought the power issue squarely in HR's court.

Briefly, the theory states that there are five different forms of power: (1) Position, (2) Coercive, (3) Reward, (4) Referent (or Charismatic), and (5) Expert. You are likely very familiar with position power. People whose names occupy higher boxes on the organization chart have power over the people whose names appear in boxes below theirs, simply by virtue of the power of the position. When you have coercive power, you can inflict punishment on those who don't comply with expectations. Police officers and judges sure have coercive power. So do some managers. The flip side of coercive power is reward-based power. When you have this form of power, you have the authority and wherewithal to reward others when they do what you want them to do. Although coercive and reward power often go hand in hand with position power, referent power is not necessarily linked to a position in the hierarchy. When you have referent power, others are influenced by your compelling personality, charisma, and other qualities that induce them to want to follow you, share your point of view, or enact behaviors that you influence them to enact. Expert power exists when the person's knowledge and skills are clearly superior to others, and that person gains trust, respect, and influence because of his or her recognized expertise.

Some HR professionals may enjoy position power. However, they often need to create and sustain power and influence through other vehicles. Even when you have position power (say you're in the top HR position in the organization), that power is usually limited to those inside the HR organization (that is, the HR professionals who are "below you" on the HR organization chart). So, for you to increase your influence and the respect you think you deserve beyond the HR organization, you need to concentrate your efforts on the last two forms of power—referent and expert.

Many HR professionals, by virtue of their knowledge, skills, and experience, enjoy a reputation of having expert power. After all, HR professionals are the experts in various "people matters," right? You are the source for expertise when it comes to such matters as employee relations, benefits plans, leadership development, performance management, and HR information systems.

Consider that expert power is necessary and insufficient for HR career success. If you rely solely on your expert-based power, you are in danger of becoming that hammer in search of a nail or that authority on cardiovascular disease consulting in the film industry. Eventually, you will find yourself in situations in which the organization no longer needs nails or can outsource your expertise to hammers that are cheaper.

What about reward and coercive power for HR? Well, we've seen this type of power backfire more times than we can say. When your customers complain that "all HR does is tell me what I can't do" or "I'm tired of HR slapping me on the wrist," these complaints very well could be a signal that you have overused and possibly abused coercive power. And when that happens, your influence will be limited and your reputation tarnished. This is not to say that some behaviors absolutely need to be punished (as well as rewarded). If you find out that a manager has acted unethically or illegally, you are obligated to inflict punishment, or at least to convince others to inflict it. If you find out an employee has done an outstanding job on a project, you should find ways for that employee to be recognized and rewarded. But as the old saying goes, "power corrupts and absolute power corrupts absolutely." When HR takes it upon itself to act as "the cop in the organization" (sometimes called "the HR police"), you may indeed get outward compliance and thus relish the thought you really have a lot of power around the organization. Chances are, however, that inwardly you are not getting compliance but rather resistance, resentment, and hostility. Sooner or later, that is likely to catch up to you. Compliance has become a major role of the HR practitioner. You just have to be careful not to abuse that role. You need to be coercive and authoritative selectively.

What we are advocating is that you seize opportunities to engage in referent forms of power to complement your use of expert power (and position, reward, and coercive power, if you have those as well). This does not imply that somehow you need to become the next Gandhi or Martin Luther King, Jr., to enhance your influence in organizational life. What we are saying is that because HR generally has less position power than others (along with less reward and punishment power), you need to enhance your expert and referent power bases. And per the preceding discussion, relying solely on expert power has its risks. We think those risks are considerable.

In addition to your own power, you need to learn about the forms of power and the ways they play out throughout the organization. If you had to create an "informal organization chart," what would it look like and how would it compare to the formal one? That is, how is *real* power *really* enacted in the organization? Who has *real* influence over *whom*? Who has the ear of the CEO and other managers? How did they achieve this position? If you dig deeply into the workings of the organization's power machine, you can find out the answers to such questions.

In addition, find out the answers to such issues as how power is acquired in the organization. How is it lost? And how is it distributed throughout the organization?

We think it likely, and can virtually guarantee, that if you obtain accurate data on these issues of power, your informal organization chart will differ, at least in some ways, from the way the formal chart looks. That is, some positions (and incumbents in those positions) may be higher up on the formal chart but in reality hold relatively little power and influence compared to their peers and even in some cases those who are further down the formal chain of command. Keep in mind that formal organization charts show only position power. We have yet to find an organization in which power is limited to its positional form. Figures 7.1 and 7.2 illustrate these differences.

The formal organization chart in Figure 7.1 is fairly typical in that it has one boss and that position has eight direct reports, with each one at the same level (the horizontal plane on which the smaller boxes rest). Each direct report is depicted by the same-sized box, indicating that these positions manage the same number of resources and thus have equivalent amounts of power.

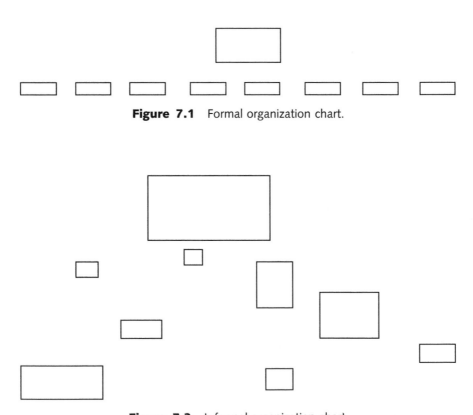

Figure 7.1   Formal organization chart.

Figure 7.2   Informal organization chart.

If you were to delve into this organization and find out what really happens and how decisions are made, you might find something along the lines of Figure 7.2.

The informal chart in Figure 7.2 depicts how things really get done in this organization. Yes, the boss is still at the top. But notice that the eight direct reports are in varying-sized boxes, and those boxes are on different horizontal positions as well. Some of the direct reports manage more resources than others (their box is larger) but have less influence on the boss and the boss' organization than other managers (their boxes are not as close to the boss' box as others).

Knowing the informal power dynamics of an organization will help you immeasurably to assist that organization with its HR issues. In other words, it's risky to assume power operates exactly in ways as depicted in the formal organization chart in Figure 7.1, and will likely limit your ability to influence (that is, your power) that organization effectively.

Customers

As the term relates to our Success Model, by "customers" we mean those groups of people and/or segments of the marketplace that the organization serves. We are thus not restricting the issue of customers to for-profit organizations. Nonprofits and government organizations also have customers—those who are recipients of their services.

If your knowledge of a variety of issues pertaining to the organization's customer base is limited, your impact is limited. After all, your customers—managers and employees—have their own customers to deal with, serve, worry about, and keep. For you to adequately serve your customers, you must know the hot issues and challenges they face with their customers.

So what is essential for HR to know about the organization's customers? Here are some guidelines in the form of questions. If you can't answer them quickly and confidently, chances are you need to bulk up on your knowledge of the organization's customers.

- What markets (for-profit) or segments of society (nonprofits and government) does the organization currently seek to serve? What future markets or segments does it hope to serve? What is the strategy for doing so? How does the organization approach its customers now? How well is that effort working?

- How does the organization retain its customers? What are the causes of attrition? Which competitors are taking your customers? What is the organization trying to do about this situation?
- What do customers want from your organization? What is the organization doing to attract new ones and exceed current customers' expectations?
- What new products and/or services are in the pipeline? What can you learn about them? How will the organization develop them? How will they be marketed and sold?
- How is the organization structured, and how is work organized to get and keep customers?

HR can play a critical role in these customer issues. That role should go beyond offering customer service training here and there or using the word "customer" in your discussions with managers and employees. The preceding questions have myriad HR implications (and they have really only scratched the surface of what you need to know about the organization's customers). Every one of those questions has implications for who you hire, train, develop, promote, demote, and otherwise assist to achieve the ultimate goal of any organization—exemplary products and services to customers. And how the organization is structured plays a crucial role in how well it delivers services and products to customers. HR needs to be a major player in organizational structure issues as well. The closer you can make your own services and programs relevant to serving the organization's customers, the more valuable your services will be.

An organization without satisfied customers is an organization headed to the garbage heap. Similarly, if, as an HR professional, you do not satisfy your customers, your career in HR is destined to the same fate. A key way to satisfy your customers is to know as much as you can about your customers' customers and then tailor your services accordingly.

Strategy

The last major element of organizational knowledge HR needs is to understand the organization's strategy. We considered using a term other than "strategy" because it is one of the most overused (and thus abused) words in the English language, especially in HR circles. "Strategy" perhaps runs a close second to "I love you" or "Trust me" in the frequency with which it is used. For decades we have been hearing how HR needs to be more strategic. More recently, the phrase "HR as a strategic partner" has come in vogue. Then there are the many variations and permutations such as "strategic function," "strategic talent base," and "strategic priority."

At the risk of contributing to the overuse of the term "strategy" or phrases containing it, in the context here, we are referring to the overall plan or goal of the organization. For some organizations, merely surviving is the basic strategy (several major airlines come to mind here). For others, cost reduction is the key driver to everything the organization does and is about. Additional examples of an organization's overall strategy include increasing efficiency, growing market share, being the low-cost producer, being the high-quality alternative to the lower-cost producers, obliterating the competition, growing through acquisitions, and shrinking to core businesses.

So what is your organization's overall strategy? If you can't answer this question instinctively, there could be a number of reasons why. Some organizations don't articulate a clear strategy. Some of them don't really know what it is. Others simply haven't found ways to communicate it clearly, or they don't want to communicate it at all below the top executive ranks. Still others have a clear strategy and have done an excellent job communicating it clearly and convincingly throughout the organization; however, their actions don't seem to align well with the strategy. In those cases, the strategy becomes meaningless and suspect. A prime example is an organization whose expressed strategic direction is to be cost-obsessive while it spends lavishly on executive perks or employee benefit plans.

Regardless of the clarity, congruence, and communication (or lack thereof) of an organization's strategy, HR professionals need to find out what the strategy is and whether one truly exists or is created in a de facto way by forces beyond the organization's boundaries. Why is it important for you to know these details?

Knowing where the organization is, where it intends to go, why it has chartered the course it has, and how it intends to get there enables you, as an HR professional, to perform a number of critical tasks:

- Increase the chances that your skills will be valued by and marketable in the organization in the future.
- Ensure the HR strategies you embark upon align with and support the strategy of the total organization as well as strategies of different departments in the organization.
- Enhance HR's overall image (including yours) in the organization because what you do is seen as relevant, necessary, and helpful to where the organization is and where it is trying to go.

The major differentiator in HR competencies, as seen by line executives and HR professionals' peers, between those that exist at high- and low-performing organizations, is strategy contribution. A 15-year-long study (Creelman 2004) found that 43 percent of HR's influence on organizational performance was related to its strategy contribution competencies. This means, among other things, that a clear line of sight exists between HR and customers' expectations, needs, and desires—a clear link between what HR does and how competitive the organization is in the marketplace. In high-performing firms, HR not only facilitates strategy, but it contributes to its formulation and execution in important ways.

What if you are in an organization where there is a major (or even minor) disconnect between the strategy talk and the strategy walk? Although it could lead to lower popularity ratings initially, it is incumbent upon HR to point out the lack of congruence between the stated strategy and its execution. If and when you see the organization or even a part of the organization (for example, one unit of one department) acting in ways that are not congruent with or even contradict the stated strategy, by not pointing this out, you are colluding in the incongruence or contradiction. Furthermore, by acting as the voice of an organization's strategy-action connection, you are adding value to the organization.

Here are a few other points you may want to keep in mind regarding strategy and your place in it. Are all your recommendations, initiatives, and actions clearly linked to strategy at all levels (group, department, division, and total organizational levels?). In other words, is what you do with a group clearly linked to that group's strategy? Is a division-wide initiative or program linked clearly and unequivocally to that division's strategy? For example, if the division's strategy is to increase market share through new product development, how are the division's HR processes and practices contributing to this outcome? How is a proposed new reward system going to help drive the creation of new ideas for products, forge new distribution channels, make better products, and get them to the market sooner? You would be advised to ask yourself these questions continually. However, self-assessment here is insufficient. A better and more complete "litmus test" of your HR-organizational strategy linkage is whether your customers see the linkage clearly and convincingly. Ideally, your customers should not need to be educated or guided by you to see this link. It should be obvious that what you are doing in service to them supports their strategy. And it should be obvious to them.

Guides to Learning about the Organization

You should now be clear about the major elements of organizational knowledge you need to possess. But just how should you acquire this knowledge if you don't have it? And how should you increase your organizational knowledge and savvy in continuous ways?

Fortunately, you are not restricted by any single learning vehicle. Multiple pathways are at your disposal. Let's review each of them in the following pages.

Print and Web-Based Materials Available to the General Public

Obtaining information about the fundamentals of organizations is easy these days with the click of a button. Abundant resources are available. They include but are not limited to annual reports, company/agency web sites, information disseminated for recruitment purposes, articles in newspapers and magazines, and materials housed in clearinghouses such as Hoovers. You can subscribe to any number of alert services as well. They are often free subscriptions that send e-mail alerts containing up-to-date information about particular companies, government agencies, and industry sectors.

These sorts of information sources are necessary for you to tap into periodically. However, by themselves, they are likely to be insufficient providers of organizational information. Keep in mind that typically these sources contain one-sided information from the organization. They do not give a complete picture of what is really going on in the organization. So consider these sources as your "Organizational Learning 101" packet.

Internal Resources

If you are an employee in an organization, chances are it has a "for internal use only" intranet. These systems typically impart and exchange information among the organization's members continuously, keeping them up to date on a variety of events, issues, trends, and initiatives. One organization we worked with was posed for a merger. It posted what it called "The Rumor Page," an informational item that contained invaluable information about the progress of the merger, pending issues to be resolved, and predicted timelines for major milestones. In many ways, a company's or agency's intranet has replaced the organization's print version newsletter. If your organization has an intranet and you are not subscribed to it, do so now. Ditto if your organization also has, or only has, printed newsletters, whether they come out weekly, monthly, or quarterly. More than half our interviewees told us that they read information on their organization's intranet every day. If you are an external consultant or contractor, see whether you can have access to these resources. If you are told you can't, ask why.

Other internal resources include data such as turnover statistics by department, exit interview data, strategic plans, succession planning documents, and the like. These resources can be very helpful for any HR professional to peruse.

Internal-only resources are helpful adjuncts to those available to the general public. However, having both these sources of information is still not a comprehensive way to continually expand and update your organizational knowledge base. Consider these two resources as "Organizational Knowledge 101 and 102."

Observation

You can learn much about your organization simply by using your eyes and ears. In fact, you can pick up quite a number of valuable clues about the organization and its culture starting in the parking lot. Does the organization reserve the closest parking spaces for executives? Customers? What shape is the parking lot in? What kinds of cars are in the lot? Good external consultants know to be observant the minute they hit that parking lot and every minute they are inside the organization's edifice.

As we suggested in our discussion of culture, you need to be a sponge because data about the culture as well as other organizational knowledge factors are there for the taking. Be a keen observer, especially of people. How are they dressed? How do they carry themselves? What facial expressions and other nonverbals do they display? Try and focus more on what people actually do (their observable behavior) and less on what they say. Most of the time, actions do indeed speak louder than words. And actions usually convey what is really going on in the organization more than what people may say is going on. About three fourths of our interviewees said that the most easily accessible source of organizational information is through observation. Our own experience in hundreds of organizations confirms this conclusion.

People

If observation is the easiest source of useful organizational information to obtain, we think it's likely that the single most helpful and informative source is through other people. There are some caveats to consider, however. Others can be a tremendous organizational information resource if

- You are teachable. If you are not willing to learn from others, they can do little to teach you anything worthwhile.
- You listen intently and intensely. If your mind is elsewhere, you are tired, or you are otherwise consumed with some other pressing matter, listening will be difficult if not impossible—and we mean *really* listening, to what others tell you, through their words and nonverbal behavior.
- You collect information and analyze it before reaching conclusions. This is far easier said than done. If you're like most people, you carry "theories of truth" in your head. Then, as you collect data—be it through observation, reading, or otherwise—you can easily and unconsciously distort the data to preserve your theories of what is true. So when it comes to important organizational knowledge—be it about customers, strategy, culture, the business of the business, issues and trends, or power—act like a good researcher. Suspend judgments until you have enough data (information) to support or refute what you think is true. And remember, it is often the case that the more people you talk with (and listen to), the more versions of "the truth" you will hear.

So who should you listen to? We think it is absolutely essential that you meet, informally and formally, with line management and employees on a regular basis. By "line," we mean those folks whose work is directly involved in the business of the organization. Of course, as an HR professional, you will be doing this anyway as you go about your work. But to learn more about the organization, you should be talking with (and listening intently and intensely to) your customers before any particular program or project is designed and launched. Suspend your own agenda, whether it is to get a program off the ground or evaluate one that's been up and running for a while. Remember to be teachable. Ask these people to lunch for help in understanding their organization. Tell them you need this information to be of maximum service to them and their organization. As you listen and absorb, ask questions pertaining to the six factors of organizational knowledge described earlier in this chapter. Then be quiet and listen again! If necessary, reframe the concepts and questions in this chapter in language that has meaning to you and your customers.

Tom Darrow, a principal with HR Connections and Consulting, LLC, and incoming president of Atlanta's SHRM chapter, made what we think is a novel suggestion concerning who HR people should talk with and listen to for expand-ing their organizational knowledge base. He suggests you find employees who have left the organization within the past year because they can give you critical orga-nizational information that current employees and managers may not be willing to share.

Part of your success in obtaining good organizational knowledge, no matter who you speak with, is your ability to be a good interviewer. Specifically, you need to be able to help people feel comfortable talking with you and opening up. You want reliable and valid organizational knowledge. Often this knowledge entails sensitive information. Even the most well-intentioned and helpful line people will not open up and give you the real scoop if you don't make it easy for them to do this. Those of us who conduct interviews on a regular basis know how important it is to talk about 20 percent of the time and listen the other 80 percent, too.

Another human source of good organizational information may be your boss. This is especially the case if your boss is part of the top executive team; then you have great access to what is going on at the helm. Several of our interviewees told us that they initiate discussions with bosses on a regular basis to get updates about what is discussed among the executive team. Although it is true that what you get may be filtered information, at least you will be getting information from someone who was "at the table."

Training/Courses

Many organizations provide in-house learning experiences pertaining to the organizations' business and/or areas that fall outside the HR bailiwick. Perhaps your organization has courses, whether classroom-based or online, that deal with finance fundamentals, an overview of the business of the business, operations management, and the like. One of us recalls taking such a course to learn how jet engines are made, sold, marketed, financed, and designed. Why? We did not intend to become an aeronautical engineer (nor any kind of engineer, for that matter). But because we were working as an HR manager in the jet engine business, we found it helpful to know the basics of the product line, customers, manufactur-ing processes, and the like, lest we became enslaved to "the HR silo." After taking the course, we could at least tell a fan blade from a second-stage compressor. And knowing a little about these things helped a great deal in terms of credibility when working on HR issues with managers and employees who designed, sold, made, and serviced these products.

Reading and Miscellaneous

Yes, we are clearly in the Information Age. And many of us are on information overload. Just trying to stay abreast of HR issues and trends through reading about them in HR-oriented publications can almost seem like a full-time job in itself. However, we think it is well worth your while to at least skim some of the things your customers read—for example, industry trade publications and newsletters. As in our jet engine scenario, you need not aspire to be an expert in the intricacies of your organization's industry (be it forest products, chemicals, financial services, or education) or even a quasi-expert. But reading about the industry will enrich your knowledge of the industry, and your customers will likely notice this fact and be positively impressed. Most of our interviewees make trade publications a regular part of their reading routine.

In addition to publications, consider attending industry trade shows periodically. Perhaps this will mean you don't attend that upcoming HR-oriented conference you have been desiring to go to for a while. There is no shortage of conferences geared specifically to this line of work. Miss one and try out an industry-related one instead. If nothing else, it will likely be very different, at least in terms of content, than what you may be accustomed to at HR-related conferences.

Your HR peers can be very valuable sources of organizational information and insight, whether they work alongside you or are in another organization halfway around the world. No one can know everything about anything, including organizations. Don't immediately dismiss the values of peers because "they work in another industry or in another sector than I do."

Find a way to get information about what is going on "at the table" (that is, at the top executive ranks). Earlier, we mentioned keeping in touch with your boss if he or she has an assigned seat at that table. If your boss isn't invited there, explore creative ways to get some information anyway. Maybe your boss' boss is at the table. Or perhaps you and a group of your peers can initiate efforts to be briefed about what is discussed at these meetings.

There are additional ways to get and stay in the organizational knowledge loop. One is through climate surveys. Perhaps your organization conducts such surveys on an annual basis, if not more often. Although these processes vary among organizations, essentially their purpose is to gauge what employees are thinking and feeling about their jobs, their future, and the organization and its management. While such surveys, like all surveys, are not perfect indicators of what is really going on in an organization, even when respondents tell the whole and complete truth as they see it, they can provide the HR professional with insights into the inner workings of the organization. The information gleaned from climate survey data is often not made public nor are the results necessarily made available to anyone inside the organization who asks for them. But as an HR professional, you can probably make a strong case that knowing at least the results in aggregate form will assist you to assist your customers more effectively. Such surveys often are part of a consulting project staffed with internal HR professionals, external consultants, or both. Volunteering to be part of the survey process (be it in survey design, distribution, data analysis, report preparation, and/or report presentation) can be a very valuable use of your limited time. In Chapter 8 you will read an example illustrating how surveys can be a vehicle for HR involvement in important organizational issues. And speaking of volunteering . . .

A consistent recommendation our interviewees hammered home to us was to volunteer on committees, task forces, and cross-functional project teams. We concur with them completely. We think such experiences are great ways to learn more about your organization and are ready-made vehicles for expanding your organizational knowledge base. But be wise and careful. These committees, task forces, and project teams do not exist primarily to educate you and other HR professionals about the organization. So don't usurp a lot of time in group meetings trying to learn more about the organization from these people through asking an excessive number of questions that don't pertain directly to the business at hand. If need be, invite one or more group members to lunch or for a separate meeting to ask more questions (and remember to then be quiet and listen).

Several of our interviewees went a step beyond volunteering for such opportunities. They obtained line jobs. One performed line functions (as an operations manager in the hospitality industry) before she entered HR, even though she knew at the time she wanted to carve out her career in HR. That is, she deliberately got line experience to enable her to be more knowledgeable, skilled, and credible after she entered the HR arena. Another person we spoke with started out in HR, was promoted several times, and then decided (with her boss' blessing) to be a first-line supervisor of blue collar workers for a few years before moving back onto the HR career path. Looking back (and yes, hindsight's always 20-20), both of these people's HR careers were enriched immeasurably by their having had some experience in the guts of the organization. So if you have been in HR a while, or are contemplating the launch of your career in HR, consider a line job at some point along the way. This experience will provide a springboard to your HR career.

Concluding Remarks

Be a lifelong learner. You hear this advice all the time. You hear it at conferences. You hear it from your boss and peers. You read about it in various publications. Gurus preach it constantly. If success in this day and age means engagement . . . no, full engagement, in lifelong learning, it is certainly true for HR professionals. And lifelong learning has to be more than learning about HR functions and trends. You simply must do all you can to be students of organizations as well.

Continuous learning about organizations can't guarantee your success in HR. However, we are supremely confident in asserting that if you do not engage in continuous learning about organizations in general, and yours in particular, your career in HR will be in serious trouble. At best, and we think we are being very optimistic in saying that remaining more or less in your HR silo will result in limited success.

How much organizational knowledge is enough to be successful? When can you cut back? What if you're already overworked and underleisured? We won't offer hard and fast answers to these questions. But they're important questions that deserve thoughtful responses.

One yardstick for you to use, more or less continually, is to discover how much time you spend in your office (or cubicle if that's where your home base is located). Don't guess. Track your time for a week or two. If you spend less than 20 percent of your time at work outside your office—observing, talking, listening, and in other ways acquiring important knowledge about your organization—chances are you are spending too much time in the comforts of your own cube or office while the organization goes on, literally without you. If what you do in HR is going to be important to the organization, then you simply must be exposed to what is going on "out there" and learning from your exposure.

Tom Darrow told us that he spent the first two weeks of every HR job in the trenches and away from his office for this very reason. In each instance, Tom told his boss, "Don't expect me to do any work for two weeks." Tom observed and listened to his customers over this two-week span, soaking up as much organizational knowledge as he could. This experience not only got him up to speed quickly, but it also helped him establish the trust and credibility necessary to be effective with his customers after that initial two-week learning period.

Similarly, John Courtney advises that, "You don't know what you don't know." As you travel the organizational landscape, you will often realize just how much there is to learn there and how much you thought you knew but didn't.

Consider for a moment those things within the HR world for which you have a true passion. Maybe you enjoy working with a client on an EEO issue. Maybe you enjoy studying the latest ideas about containing health care costs? Or attending an HR conference? Or perhaps designing or delivering a customer service training program? Whatever that passion is, it is probably second nature to you. It takes little effort, in part because you enjoy it so much. The thought of sacrificing some of the time you would have spent doing those enjoyable things to engage in some "organizational learning" seems quite unappealing. And rightly so, in a way.

Many of our interviewees admitted it's tough for them sometimes to resist working on that favorite HR project so they can attend an industry trade show, have lunch with someone in accounting to learn more about the budget, or scan the intranet to see what competitors are up to these days. Thus, doing what's important for the business, whatever that business happens to be, can often involve delaying your short-term gratification and replacing it by investing in enhancing your longer-term value and marketability. Value and marketability for those in HR have always been important, but never more so than now. So when you are faced with a choice of immersing yourself in that favorite, fun, interesting, and challenging HR task or learning more about your organization, you might ask yourself whether you are trading long-term success for short-term pleasure.

If you truly see yourself as a student of organizations, know it is a continuous venture. Contrary to the adage that admonishes "Never say never," we urge you to never graduate from the school of organizational knowledge. If you walk down the aisle and pick up your diploma, you do so at your own risk. And we are convinced, as are many others, that the risk is profound.

OK. Enough preaching. Let's just take a brief (and nonpreaching) look at some of the reasons why HR professionals resist engaging in organizational learning activities in addition to the lack of desire to delay gratification.

The one form of resistance that we've alluded to already is T-I-M-E. Who among us has too much discretionary time these days? Or even almost ample discretionary time? As you move, bob, and weave among projects, clients, deadlines, crises, problems, proposals, meetings, reports, and the usual smattering of unexpected but still commonplace eruptions and obstacles, who has time to even think about learning more about the organization? You may be wondering when you are going to find any time to scan the company's intranet, annual report, or newsletter, much less dive into a trade publication or have lunch with some line folks.

The good news is that you have time. The perhaps not-so-good news, or unwel come news if you are already feeling overworked and every minute of your existence seems tied to important commitments, is that it is up to you to make the time.

We are not advocating workaholism. We are not advocating working all weekend every weekend. We are not advocating letting go of a personal life that is fulfilling. We are not advocating pitching "down time" out the proverbial window. What we do promote is prioritizing. And, as one of our interviewees, who has a very demanding job in addition to raising three young children, said, "Be true to your priorities once you define them." Being a lifelong learner of organizational knowledge will likely mean something will have to give. Perhaps it's that favorite pet HR task that can be put off (but not dumped for good). Maybe it's cutting back on spending fun though not necessarily highly productive time with people at work you simply like hanging out with.

As confident as we are that continuous organizational learning is an essential part of your HR career success, we are also confident that you will be able to find the time and energy to make it happen. We are also supremely confident that you will find ways to carve out time to be a student of the organization without sacrificing the quality of your HR work, your personal life, and your health. Others have done it. So can you. But the first step is to buy into the notion that organizational learning is indeed an essential component of your success, today and tomorrow.

In addition to time constraints, another fairly common form of resistance to organizational learning is procrastination. You can easily take the Scarlett O'Hara approach of "I'll worry about it tomorrow." Too often, tomorrow never comes. Can you delegate or outsource some tasks to others, especially those things that are not strategic? If those options aren't available to you, perhaps you can simply put off less essential or nonstrategic tasks to free up some time for organizational learning (which, as you no doubt have guessed by now, is highly strategic in our minds).

Over the years we've heard many HR professionals state, "Line people are busier than I am, or at least as busy as I am. They won't want to meet with me. And even if they do, they want their issues addressed. They don't want to teach me about their organization." Well, that may be true. But in our experience, this line of thinking is more of an excuse than an explanation. First, if you take this stance, you are probably making an assumption. How do you know "line people won't want to talk with me so I can be more savvy about the organization"? Have you asked them? Have you asked *all* of them? Suffice it to say, if not one person in the line in your organization has any willingness to talk with you about organizational matters, something is seriously wrong with the organization, with you, or both. It is a rare organization indeed that has no employees in its midst who enjoy talking about themselves, their organization, their challenges, their headaches, their opportunities. Furthermore, if you can frame a meeting or informal conversation in terms that clearly show what they will get out of spending time with you (for example, they may just need a gentle reminder that you will be more helpful to them in the future the more you can understand their business now), chances are at least some folks will be more than glad to devote some time for you. In essence, when you try to convince them that the more you know about their organization, the more you can help them with those things that are important to them, little more than gentle persuasion will be required to get some time with them. And when you do spend time with them, make sure to ask who else in the line organization might be available for you to see. This approach is not unlike networking when you are looking for a job or a consulting engagement. You are more likely to catch more fish when you increase the size of your fishing net.

Here's another form of resistance we hear quite frequently: "I'm probably going to be laid off from this place, so why bother learning more about it now?" People get laid off for many different reasons. But if it truly appears that you are in the line of fire, then ask yourself that painful but necessary question, "Why me?" Could you have positioned yourself in ways that would have possibly enhanced your value to those who decide who stays and who goes? Maybe if you had more knowledge of the business, culture, power, and the like, then you would have been seen, and rightly so, as a more valuable member of the organization. But even in cases in which losing your job truly is "just a business decision/it's not personal," there remain abundant organizational learning opportunities for you. (And really, it wasn't your job in the first place; if it was, how can you lose it?) Being laid off may indeed not feel like a great opportunity, but just observing, hearing, and seeing how the organization approaches layoffs and downsizing can be valuable to you in the future. After all, by definition, layoffs and other forms or shrinkage involve people, so there are certainly many implications you can take with you in your next HR role.

A final form of resistance we keep hearing over and over goes something like this: "I'll learn the buzz words and the jargon so people will be impressed with how much I know about _____." The blank may be about a product, a service, markets, finance, whatever. There have been countless calls for HR to learn the language of business, finance, operations, marketing, sales, ad infinitum. And then somehow, the implication, stated explicitly or not, is that when you have a handle on some words and phrases, your credibility within the organization will blossom.

Another caveat: Most people we have ever met are not stupid. If your knowledge of the organization is limited to some choice words and terminology, people will see through this facade eventually. Most will see it rather quickly. Learning the language of the organization is important for many reasons. Just don't stop at the superficial level.

A recent meeting about the future of HR was attended by senior HR executives, HR thought leaders, and chief executives of private and public organizations. An eye-opening and rather disturbing outcome transpired when the chief executives and HR people exchanged ideas and perceptions about the future of HR. The two camps were looking at the same issues and trends from completely different perspectives. It was as if the HR and line people were from two different universes (their being from two different planets in the same universe would have been less of a chasm between them). Keep in mind these were senior HR people and thought leaders of the field.

A key outcome for HR from this meeting was the imperative for HR professionals to "get inside the heads of CEOs" if HR is going to be a valuable function. This means more than "learning the language of business" or "adapting the phrases CEOs are fond of using." To get inside a CEO's (or anyone's) head, you must study and learn about that person's world and how he or she sees it. In other words, you must be students of organizations. And in that process, you uncover ways HR professionals are uniquely positioned to help these organizations and the people employed by them. See May and Kahnweiler (2002) for a complete description of this meeting, the lessons learned for HR professionals, and ways you can apply those lessons in your daily work.

For us, learning about organizations has been intriguing and stimulating. Sometimes it has been frustrating, confusing, aggravating, and even joyless. But more often than not, the work is intensely interesting because people and the organizations where they labor are fascinating, unpredictable, not totally rational, and anything but boring or meaningless. If you are crafting an HR career, chances are that you, too, find people fascinating (as well as other qualities, some not so complimentary). And chances are, if you find people fascinating, you will be drawn to organizations—those curious entities composed of groups of very fascinating people. We sincerely hope your interest in organizations never ends, either. And after all, when you find something so fascinating, don't you want to keep learning about it?

References

Creelman, D. 2004. "Interview: Dr. Wayne Brockbank. New Findings from HR Research." HR.Com. http://redir.hr.com/c.asp?s=24798472&l=123168 (accessed May 2004).

French, WL, and CH Bell. 1990. *OD: Behavioral Science Interventions for Organizational Improvement.* Saddle Ridge, NJ: Prentice-Hall.

French, JRP, and B Raven. 1959. "The Bases of Social Power." In *Studies in Social Power.* Ed. D Cartwright. Ann Arbor, MI: University of Michigan Institute for Social Research.

May, GL, and B Kahnweiler. 2002. "Shareholder Value: Is There Common Ground?" *Training and Development* July: 44–52.

Meisinger, S. 2003. "When You Talk, Do People Listen?" *HR Magazine* 48, no. 9: 8.

Peters, TJ. 1999. *The Circle of Innovation: You Can't Shrink Your Way to Greatness.* New York: Knopf.

Schein, EL. 1999. *The Corporate Culture Survival Guide: Sense and Nonsense About Culture Change.* San Francisco: Jossey-Bass.

Vosburgh, RM. 2003. "The State of the HR Profession in 2003: An Interview with Dave Ulrich." *HR Planning* 26, no. 1: 18–22.

8

Achieving Results: Pathways to Success

What does success look like? Throughout this book we have discussed the HR Career Success Model and ideas, strategies, and tools to support your growth in this dynamic profession. Our goal has been to provoke your thinking and offer you a reality-based perspective of what it is like to practice HR in today's organizations.

This chapter contains examples and analyses drawn from our 60+ years of experience in HR plus the wealth of experience our expert interviewees shared with us. These examples do not portray perfection but rather are reality-based illustrations from which you can learn. What are the challenges you meet when getting out there and applying knowledge? What positive outcomes can you reach, and how do you actually achieve results?

Organizations are living, breathing organisms that are unique and ever changing. Even though your situation will vary from the prototypes described, we think you can learn important universal lessons from these stories. As you read this chapter, focus on the lessons learned in these scenarios and ask yourself how you can apply them to your own career. Think about the goals you want to achieve in your career and focus on the stories or examples that resonate with you. If you are aware of the goals you want to focus on, chances are you will be more receptive to multiple strategies for getting there.

Achieving results is measured by a number of key outcomes: (1) Win-Win—Achieving satisfying results for you and your clients. Customers truly partner with you. (2) Passion—You have a deep commitment for the work you do and the people you serve. (3) Marketing by the Customer—Customers seek out your expertise and do your marketing for you. (4) Demonstrated Impact—Customers demonstrate and use what they have learned from you in their work. (5) Values Conflicts—Differing agendas and priorities that must be confronted for mean-

153

ingful work to take place. If these conflicts are not dealt with, little impactful work is probably taking place. HR professionals directly contribute to organizationally valued outcomes, and you are seen as value added.

Let's peel back the layers on each of these outcome measures to see what they mean and how you can achieve them. In this first section, we will provide some specific cases of successful win-win situations.

Win-Win

Creating a win-win situation means that both parties are getting what they want. You, as the HR professional, are gaining satisfaction in the work you are doing and at the same time you are delivering benefits the organization values. Let's look at how this plays out in several different situations.

Bringing in the Experts Who Are Already There

In reality, what does the picture of win-win look like? Consider a scenario one of us faced as an internal HR professional in a large heavy manufacturing facility of a Fortune 10 company. Most of the 1,000 first-line supervisors had risen through the ranks. Although competent in the technical aspects of their work, they seriously lacked management and leadership skills. Employee grievances were rising, and it became increasingly apparent to Human Resources that the root cause of the problems on the factory floor was related to poor or out-of-date management practices. The decision was made to implement a five-day company-wide supervisory course for this population. There was initial resistance to the idea, especially when it meant time away from the floor. In addition, production expectations were at an all time high.

The HR team, in collaboration with a newly appointed director of supervisor training, decided that they could minimize resistance by going for a strategy of teaming with line supervisors. They co-designed the training program. The HR team acted as the subject matter experts while the line supervisors knew the audience and the teaching approaches that would likely be most effective. Perhaps most importantly, the director and line supervisor co-trainers brought a tremendous amount of credibility to the project. When it came time to deliver the training, the audience was already sold, and the program received high reviews. This approach was successfully replicated in other company locations.

In this case, the training program was well received, and the company achieved its objectives. Note how earning the trust and credibility of the customers (the supervisors) was so critical here. In addition, the HR staff showed that they under stood the appropriate role to play. Instead of highlighting their role as "experts" in management training, they tapped a key source of the expertise. By creating a program that involved and engaged key representatives from the ranks, they scored points. They showed their value by understanding their customers. In addition, they applied their knowledge of the organization by understanding what it would take to gain their stakeholders' acceptance and support.

Giving Them Something Extra

Consultant Linda Kammire-Tiffin aims to have interactions with her clients that are "deep enough and rich enough so that we both walk away having learned something." When Linda meets new clients, she lets them do the talking and sees her key role as asking good questions. As a result she gets people to divulge their passions, their philosophy, and the way they approach their business role. She uses this information when collaborating with them to come up with viable solutions.

Linda will often look for opportunities to demonstrate her value by doing something "extra" for clients. She shared such an example with us. "A prospective client of mine was preparing an announcement for managers about the focus and purpose of an upcoming management retreat. She needed something that was informative and offered a good incentive to attend the meeting. I drafted a sample announcement that she (the client) used nearly verbatim. It made her life easier during a high stress time. The prospect was surprised and very appreciative to receive the help, and ultimately did business with us."

Linda believes that this strategy results in prospects feeling that she is not just "selling them." She gives away some of her expertise to develop partnerships. The same approach of giving away resources can also be applied successfully in internal consulting situations. If you focus on helping others and not just seeing what you can get, this approach reframes the relationship. You are more likely to have people reciprocate when this occurs.

Partnering for the Long Term

Dianne Smith found herself in the midst of a major reorganization at her university library. She contracted with an outside consulting firm that specializes in organizational redesign. The company introduced Dianne to a model of organizational intervention that helped her to focus and move forward with effective changes. Though she described the process, which lasted several years, as both exhausting and exhilarating, she found this partnering (with the external consultant and her clients) to be a win-win for her, her constituents, and the organization. The library achieved the restructuring with a minimum of pain, she said. The project also had the significant impact of raising the visibility of HR. Another key result for Dianne was that she learned that she had a lot of expertise and skill to bring to the table.

Dianne knew that showing value was important in influencing people over which she did not have authority. By calling in additional expertise to supplement hers and by using her consulting skills, she was able to achieve a win-win situation.

Demonstrating the Benefit of Face Time

One of our interviewees designed a multi-rater feedback system and rolled it out to more than 100 managers. In reflecting back on the successful results of this project, he shared that the "face time" he had with these individuals helped him gain acceptance and respect. He was able to earn trust and credibility by networking and building relationships. He also demonstrated his value by producing a high-quality process that encouraged managers to be open and honest with him. His win was in gaining great satisfaction in seeing "how I helped them." The managers gained a deeper understanding of their "blind spots," or what behaviors and actions they could improve upon with their teams. With the help of this individual, they were able to also see what strengths they could build upon in their managerial repertoire.

Achieving Win-Wins with the Boss

A vice president of HR at a large bank sees achieving win-wins between himself and his manager as vital. His victory emerges when he provides two to three viable solutions to his boss and does not just present the problem. To do this, he needs to dip into his knowledge base. Sometimes it involves research about his organization and the approaches that will work in that culture. At other points his solutions might push him out of his comfort zone, and he might present a new and different approach to a problem (for example, telecommuting is one solution that has emerged in some traditional companies as a way to offer cost savings). The vice president's research may even involve accessing knowledge about best practices in HR. How have other companies handled similar problems? Being able to access this knowledge helps him prepare more impactful solutions to present to his boss.

Making a Difference with Employee Surveys

What follows is an example of one area in which HR professionals have an opportunity to achieve true results for an organization and use the win-win approach to get there. A recent article in *HR Magazine* (Garvey 2004) highlighted the increased focus of employee surveys on employees' connection to and perception of their employer's business. With an emphasis on turning this feedback into actionable goals, employees are asked for their input and ideas. As Craig Ramsey, a senior HR manager at Intuit, one of the profiled companies, said, "We encourage our leaders to hold their managers accountable for moving the score in the right direction" (p. 75). Active support for this focus on performance by the senior team has proved to be critical. The potential for achieving business goals and increasing employee satisfaction and retention are tremendous in well-executed survey initiatives.

Like the conductor of an orchestra, the HR professional leading survey efforts has the opportunity to access knowledge of self, the field, and the organization. High social competence is needed to navigate your way through all the constituencies and their competing agendas. Self-knowledge is also required to understand where you may need to supplement your skills and rely on team members to help you interpret data or present reports. You will need to choose appropriate roles by looking at the big picture and deciding how you can best help your clients. The challenge will be to stay focused and clear about what your role is. Perhaps it is to facilitate a team action planning session, or maybe it is coaching a manager on performance improvement. Or maybe the best role you can play is to consult with the CEO on the most effective way to communicate the results to the organization. By doing this, you are showing your value to the organization. Like the previous interviewee who relished the "face time," you will continue to gain trust and credibility in this role.

Another element of Applying Knowledge, honoring boundaries, is certainly at play here. In any large visible initiative like employee surveys, you can easily lose focus and become overwhelmed by data and deadlines. Remember that you are the conductor, which means that you are facilitating the project but are not playing each instrument. You do not "own" the entire project. When you are keeping your boundaries in mind, being able to say "no" is especially helpful in setting limits.

Passion

Passion is the belief that what you do matters to yourself, your organization, and the people you serve. This sometimes elusive element can be seen in the examples that follow.

Black Belt Boot Camp

Several years ago we were involved in the launch of one of the first wide-scale implementations of Black Belt training at GE Capital. This was part of a transformational quality improvement initiative, which was to have far-reaching implications. The goal was to decrease the number of defects in the company and revamp these service-oriented businesses into highly cost-effective and cost-efficient enterprises. The term "black belt" refers to a certification in this area that is granted to individuals trained in the processes of Six Sigma (an approach to quality). The company invested a significant amount of resources toward its execution.

The Opportunities and Challenges

Our training team of four experienced internal consultants entered into this arena with a mixture of excitement and anxiety. On the one hand, as internal consultants, we had the opportunity to ride the crest of this emerging methodology and establish a serious place for ourselves in a core business of the company. We could also make a direct contribution to bottom-line results. This new, more quantifiable approach to doing business yielded great business potential.

On the other hand, the task was daunting. We faced tight preparation and delivery deadlines, mixed receptiveness from our participants, and the need to learn new and challenging content.

As the weeks went by, we rallied as a team and divided up delivery segments. We coached each other in content and delivery and practiced smoothing out the kinks of co-facilitating. We negotiated course deliverables with our highly supportive manager and worked closely with outside consultants, some of them the top names in the field of quality improvement. We shadowed these experts, co-taught with them, and received intensive coaching and feedback.

As we sweated it out around conference tables and on airplanes, our team bonded and focused on our common objective. We aimed to deliver the highest quality training program possible to our business. We led numerous "boot camp" experiences. We delivered a compressed week of interactive training for intact teams, whose members were all responsible for a process. Often the team members were composed of people from different departments.

The training sessions included drilling and testing in the principles of Six Sigma. They also covered work on team building and the change management process. Teams arrived with challenges to address, and we helped them apply the theory to their issues. We made presentations and also facilitated the small group sessions in which our skills at managing group dynamics came into play.

As consultants, we also became strong believers in this approach as we saw creative solutions emerge and action plans start moving. We watched people step out of their comfort zones and move into team leadership roles. Although our formal role did not include follow-up, we were able to learn about successes when participants returned to the workplace, and this news was very gratifying.

Achieving Results

How else did we know the sessions were a success? Metrics were instituted, and a large majority of our participants "passed" the course. That is, they had the basic knowledge of Six Sigma tools to make it happen. We knew we had met our objectives, however, when we received more-than-high "smile sheet" (course evaluation) rankings completed at the end of the course.

The teams emerged with newly designed and more effective ways of conducting business. Procurement teams eliminated stubborn bottlenecks in the purchasing process. HR teams designed ways to reduce steps in the turnaround time to their internal clients. Customer service groups created new strategies to increase customer satisfaction. By working together across departments, team members understood their work from a much broader perspective and began to take ownership of their work. We also observed many of them exhibit passion for the improvements they were moving toward.

Of course, not all the projects were successful. Some fell apart before the week was even over. We tried to learn from those teams and practice our own quality analysis of what worked and didn't in the training that contributed to those results. In some classes resistance was high because of the organizations the team members came from; in these cases, no amount of training or passion on our part would break through that resistance.

The truth was we also developed passion for our work. We were motivated to do the best job we could possibly do, we knew how important this work was to our organization, and we wanted to transmit that enthusiasm and knowledge to our customers.

How did we succeed in this work? We applied our knowledge in a number of key areas in this scenario. First, we had to access knowledge. We had to be organized and know how to get to the tools and resources we had at our disposal, including numerous books and manuals. Knowing what content areas needed beefing up, determining what additional knowledge we needed about the teams and their work processes, and understanding how our work fit into the direction of the corporate learning center all were important. In addition, we had to use self-knowledge to recognize our limitations and strengths in assigning work among our team.

We also had to choose appropriate roles. We needed to know when to play the role of guide versus that of expert in facilitating the training teams and we had to know when to push back and when to let the process evolve. We showed value by playing a consulting role throughout the training program and, as mentioned, following the on-site work. We also learned to work in partnership with our external consultants who were able to field many questions we were unable or unqualified to answer. Rather than fake it, we referred these queries out to them (and listened to the responses so that we could continually add to our knowledge capital). We increased our trust and credibility with our constituents by proving our competence and expertise. Finally, we built strong relationships across the company and connected people on our team with one another.

Passion Is Contagious

Many of our interviewees spoke about passion as a key motivator for themselves and their work. Kay Yoest, Vice President of Human Resources at Munich American Reinsurance Company, feels strongly that you need to have passion and a belief that your work is important. To be engaged, she puts herself in the shoes of her clients. When they know she is relating to their world, they are more likely to partner with her. She also shows value by finding out what her clients need and demonstrates how she can help them. "I have to be genuine," she says. When you lack commitment and energy, then you are simply going through the motions and your clients can see right through your overtures.

Kay also indicated that creating and designing programs, and not just executing them, led to strong passion for her work. We agree that when you are involved and stretching yourself, you are more likely to gain energy and enthusiasm, which transmits to your clients.

Dave Potts, a director of OD and Training, described passion as a key outcome measure for his work. In answer to the question "How do you measure success?" he said, "Clients enthusiastically take action based on my work with them." Another senior-level HR manager in banking said, "If you are not enjoying the work and having fun, get out and do something else." Having a drive and excitement about what you do will be contagious. Such fervor is probably the best-selling tool you have for your work.

Marketing by the Customer

Let's look at the next benchmark of achieving results: marketing by customers. When your customers or clients do your marketing for you, you can give yourself some credit. This behavior usually means that they have benefited from working with you and want to pass on your name as a resource. Sincere client testimonials are strong indicators that repeat business is forthcoming.

We don't typically take courses in marketing or selling. However, as many in the HR world have come to learn, promotion and selling can make up a large part of what HR professionals do. Often what we call "selling" is an educational process. For instance, highlighting the benefits of Six Sigma to the teams described earlier and influencing managers to get behind a 360-degree feedback program are both examples. If you do your job well, marketing becomes easier each time. Your customers are more receptive to what you can offer them. As happens with a great restaurant that you tell your friends about, the word about your performance will spread quickly and will either be greeted with open arms or avoided like the plague. Consider the cases described next.

Partner Relocation Assistance: An Entrepreneur Learns Important Lessons

Back in the late 1980s, one of us took a leap into entrepreneurship and began a consulting firm. Research had told us that there was a need for partner relocation assistance with an emphasis on job search support in recruiting and retaining brand managers. Our first client, a large consumer products company, asked us to develop and test a program that provided career assistance counseling for this target group. The program proved to be very successful in helping these partners land positions quickly, and we quickly had more business than we could handle.

Simultaneously, we developed a solid business plan, financing and marketing support, and a strong team of advisors. We also were excited about our work, a contributor to business success. Boosted by this commitment from a Fortune 50 company and our own drive, we were poised for more clients to come in the door. Can you guess what happened? You are right if you say the cycle of life took hold.

Business was steady in the first few months, and our stories of satisfied individuals multiplied. Though our key internal customer continued to market us throughout the organization, we faced a few initial challenges. First, we had not factored that the company was involved in active recruiting for only four to five months a year. Second, we found that even though our internal organization champions were giving us testimonials, this wasn't translating into volumes of business. These HR partners agreed that the service was needed and an important endeavor, but they needed to convince their clients, the brand managers, to use it.

We decided we needed to jump in and increase our communication and marketing efforts with these individuals. With the collaboration of the internal HR team, we created several one-page memos, the accepted format for communicating in this company. We presented the brand managers with statistics about our placements and gave updates to the HR team. We shared our testimonials and encouraged spouses and partners to communicate their positive feedback directly with the company.

We also secured local press relationships and fed stories to local reporters. Because this field of dual-career couples was a new emerging area, we pitched stories related to our expertise to media outlets. We became known as the "go-to" firm in that city for career consultation, dual-career issues, and many human resource topics.

After a few nail-biting months, our efforts paid off in an upward trend in referrals. We increased the number of referrals from this company and branched outside. In some cases, the HR team members marketed us to their peers in other companies. Our client list expanded through these referrals and our own concerted and persistent marketing efforts. These relationships eventually grew to encompass a national client base.

After we had developed our client relationships, our customers approached us about some of their other needs. For instance, we created a career assessment program customized for their management trainees as well as an outplacement program for those new hires that didn't fit into the organization for one reason or another. We even added personally guided tours for recruits the company was trying to attract to the city. We reached our financial goals at the end of the first year and stayed in the black until we sold the business for a profit several years later.

How We Achieved Results

We applied knowledge of the client in shaping interventions to meet their needs. In the case of the consumer products company, we learned as much as we could about the company to understand the key concerns of the HR group. We shared our successful results with the client to make this partnership work and continue to listen and respond to their needs. In this way we showed our value. We used our relationships and networking throughout the organization and community to build bridges and establish our brand. Out of these relationships grew trust and, of course, credibility, as we delivered on our promises.

Another key lesson we took from marketing was to diversify our client base and avoid relying on one client to meet all our needs! We also learned an invaluable lesson about the way organizations work. We continued along the entrepreneurial path for the next 20 years and reflect back on that first venture as a pivotal time of learning and growth—especially about what it takes to succeed in doing business.

Marketing from the Top

A director of Human Resources at a large metropolitan hospital told us how he had become the confidante of a senior vice president. It is commonly known that the higher up you go in a company, the lonelier it can be. There are not many people with whom you can share your challenges. Another HR generalist rode in the car with the CEO and provided counsel to him away from his inner circle. The CEO could let down his hair and share his fears and challenges in an open and honest way with this person. As the hospital director shared, "The Senior Vice President gave me credibility and expertise, and I got more business from his marketing of me."

Both these professionals demonstrated their value and didn't need to worry about selling themselves to their clients. They had shown their value and earned trust and credibility. Thankfully, their selling was done for them by performing well in these key coaching roles.

Another interviewee who was a senior HR manager in banking found his marketing came from the highest levels of the bank. The senior executive team knows that he is "someone they can put in front of the Board of Directors and be confident that I will perform." To achieve this level of confidence, he had chosen appropriate roles in interacting with the senior team. He demonstrated competence so the team knew that he could think on his feet and represent their views to the key decision makers in the company. Again, this was a case in which trust and credibility were at an all-time high.

Acting as Business Advisor, Not Order Taker

Tom Darrow, a successful recruiting consultant mentioned for his networking prowess in Chapter 5, has a central way of gauging his impact. He observes how much clients actively solicit his opinion. As a business advisor and not "an order taker," he helps out clients even when he is not billing them. As referrals come his way from those clients and others, he knows that he has satisfied their needs. He also judges his results by the number of repeat referrals he receives. People seek out Tom because, like the other professionals in this section, he has proven his trust and credibility, shown his value, and selected the appropriate roles to use with these clients.

So is marketing by the customer the only way you obtain new business? Of course not. The bottom line is you still must educate prospective clients about ways you can help them solve problems. However, we have also tried to illustrate that good work sells. You will end up getting repeat business and referrals for new business when your customers are pleased with their results.

Demonstrating Impact

If you are making a difference in your organizations, your clients should be clearly demonstrating and applying what they have learned from you. You should be contributing directly to organizationally valued outcomes. This is what we mean when we say that HR must be "at the table." The question is, "How are you truly making a difference in a way that is connected to your organization's success?" Let's look at some sample cases.

Shifting Perceptions of HR

In her work as an internal HR consultant for a large telecommunications company, Margaret Brake seized the opportunity to work with a senior executive who had just taken over a new department in need of change. He brought with him the reputation of being difficult to work with but also came with a strong drive to improve the team's performance. Though he didn't ask for her help, Margaret jumped right in and offered to partner with him in his change efforts. She knew that she could leverage her organizational design expertise and experience and, if necessary, bring in the appropriate resources to assist with other HR functions.

Margaret decided to put rumors of his personality aside and confidently approached the manager. She offered to help him plan and execute a two-day strategy meeting. He accepted her offer. Together they planned a successful strategy retreat with the department where they analyzed their current and desired future state. They created a mission and vision plus looked at roles and ways to satisfy customer needs. The manager wisely followed Margaret's suggestion to involve other members of the leadership team. The two of them asked the team to help plan agendas and encouraged their input in planning sessions. Most of the team participated willingly in this process. Margaret also involved other HR team members to assist with aspects of the project. However, she did experience resistance from some members of the team she believed were uncomfortable with an external HR team member being the boss' confidante.

Despite this challenge, the reorganization project was a huge success. Margaret and the executive partnered on a number of subsequent projects also geared toward reaching tangible business goals. He actually ended up nominating Margaret for an achievement award and told her boss that "in all my years of work, I never had an HR person like this before." She was very pleased to be able to contribute by doing work she loves, and her client, thankfully, gained a new appreciation for what the value of HR could be.

How She Achieved Results

Margaret demonstrated many aspects of the HR Career Success Model in this scenario, including drawing upon her knowledge of self. For instance, she took initiative and applied her experience and skills. She had the self-confidence to take a risk and approach a manager whom many avoided. Yet she continued to be proactive in working with this manager and collaborated with him because she knew she could add value to his leadership.

Margaret also accessed her specialized OD knowledge by planning and executing consulting interventions. She was client driven and knew she needed to refer work to specialists in compensation and job design because this work was outside her area of expertise. Margaret showed tremendous value to her customer as indicated by her award. High Emotional Intelligence allowed Margaret to build a relationship with this executive, and she continued to offer him consulting services as his needs evolved.

Investing in Talent

Erin Hand, Director of Leadership Development at her company, measures her success by how it directly impacts the business. In the leadership development program she spearheads, one key measure she looks at is the number of people promoted. In addition, she reviews data that indicate how well their knowledge is transferring to the job. Erin also indicated that her goals for the business and for the growth of human beings are intertwined. She says that when she sees the participants in her development program grow and also do what they love, she knows that this is making them better people both at work and at home.

A Failure If They Leave

A vice president of Human Resources at a financial services company puts a priority on developing a strong talent pool for her organization. She assesses the people skills of managers, conducts 360-degree feedback appraisals, and coaches them toward improvement. She also sees her role as championing strong individuals for promotions. Though some might argue that she is taking ownership for outcomes she can't control, she takes this role very seriously and says, "I consider myself a failure if they leave (the company)."

Selecting the Successor

Carol Dubnicki, Director, Human Resources, Shell International Exploration and Production, values the success she achieves through influencing others. She said that her most gratifying experiences have involved having someone selected as the successor to the CEO and being able to help positively impact leadership behavior.

All three HR professionals just discussed indicated that they build trust and credibility with their clients by aligning with business goals. By understanding the changing direction of their organizations, they are working on priorities. That is, they are actively contributing to the retention of high-level talent in their organizations. What better way to demonstrate impact than rolling up their sleeves and focusing on these individuals? Their impact is clearly demonstrated.

Demonstrating Results in a Government Setting

One interesting project we were involved in as external consultants illustrates how HR professionals can demonstrate impact in other ways. Several years ago, we were faced with the challenge of creating a career and training center for 200 employees of the regional office of a federal agency. Starting from scratch, we worked closely with a very proactive and supportive HR manager and staff member who were creative, "out-of-the-box thinkers." They both strongly believed in collaboration and finding innovative ways to get things done. In addition a strong group of union representatives had input into the process.

This group had a vision of providing a place where all levels of staff could grow their careers and receive coaching support. Fortunately, the imperious walls of bureaucracy did not stymie the leadership team. Our clients asked us to use our expertise to make this vision a reality and supported us in finding resources, fighting organizational obstacles, and advocating on our behalf.

We went to work and put some processes and programs in place after conducting a thorough needs assessment of each department. We also took time to get to know the key players and those among the ranks. Through interviews, observation, and surveys we were able to develop a strong mission and strategy for the "Skill Clinic." Programs such as a leadership development series and executive coaching, a variety of skill based training programs, computerized career assessment and counseling, facilitated team-building retreats and staff meetings all grew from this mission of providing career and leadership development for each employee.

As word of our service spread and strong reviews came in, we were asked to provide more and more services. In response to this need, we hired some local graduate interns and put them to work. We also found that people sought us out for a variety of other human resource development questions. We found ourselves having to put some limits on the amount of time we could spend on different activities such as individual counseling sessions.

We were sure to stay closely connected to organizational changes within the agency so that our programs reflected these priorities at the local level. For instance, when it was discovered that more qualified candidates were needed for certain positions, we worked with employees to help them prepare Individual Development Plans and ramp up in the required skill areas.

One major result of our three-year involvement with this agency was formal recognition of the program by the headquarters agency. The program was replicated as a best practice throughout the country, and we were brought in to teach other branches how to adopt our approaches. The Skill Clinic model thrives today.

How We Achieved Results

How else did we achieve results? We accessed our knowledge from a variety of the past venues we had worked in as well as from our own knowledge of organizational development. We also worked hard as outsiders to earn the trust and credibility of our clients and found that they did much of our marketing for us. Stepping into the world of government work from the private sector is a real transition. Choosing appropriate roles by learning the culture, including the many acronyms and forms that are used, was a feat in itself. As our part-time schedule filled up with clients, we had to know our limits and say no to clients who wanted to know if we "just had a minute."

This example illustrates multiple signposts of success. Marketing by other satisfied clients and win-win outcomes were prevalent. At the same time, what made all that possible was the impact of our efforts on people and the organization. In serving as an internal consultant, we facilitated changes in the management behaviors of some key managers. We also assisted in helping them create more positive work climates. Employees reported being more motivated to enhance their skills and progress forward, knowing that resources were there to support them. Increased responsiveness to the agency's constituents as indicated by their feedback and service use was a particularly rewarding impact of this scenario.

Proving Your Worth When It Counts

Learning Technologies Manager John Courtney was giving a presentation on performance management when he was thrown a curve-ball question by one of the participating managers. He answered by thinking on his feet. He soon found himself a consultant to this manager who respected John's wisdom and insight. John clearly showed his value. He chose the expert role in coming back with his cogent answer in this training session and transitioned to the role of guide for this manager who trusted his opinion. John had but a fleeting moment to demonstrate his value and he hit a bull's eye. You never know when such a moment may surface, so you need to be vigilant and seize the opportunity when it appears.

Using Numbers to Measure Results

Sometimes HR professionals are able to quantify their success to demonstrate their impact. As an example, client surveys and 360-degree feedback appraisals are commonly used to provide concrete data about the effectiveness of interventions. Jonathon Dawe, Director of Safety, Training, and Development at The Simmons Company, took on safety because he knew that it was a key results area for his company. In this role, he had the opportunity of working with all people "from the floor sweeper to the CEO," Jonathon believes that it is important to get out of the HR silo and "earn your rewards daily."

He implemented an internal national safety audit process, rigorous accident investigations and workers' compensation claims handling, behavior-based safety training and detailed regulatory safety training, and a slew of other key initiatives. In addition, he focused on a targeted prevention initiative that emphasized such activities as company-wide campaigns on wellness topics and company-sponsored health club memberships.

In the safety arena, Jonathon proudly reported that his company reduced OSHA error rates by 400 percent in two years and his company fell significantly below the industry average. Another tangible number he cited was a tenfold reduction in workers' compensation claims. By taking on a high-visibility area where he could influence change, Jonathon demonstrated leadership. In moving into an operations area, he also established trust and credibility with the plant managers with whom he was collaborating. And the numbers spoke for themselves. Being able to validly and legitimately capture the results of your work quantitatively goes a long way in planting the seeds for a successful HR career path.

Confronting Resistance Head On

You often learn the most from the most complex projects. The project described next deals with the way resistance must be dealt with before you have any hope of achieving results.

Background

A large media and entertainment organization desired to revamp its performance management process and increase employee involvement. The rationale was to achieve higher levels of performance and increased productivity in an increasingly competitive marketplace. HR was charged with implementing a company-wide program that would translate this objective into reality. The HR team members were charged with encouraging employees to take ownership of their work. They also wanted to develop the coaching skill set of managers so that the managers could become more effective at leading and motivating their employees and not just managing the work.

The HR team partnered with our group of external consultants to design and execute a performance-based coaching process targeted at managers and employees. This initiative focused on a number of components to support this wide-scale change including redesign of the entire performance management system. The decision was made by senior management to roll out this program across the organization, so a training initiative was launched. Mandatory training classes were scheduled for managers and employees.

The management programs focused on the rationale for this change, demonstrating how this performance management approach aligned with the company's direction, challenging participants to directly link their individual and department goals with those of the organization. The classes provided many tools and approaches to help managers build coaching and leadership tactics into their roles. They were positioned as the catalyst to motivate and move their teams toward reaching stretch objectives. These classes also focused on sharpening communication skills.

The employee programs covered some of the same content and were tailored to encourage employees to take ownership of their work. They were also designed to equip employees with skills to become more proactive and involved. In addition, they taught the employees techniques for coaching and mentoring their peers to achieve results.

In company-wide change interventions like this one, we have learned that many variables can influence outcomes. Support from the top, clear and ongoing communications about the change, past changes and their outcomes, and the financial health or stability of the company can all be factors. When we joined the project in the early months, the jury still seemed to be out on how committed the company was to changing the leadership focus to one that was more performance based. There also had been several recent mergers and an impending acquisition, so uncertainty and anxiety were high among participants.

Classes were designed to occur over a four-week period with practice assignments built in between sessions. This homework usually involved a discussion with the participant's manager to apply learning from the class as well as a skill practice exercise to apply on the job. At the first session of the management class, it was our standard practice to introduce the goals and objectives and surface the perceived barriers. In other words, what did participants feel would impede them from getting on board with this new company direction? Answers ranged from lack of time to commit to the new process to concerns about their managers, some of whom they saw as nonsupportive of the new way of leading.

As facilitators, our team first validated these concerns by writing them on flip charts. In some cases, we had enough knowledge about the concerns to provide answers on the spot (for example, Question: "How will we be able to leave our jobs to come to class?" Answer: "Your manager must give you the time off as it is company policy"). Sometimes, other participants who were having successes or had previously had some success using these coaching strategies offered testimonials for applying some of the tools of the course (for example, "Being able to delegate work to my peer and ask in a direct way really was effective").

We didn't try to "fix" all these concerns and asked the project leaders to help us respond to questions we could not answer. We made sure to address those in the following class or by e-mail to the individual involved. We also reinforced the expectations of the senior leadership that the company was indeed transitioning to this new approach of performance management and that our HR team was there to help participants succeed.

Classes proceeded, and we received mostly positive results. As people experimented with new techniques such as active listening and asking open ended questions, they experienced small successes. Some managers reported having a dialogue with their managers for the first time. Employees shared how setting goals forced them to ask important questions of their internal and external customers. The answers often led them to fix processes. One technical manager gathered his team together for regular team meetings and actually listened to their improvement ideas. He reported a changed work climate. Participants relayed anecdotes to the class and in turn received valuable feedback about ways they might handle these tough work situations.

Of course, as in many of our experiences in HR, resistance raised its high and mighty head. The most challenging experience came when we were assigned to facilitate the in-house attorneys and their staffs in one of the leadership classes. From the beginning, a number of them argued with the premise of the class. They saw no reason for changing how they operated. Instead of engaging in arguments, we decided to bring in some credible leadership to address their issues directly. We explained the "push back" to the chief counsel and asked her to address the group in the next class. She made a persuasive case for the company's changes, referencing increased company earnings and cost efficiencies as central drivers. She also made a strong personal case for her own transformation in switching to a more participative leadership style and shared some of the key results of this transition. Although not everyone in the room agreed with the idea of attending these classes, everyone had a chance to debate, ask questions, and be heard. In addition, the chief counsel decided to fully participate in the classes and, by doing so, modeled the type of behavior that she wanted her team to exhibit.

The remainder of the classes proceeded without great drama. Most people actively participated, although some appeared to "check out" by not completing assignments and conducting sidebar conversations in class. We chose not to focus on this. We prepared illustrations of the principles and conducted skill demonstrations using familiar scenarios. Role plays were encouraged. Stimulating discussions often went to the core of some of their toughest leadership issues, such as motivating employees, handling discipline, and so on ("Why should I involve my employee when I know the answer to the question?").

What we discovered was that most of the attorneys had had little management training and were actually uncomfortable in this area of managing performance and coaching. Aside from their not valuing the emphasis on "soft skills," we think that their overt and more passive resistance arose from this lack of confidence. As they experienced some success in their coaching sessions outside the classroom, we saw some positive change in the classroom. This wasn't true for everyone, of course. The classes received strong ratings, and follow-up feedback indicated that the new system was being implemented across the department. In addition, the Chief Counsel was pleased to report that she thought the class had achieved its objective and also knew she had further work with her group.

How We Achieved Success

Against a strong background of resistance, we achieved our targets and met the expectations of our client. What factors helped us to achieve results in this training scenario? There were several: (1) We accessed our knowledge base by learning as much as we could about the reasons for this organizational change. Understanding what was driving the cultural shift, who the players were, and what the rationale for the changes were critical in demonstrating competence to this group of attorneys who place a high value on expertise and knowledge. (2) We also learned as much as we could about the challenges and problems of the legal department by talking with members of our internal HR team as well as the General Counsel throughout. We found out what they were most concerned about (for example, making a case to the legal department and providing them with a foundation of skills). (3) We worked in partnership with the General Counsel and encouraged her to tie the HR efforts to organizational outcomes instead of asking us to do all the convincing. We knew that this was a key strategy to use with this population of attorneys. (4) Preparing our content (sometimes overpreparing) was necessary so that we could feel confident before leading these classes. We sometimes even role rehearsed the lecture portions to be absolutely prepared. (5) We also had to draw upon our knowledge of the training field and our experience in handling resistant participants. Using approaches and techniques to avoid alienating participants and effectively meet and channel resistance was critical. Otherwise, we risked losing the respect of the entire group. (6) We accessed our knowledge of self. Understanding that our style was a more collaborative one meant that we had to shift to a more directive, at times combative, style in order to be heard. At other times we had to use our inner strength and self-confidence to avoid taking some strong comments personally. (7) We also knew that honoring boundaries was important in achieving success in this scenario. By not taking ownership of their resistance, yet validating their concerns, we allowed them to move forward at the pace and manner which worked for them.

Values Conflicts

We believe that all HR professionals experience values conflicts in their work. If you are not questioning the work you are doing and how it is being done, then you are probably not doing meaningful work. Values conflicts are a normal and necessary part of how you conduct business. Although there is no roadmap for ways to handle all conceivable situations, you can learn from the experiences of your colleagues.

Walk the Talk

As external consultants to a large, growing metropolitan hospital, we were involved in the wide-scale implementation of a new performance compensation system. Our reporting directly to the CEO was beneficial in that the implementation was turned around quickly due to his firm verbal and financial commitment to the project. Interestingly enough, however, shortly after the system was launched, we realized that the CEO was neglecting to use the tools and processes with his own senior team. The consultants saw the futility of their work when the leader was not "walking the talk" of this program that he was verbally promoting so strongly. There was a strong disconnect as more members of the organization became aware of his lack of participation and questioned why they should change at all.

At this point, we had already been paid for the bulk of our work with the hospital. It would have been easy to walk away, happy with our take. However, we felt that it was important to bring up our concern to the CEO about the lack of consistent behavior between his vocalized and actual behavior. He was a stubborn individual, and we knew that we might risk his wrath and even future work with his organization. To our surprise, he did respond favorably and even asked us to coach him as he transitioned to this new process.

How Our Values Came into Play

The CEO was consumed with a multitude of other concerns, as any health care executive should be. He simply had unintentionally overlooked how important it was for him to model the behavior he wanted emulated. We could have easily avoided the confrontation and rationalized this fairly easily (Why make waves?). However, we decided to bring up the issue for one major reason; walking our talk—demonstrating integrity—is a value that we embrace. We felt it important in doing work with this client that we put our cards on the table. If he had not reacted positively to our feedback, we would have had much less respect for his change efforts. We would have questioned his true commitment and our own in working with him in the future.

We had the courage to be assertive and stay true to our values. We also knew that by doing the right thing (in naming what we observed) we were also increasing the chances of success with the program. Another unintended result of this intervention was that the HR team became more responsive to us and began to take on more initiative in driving the new compensation system.

Conflict of Interest

Anybody familiar with college recruiting practices knows that it is fairly common for organizations seeking the best and the brightest to invite college placement representatives to their sites. They hope to give these advisors a first-hand look at their companies and create a buzz about working there. On one such tour of a large computer software organization, we were particularly impressed with the "show" that was put on. We experienced all the bells and whistles from dinners in upscale restaurants to a tennis tournament at the local country club. We even were given a chance to visit with the celebrity CEO. With drama and flair, he flew in on his helicopter to a pad outside the office. It was hard not to believe that every one of our graduating students would be anything other than thrilled to work at such a "cool" company.

After we returned home, we were able to put the trip into some perspective. We learned more about the software business and, in particular, the culture and direction of this company. We also realized the kind of student who might be a good fit for this organization and, likewise, the type who might be miserable working there. We attempted to provide objective information to our student clients by doing research on the company's competitors and did our best to share our knowledge with students about how these companies differed from each other. We also encouraged students to view us as a sounding board in weighing their decisions. We avoided being a cheerleader for the company to each and every student who expressed an interest in opportunities there.

In this case we needed to put our Emotional Intelligence and, in particular, self-awareness to use. We could have been seduced by this company and influenced many students to go there. Instead, we had to be aware of our emotions and reactions and remain objective. In addition, we honored our boundaries by not allowing a "suitor" to impact our professionalism.

Work/Life Balance—An Elusive Goal?

Probably no other area raises as much angst for the HR professional than the topic of work/life balance. We addressed this topic in Chapter 5 when we discussed values. It resonates with us because we know intellectually and from three decades of working that it is important to have a life outside work. It also is a constant challenge. However, the reality is that the workplace and the HR profession have become more demanding. HR roles are intensive and all encompassing, and you may not be sure how to make this balance happen. It often comes down to the question, "Where do my loyalties lie? Are they more to the company or to me?"

Work/Life Balance Strategies

Our interviewees gave us indicators that they continually work on the issue of work/life balance and that they have no clear-cut answers. How do they approach work/life balance and the conflicting values they face? Several said they set priorities. One respondent said, "Here is my order: myself, my family, and my job. I work to schedule my time in that order." Others make time to exercise and schedule nonwork events onto their calendar. "I don't take my computer on vacation." This same senior HR professional admitted that work/life balance was hard on members of the executive team. She believes in modeling work/life balance for her staff and goes home at 5:00 p.m. no matter what occurs as she is going out the door.

What we also found interesting is that there seemed to be a fine line between passion and obsession for our interviewees. It was apparent from our interviews and from our discussions with peers that many of them have a hard time turning down the juice. "I love what I do and it's hard to slow down" was a common refrain. At the same time, several said that loving what they do means that work is play, not work for them. Of course, you must create your own definition of work/life balance for yourself. We also believe that this picture ebbs and flows as changing needs (job, family demands) emerge in your life. As one HR manager said, " I work as much as I have to and as little as I can."

We were disturbed that several interviewees admitted they "wore out" before they recognized the need to cut back on work. This is a clear case in which honoring boundaries is essential. Of course, sometimes you need to sacrifice personal and family time for the sake of the job. The picture of juggling many balls comes to mind. Some of those balls are crystal and if you let them soar in the air too high and too long, they will eventually break into many pieces. You need to juggle your life with care in the same way and keep your eyes on that crystal.

If you are continually drawn into the work dramas, short-term satisfaction, and demands of your work, you will never have a chance to breathe. The consequences of "burnout" are mental and physical in nature, so being aware and dealing with your work/personal value conflicts as they emerge will head off problems down the road.

Concluding Remarks

This chapter focused on the five key results the HR professional can achieve by gaining knowledge and applying it to achieve: (1) Win-Wins, (2) Passion, (3) Marketing by the Customer, (4) Demonstrated Impact, and (5) Values Conflicts.

We presented actual cases and scenarios from the world of Human Resources to demonstrate the many twists and turns you can face. We analyzed those cases by looking at what elements of acquiring and applying knowledge were instrumental when achieving those results. Following are some themes to keep in mind as you take these lessons and plan for your own successes.

Understand the Nature of Success

Be your own teacher. After a project, be honest with yourself and ask how you did, regardless of how the client said you did. Don't rely solely on others' evaluations, be they formal or informal evaluations, as the yardstick of your success. And face up to less-than-successful efforts on your part, learn from them, and try to do better the next time.

Resting on past laurels is easy. Organizations that have done that are out of business. So celebrate success for sure—and don't use it as an excuse to avoid continuing efforts to achieve more of them.

Know What You Can Control

Stay in touch with what you can control and influence and what you can do virtually nothing about, and keep those distinctions clear. Note that the results factors all involve other people to one degree or another. You can do only so much about what other people think, do, and feel about you and your work. Choose your battles strategically. No mere mortal can satisfy some clients. If you know that going in, you can do what you can to build on prior successes.

At the same time, consider success an "inside job." If your work was reflective of the best you had to offer at the time and your customer wasn't thrilled with it, do you consider this outcome a success or not? Why or why not? Measure your success in baby steps to avoid discouragement or inertia. Maybe that means, for example, that you do work you have a passion for and your customers aren't ready or willing to market you and your services . . . yet. Or maybe you help a customer get a win, but you don't (yet) feel as though you've won much. Keep on truckin'. Don't wait to celebrate until big successes materialize. Celebrate and embrace small successes. Often, they lead to bigger ones. None of us hits home runs daily, either.

You will likely, especially as an internal, choose to take on projects that have small, if nonexistent, chances of your achieving any of the results in the model. Maybe you really have no choice unless you are willing to be accused of insubordination. Or, part of your job, like most jobs, entails some mundane, unsexy tasks no one else wants or is willing to do. Even as an external, you may choose, and rightfully so, to take on projects that have low chances for success, as we are defining success in this chapter, just because you need the income or you hope that by taking on that work it will lead to better work with that organization. All of this is OK. You just don't want *all* your work to be like this (either mundane or low risk/low reward work) throughout your career.

Avoid all-or-nothing thinking on these key results. We think it likely you won't have strong passions about each and every piece of HR work you do, each and every client you serve, and each and every organization's business that you try to assist. You likely won't have all win-wins. Values conflicts may not arise, and you still can achieve success. As noted earlier, HR's impact is very difficult to demonstrate reliably and validly, so you will have successes even though at times you really can't say what impact you've had. The last thing we want is for you to believe you haven't succeeded unless and until you can be confident you've achieved all five results with every project.

Think Before Acting

It's relatively easy to look back on your own successes as well as learn about other HR people's successes and tear apart the fabric of that success to see what caused those successes to occur. This is easier than when you are faced with situations in which it's unclear what to do with whom and when. In this case, the HR Career Success Model can help you focus your finite amount of energy and time. The model should help you raise questions to ask of yourself (and perhaps to others as well) and then to think through what the answers are *before* you invest heavily in any given project or job. For example, do you have a passion for the work? Does the organization value your work significantly? What values within you is the work drawing on? Are you being thoughtful about the best role or roles to play?

Multiple Results Are Common

We grouped the scenarios by the five results factors in the HR Career Success Model factors by design: to help you visualize how each of the factors works in practice and why they work. At the same time, HR professionals achieve results in ways that are hard, if not inappropriate, to categorize in a single result factor bucket. Some of the stories illustrate this point. For example, you can achieve a win-win while also having the client do much of the marketing. In another example, you can confront values conflicts and in that process add passion to the work you are doing and, in turn, that passion helps produce results valued by the organization. And in still another example, multiple results are the case: You can demonstrate the impact of your work, and that work impacts issues important to your customers. In turn, your customers promote your value to others in the organization.

Share the Credit

Be willing, especially if you are in an organization that has developed a sophisticated HR metrics system (e.g., balanced scorecard), to take the responsibility when things don't pan out completely as planned and intended, along with any credit that is due you. But more importantly, be less concerned with taking credit for outcomes than doing all you can to help produce those outcomes. Include your clients, if not credit them, with any successes that come your way. Their success is *your* success, isn't it? It's far better to be *given* credit than to take it.

Reference

Garvey, C. 2004. "Connecting the Organizational Pulse to the Bottom Line." *HR Magazine* 49, no. 6: 70–75.

9

Your Future in Human Resources: Career Development Planning for the Savvy

The Case for Development

In leading training seminars over the years, we have found that there tend to be three groups of participants. The "vacationers" are the ones who come for a few days off work. The "prisoners" are the ones who were told they had to be there. Finally, there are the self-motivated "learners"—those with initiative and drive who take their learning seriously and put their lessons to use. We know that everyone can fall into any of these categories at one time or another. The important point is that you must become a "learner." If you are to survive in this evolving field, you must drink up knowledge and apply it continuously. So although you might not always be motivated to attend seminars or engage in the many other learning strategies we recommend in this chapter, we hope you give them strong consideration.

Consider what Gautam Ghosh wrote in an article titled "HR's Evolving Role" (2003). He said, "HR's learning curve has to take into account not just today but tomorrow, while keeping an eye on what yesterday has left behind. It has to focus on processes, customers, employees and discontinuous change. The question they constantly need to ask themselves is 'what if all the knowledge and skills I hold becomes redundant tomorrow? What then?' and build a mindset in their organization where everybody asks this question about themselves."

Getting Motivated

We hope we have made a case for continuous learning throughout this book. To remain a vital contributor and have career options, you need to stay on the leading edge. Our successful interviewees cited learning as the key reason they remain and will continue in this challenging field.

Engaging in ongoing development requires that you search for your own internal motivation. Even if you consider yourself a "prisoner," we ask that you take a look at your resistance. Ask yourself why you haven't made development a priority. The reasons for avoiding it or reluctantly moving ahead can vary. Being out of your comfort zone is often the source of your resistance. For example, we go kicking and screaming to each finance and accounting course we enroll in. Over the years, the screaming has been reduced to a sigh (never a shout of delight!) as we have emerged with a better, faster way of managing finances.

You also need to see the reason for the development. Are you are being asked to make changes in the way you operate or increase your skills? How will the cost of time and effort spent pay off? How will engaging in the development effort impact your ability to perform at a higher level or expand your knowledge base? Posing these questions to the managers and vendors involved with your development is a legitimate course of action. Although we can't predict total career impact, we have found that understanding the connection to current or future job performance is essential to our motivation.

In addition, you should review your personal career goals on a regular basis. Does this development effort bring you closer or further away from where you want to be moving? What will encourage you to sign up for that needed training course or networking event? What incentive do you have to risk rejection and approach someone to be your mentor? Most likely, you will want to discuss your development plans with your manager or, even better, with a trusted coach or mentor (more later on this topic). You can then translate these plans into internal motivation as the What's In It For Me (or WIIFM) principle takes hold. Moving from the "prisoner" mentality to the "learner" mentality will make a huge difference in the way you engage in the learning process and, of course, what you ultimately gain.

We also believe in taking action or just doing it! Inspiration might just never come. You are more likely to get energized after you roll up your sleeves and take action. We have seen this with our clients who are interested in making a career change. We put together a workable plan with every client. Those who follow through on self-assessment exercises and engage in information interviews are usually more successful in finding the right career fit. We still hear from some individuals today who are waiting to get motivated. John Lennon is said to have written, "Life is what happens when you are busy making other plans." So take action and don't worry about doing it 'perfectly.'

Anticipate other potential roadblocks. Be sure to make development a priority by saying "no" when necessary. If you have signed up for a training opportunity or have a mentor meeting scheduled, nothing, short of a family emergency, should get in the way. You may need to delegate more tasks or push back on some deadlines. Do what you have to; otherwise, the days, weeks, and years will go by and you will wonder why your career is stagnant. Take assertiveness training classes and practice saying no. But, at whatever cost, learn to say it. You will thank yourself later!

Planning for Your Development: A Place to Start

If you buy into the idea that you are responsible for your own career development, where do you begin? Someone once said that if you don't know where you are going, any road will get you there. You need to figure out the general direction you want to steer and decide what you need to get there.

We suggest using the HR Career Success Model to start the goal-setting process. Earlier in the book, we said that the model needn't be worked sequentially, but that you could start at any "leg of the stool." Consider beginning with the "Achieving Results" component. Ask yourself the question, "What results do I want to achieve?" These desired results can spring from your own self-knowledge and assessment (see Chapter 5). What experience, skills, traits, values, likes and dislikes, and areas of Emotional Intelligence are you strong in?

When crafting your goals, you can also refer to the model by considering what organizational and field knowledge is necessary to make you a valued player (see Chapter 5). For instance, say you decide that your goal is to be a strategic business partner in your organization. Decide what that role looks like—providing consulting on business processes, coaching managers on employee challenges, initiating compliance programs, etc. Discover what is required to become proficient in those areas from research and discussions with knowledgeable people you respect. See the HR Skills Assessment in Appendix A. Coaches and mentors can be vital in this regard.

Then it is time to go to work. Here are some specific suggestions for putting a development plan in place:

1. Write down your goals. Salespeople tell us that if you write down your targets, you are *much* more likely to reach them. See the sample developmental action plan and goals in Appendix A. You can design a format that works for you. You just need to do it.

2. Know that your developmental goals will change over time, so be prepared to be flexible and revise them as needed.

3. Devote priority time to planning. Set appointments with yourself throughout each and every year and to write long-term and short-term goals. Use these sessions to assess your progress and close any gaps.

4. Use the SMART formula when crafting your goals: S = Specific (say specifically what you will do), M = Measurable (put some measures in place to measure your success) A = Achievable (make the goal a stretch goal but also one that is possible to achieve, R = Realistic (are the conditions in place for you actually to work on this goal?), and T = Timed (when you will complete the goal by). (see FigA.7 for an application of a smart goal on a Development Action Plan.)

5. Contract with another person to complete your goals and devise a check in strategy. You can even use the buddy system and also help your colleague achieve his or her goals.

Be sure to celebrate success. Taking the time for yourself to learn new areas and stretch yourself is usually not very easy and takes commitment. Although the rewards are many, in our opinion you still need to give yourself a pat on the back. You moved forward, took action, and didn't wait for doors to open. You probably learned a lot about yourself along the way.

Key Trends Affecting Human Resources

Some trends come and go. Just as fashion trends re-emerge in the next generation (we should have saved all those bellbottom blue jeans!), organizations recycle structures and transform themselves only to recycle back again. Today you can see some of that as HR moves from decentralized functions, back to centralized structures, and then back again. However, many experts agree that transformational changes occurring in today's organizations are new and different from what has transpired before. As you think about your own developmental steps, keep these current and emerging trends in the background. You will avoid becoming obsolete. Be sure to take these trends with a grain of salt. World events are unpredictable. For example, prior to 9–11, who would have predicted that security would be at the top of our minds?

In the following sections, we summarize five major trends we think are important for HR professionals to know. They are the impact of change, technology, talent management, diversity, and outsourcing. Of course, many more changes are on the horizon, such as the increase in the amount of legislation and the number of compliance issues. Refer to our web site and the list of resources in Appendix B for updates. Sites such as www.HR.com and www.shrm.org with their options for newletters and alerts can also keep you up to date on trends as they emerge; using this information will help you to adjust your development plan accordingly.

The Impact of Change

Managing and overcoming change will be key factors in your success. You've read the stories of our interviewees who led changes and learned tremendously from their change efforts. In a 2004 study commissioned by the American Society for Training and Development (ASTD), several existing and emerging trends were identified as driving change in the workplace. Specifically, the organization found that uncertain economic conditions are causing organizations to rethink how to grow and be profitable. It also found that transforming organizational structures are changing the nature of work and that the rate of change is doubling every 10 years. The Herman Trend Alert (2003) also forecasted that companies would re-create themselves to be more agile, nimble, and responsive to customers and employees.

A job listing we came across in the Career Masters Institute newsletter (2004) highlighted the importance of change in the world of HR. Here is what it said: "The University of _____ is currently recruiting for an HR Transformation Director. The ideal candidate will have 10+ years experience in HR leadership positions, experience with instituting change management and organizational transformation efforts, and the ability to operate at the strategic level." Will we see more of these types of positions in the future? As one of our grandmothers used to say, "You can bet on it, Mister!"

Another aspect to consider in career planning is the growth of different fields and their impact on your career. Consider, for instance, that fast-growing occupations such as health care, insurance, security, and technology will offer opportunities for HR professionals that didn't exist before.

So if change is the only constant, how do you increase your resilience to change? Consider learning more change management practices and skills to help yourself and others in the organization be more adaptable and nimble. Consider other cost-effective and efficient ways in which work can be redesigned to benefit your organization. In the competitive marketplace you work in today, you cannot afford to sit back. The question is, how will you up your "Change Management IQ?"

Technology

Technology has, according to the 2004 ASTD study, "transformed the way we work and live." Few would dispute this fact. In all the literature on HR that we reviewed, we found that being technically savvy is a core skill. Learning to use technology personally to perform your role more effectively and understanding how you can utilize technical solutions to solve organizational challenges are critical. Becoming skilled at using your calendar program can translate into more efficient and effective use of your time. At the same time you need to avoid becoming a slave to your technical "toys." Being constantly accessible can create unnecessary stress levels and can feed into the false notion that you are indispensable.

Talent Management

Many of the gurus of HR management have been raising the flag on projected skills shortages. Predictions indicate that employers will face the most severe shortage of skilled labor in history. Employers are facing questions about how they can help aging workers stay healthy longer and where additional workers will come from to fill the skills shortage gap. It is believed that HR can take a lead in planning for these and other recruiting and retention efforts. Recently, we received a brochure invitation to attend a "Boot Camp" seminar taught by "HR Generals," a.k.a. recruiting consultants. All participants were promised intelligence, strategy, and a sample battle plan to ensure success in the impending war for talent. You can expect many more of these types of offers down the road. Be sure to study them carefully and choose the best programs for your needs.

In addition, leadership development, a trend more prevalent in the 1980s, lost its luster during the economic swings of the 1990s. A return to an investment in leadership training and coaching is on the horizon if talent is to be kept and nurtured. The Herman Trend Alert predicted that up-and-coming managers will be expected to once again learn and practice leadership skills before assuming new positions. In fact, we have even caught wind of a desire to bring back "micromanagement" from some Gen X'ers (fortysomethings) we know!

Diversity

A more diverse workforce means that you must accommodate new attitudes, lifestyles, values, and motivations. Anybody who has been around workplaces lately can't help but notice the wide-ranging mix of generations; genders; ages;

and cultural, racial, and ethnic compositions. People with disabilities are yet another group.

This diversity has brought richness to the work landscape. Everyone can benefit from new ideas and perspectives different from his or her own. The road to harmony is not always smooth, however. The HR professional is faced with hiring the right mix of employees and avoiding legal challenges to hiring and firing decisions. The Equal Employment Opportunity Commission (EEOC) warned employers of the rise in national origin discrimination claims. The HR professional's responsibility increasingly includes developing clear discrimination policies, training employees in avoiding even the appearance of discrimination, and instructing supervisors in documenting employee problems. Companies are increasingly putting diversity high on the radar screen. Their diversity goals extend to hiring minority and women suppliers and targeting diverse customers.

Being on board with this direction will continue to be important for the HR profession. You need to start with yourself and be willing to question your own ingrained assumptions. Coming to grips with your own biases and making an ongoing effort to understand and learn about others must become an ongoing part of your development. You can gain experiences that will expose you to people different from yourself. You also can get the training that helps you to expand your awareness and increase your sensitivity.

Outsourcing

The outsourcing trend affects whom you communicate with in the marketplace and in the workplace. Organizations increasingly are turning to domestic and international resources to take over transactional HR functions. Driven mostly by cost, organizations are implementing processes and technologies to drive down transaction costs. Terms such as "OBA" (Outsourced Benefits Administration) and "HRO" (Human Resource Outsourcing) are commonly discussed at HR conferences.

A recent survey by the Conference Board and Accenture revealed that the majority of U.S. companies (more than 87 percent) currently outsource major HR functions. You will see outsourced opportunities increase for smaller companies and individual contractors. Some people feel that outsourcing has gone too far, with too many jobs going overseas. Despite the backlash, most experts believe that it is not going away.

Learning more about the benefits and barriers to outsourcing will help you to offer guidance to your clients. You also may want to consider the increasingly attractive career option of becoming an external HR consultant. This career path can offer financial awards, challenging work and a more flexible lifestyle. See Chapter 3 for a more comprehensive view of this role in HR.

Development Steps to Take

Recently, an HR client called us and excitedly shared that she had taken several steps since our last career counseling session to explore some new career directions in her organization. She had attended a project management class, learned more about project management from her classmates and teacher, and started networking with trusted associates. We could just hear the excitement in her voice as she considered building on her HR background in new ways. We hope that, like our client, you have some ideas of what you can do to shake your branches loose and commit to taking some new development actions. We look at development as on ongoing journey, and because you need to begin somewhere, we hope you'll consider the following additional suggestions we have used ourselves and gleaned from the successful HR professionals cited in this book.

Self-Assessment and Feedback

Ask yourself every day what you have learned and how you have helped your organization. Complete the assessment exercises in Appendix A and revisit them at least every year. Keep a portfolio of your achievements that you can bring out at your performance reviews.

Ask for feedback. Our interviewees came out strongly in favor of taking this step. Seek feedback from your team, manager, clients, vendors, and customers, they all said. Asking for feedback is not easy; in fact, giving the feedback is easier. We like the bumper sticker that consultant Steve Hewitt (2004) quoted, "The truth will set you free, but first it will piss you off." Everyone has blind spots, and the only way to see through them is to hear what others have to say. Remember also that the further you go up the ladder, the less likely you are to hear honest feedback, so learning to seek feedback will help you throughout your career.

Networking

There is no magic to networking. You need to cultivate a dynamic and varied network. A good networking contact is knowledgeable, well connected, and interested in helping you. Who do you know who fits into that category? Who do you want to add to your network? One of the weak links occurs when you become involved in your job and forget to give your network some care and feeding. Then you come out of the woodwork and ask for help. To counteract that natural tendency, keep your contacts updated about your career and your life and send them information and resources that might be of interest to them. Do this especially when you are okay with your job situation. The law of reciprocity says that when you give people something they will insist on giving even more back to you (Baber and Waymon, 2002). You will be making deposits in the bank of good will.

Knowing where to network is important. You should build a wide base of relationships but don't forget the people under your nose. Seek out individuals in your own organizations. Consider starting a group of people with similar interests and needs for support (for example, working moms). If you are not currently a member of a local chapter of a professional organization, then what are you waiting for? Get involved in a committee that interests you, and you will reap rewards from your membership investment. Perhaps you could write an article for the association newsletter, as doing so will also give you credibility and something to send to people when introducing yourself.

Also, research community groups and trade associations that can expand your contact base. Several of our interviewees found a huge and unexpected career payoff in serving on the boards of recognizable nonprofit organizations (such as Big Brothers/Big Sisters) in the community. This experience gave them a legitimate reason to contact people (for charity fund-raisers, etc.), and they also were given access to important community news outside their organizations.

People will get to know your capabilities and build trust with you when you provide service. When the time comes for you to cash in on your contacts, you will have already established a track record of success. For more information on networking, visit our web site at www.myhrsuccess.com.

Getting Out of Human Resources

In making a case to get out of HR, consultant Alan Weiss said, "Spending a career in HR is like watching only foreign movies with subtitles. You actually begin to believe that no one speaks English other than yourself" (2004). Our successful interviewees also stressed the importance of getting out of the office and the HR mindset. They felt strongly (as we illustrated in Chapter 8) that this was absolutely essential in creating value. This way, you are able to bring back fresh ideas and a deeper awareness of the challenges you face in doing your work. From a career progression standpoint, you are visible. People hire people they know, so when that next career opportunity emerges you will be, as is said in marketing, "Top of Mind" (and not "out of sight, out of mind"!).

What are some other actions you can take to broaden your view beyond HR? Seek out cross-functional task forces in which you will have the opportunity to work with other departments. Find out who the "winners" are in the organization and try to meet them (you'll find more details on mentoring in the next section). Many interviewees recommended working for different organizations as one of the best career strategies they have found. You can take best practices from one environment or industry and adapt them to your current one. Because a major part of your perceived value is how innovative you are, you will score major points by doing this. In addition, taking this approach keeps you fresh, alive, and continuously learning.

Be a sponge when you are reading, doing Internet research, or listening to TV, radio, etc. Get out of your comfort zone and explore new areas. Expand your mind and allow your brain to stretch. As with the benefits of a good liberal arts education, you will be bringing back new perspectives and gaining ongoing knowledge of important global and business trends, which will contribute to making you a more broadminded and thoughtful person—just the kind of HR professional being called a rare find today.

Mentoring

Called a critical component of career advancement, mentoring has taken on an aura of its own. The concept of mentoring has expanded from the days of the ancient Greeks when an elder took a young man under his wing to show him the ways of the world. Today the practice of mentoring has transformed into the idea of a learning partnership in which one person shares his or her experience, skills, and insights with another receptive person. The mentor can vary in age and gender and other characteristics from the mentee, and serves as teacher, sounding board, friend, cheerleader, and coach in varying degrees. Mentors can be drawn from the same organization or from outside the environment, and there are benefits for both. We and our interviewees can document great benefits from this form of learning.

Several success factors make the mentoring investment worthwhile. Know what your desired outcome is when selecting a mentor. We and our interview subjects have mentored individuals on work/life–balance questions, corporate politics, gender issues, and specific topics such as facilitating meetings. The key is to figure out what area you want help in and to go after it. Heather Schultz (2003), author and mentoring expert, advocates going after the person or persons who are the very best at what they do. She is a living example of what she preaches. When Heather wanted to enter the consulting field, she sought out the mentoring of Tom Peters, renowned management consultant. She eventually became president and chief operating officer of his company!

You also should be sure to look for opportunities to mentor others. Most people who engage in mentoring say they feel as though they learn more than their protégés. This experience is personally gratifying and helps you to clarify and assimilate what experience has taught you. In sum, it is a very rewarding way of providing service. To keep the HR profession vital and thriving, you need to nurture multiple learning partnerships. Less-seasoned and younger individuals have served as our mentors in technology and in better understanding generational differences. You need to decide in what areas you want to get mentoring and select a mentor to help you in those areas. That person will be impressed that you have taken the initiative and that you are focused on your goals. You can also find out whether your organization has an internal mentoring program. If not, consider starting one. For more information on this important career strategy, refer to the resources in www.myhrsuccess.com.

Education and Training

As you craft your development plan, consider what kind of advanced training and education you want to incorporate. We discussed choosing a degree program in Chapter 6. We believe that in addition to gaining valuable skills and knowledge, another key driver for earning a degree, obtaining certifications, and enrolling in training classes is to increase your career options. Ask your mentors and network contacts what training they recommend to move you closer to your career goals.

Professional associations such as SHRM offer certifications, continuing education credits and excellent workshops at their local, regional, and national meetings. Conferences also provide you with the opportunity to hear about current and future trends and best practices in the field. Walking through the exhibit area can be overwhelming but also revealing about what is on the horizon. By interacting with vendors, you can learn about areas you might want to pursue (such as the e-learning explosion and Human Resource Outsourcing). A recent HR conference catalog revealed a wide range of titles from building an employee brand to making effective communications. Be sure to budget for these opportunities and make a business case to your boss if necessary.

If you are an external consultant or an internal on a small budget, you will probably have to be creative in finding training opportunities. Look at local universities and colleges for continuing education classes taught by experienced professionals. Increasingly, training classes and degree programs are now offered through webinars (seminars offered through web based technologies) and blended learning (those using both classroom training and e-learning delivery) formats. Depending on your learning style, time availability, and budget, the choices are abundant.

Before you attend a learning seminar related to your work, review the objectives and discuss mutual learning goals with your manager. Soon after you return, offer to meet with your manager and your team to discuss key points you learned. This approach is a great way to reinforce concepts and demonstrate that the organization's investment in you has paid off handsomely.

Conclusion

We want to end this book as we began, with a message of hope, enthusiasm, and passion for the profession of Human Resources. As we have tried to demonstrate, there are easier professions to enter. We know of none, however, that stretch and teach you as much about life as this one. We hope you will continue to develop the confidence and competence to manage your career and that your passion will be contagious—that is, your infectious enthusiasm, willingness to perform at your best, and eagerness to take risks will be evident to all who interact with you. We also hope that you will continue to learn and challenge yourself. Alfred North Whitehead once said, "I think it is a mistake to cling to a region because it has given you a delightful experience once. You merely accumulate dead possessions. Don't cling to the old because it made you glad once; go on to the next—the next region, the next experience. We have left behind us the most extraordinary succession of delightful dwelling houses, each of which in turn once meant everything to us, but not one of which we now regret having left."

References

American Society for Training and Development. 2004. "Mapping the Future, Shaping New Work Place Learning and Performance Competencies." www.careerjournal.com/hrcenter/astd/features/20040014-astd.html

Babcock, P. 2004. "Slicing Off Pieces of HR." *HR Magazine* July: 71–86.

Baber, A. and Waymon, L. 2004. "Make Your Contacts Count", AMACOM, 2002, 117–132.

Bernard Hodes Group. 2004. "Are You Prepared for the New War on Talent?" Brochure. May 18.

Career Masters Institute newsletter. 2004. Job listing. www.cmi.com

Ghosh, G. 2003. "HR's Evolving Role." www.HR.com (accessed August 11, 2003).

Herman Trend Alert. 2003. *Workforce and Workplace Forecasts.* www.hermangroup.com (accessed December 21, 2003).

Hewitt, S. 2004. "Bumper Stickers and Self-Awareness." www.HR.com (accessed June 21, 2004).

Schultz, C. 2003. "Discrimination Claims Threaten Struggling Businesses." *The Human Resource* March: 10.

Schultz, H. 2003. Personal communication.

Weiss, A. 2004. "The Seven Sins of HR (and how to correct them) *www.hr.com*

Appendix A

Exercises to Gain Self-Knowledge

This appendix includes a number of self-assessment and career research tools to use in this important phase of career development. We have provided spaces for you to record your responses. Make some time and carve out some space to engage in this reflection. Now would also be a great opportunity to start writing in a career journal, which will allow you to explore your responses. We also suggest you reference Chapter 5 for more background information on self-assessment.

See Figure A.1 for a template called your "HR Summary." As you complete the exercises in this appendix, we suggest you record a summary of your responses in

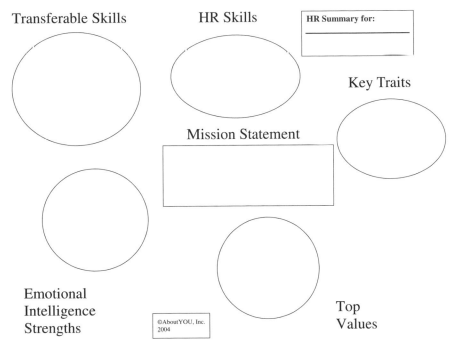

Figure A.1 HR Summary.

each oval. This summary will provide you with a concise view of your key "must haves." Think of it as map to use when evaluating career options, projects, and development opportunities. Your likelihood of finding a suitable fit will be greatly enhanced by referring to this template.

In this appendix, you will also find exercises that assist with identifying HR skills, values, and Emotional Intelligence strengths. We have even included a "Personal Mission Statement Worksheet" to help you steer a course for your exploration. Near the end of this appendix, you will also find a section titled "Essential Tips for Networking Interviews." As we have mentioned often in this book, networking is an important aspect of your development. It is also the best way, hands down, of finding out about career paths in HR.

HR Skills Assessment

Step I: Describe Your Accomplishments

Think back over your life. In the 10 spaces provided, describe your accomplishments. What were you most proud of, and what did you enjoy? Don't be concerned about the size of the accomplishment or what others might think. You can draw from both your work and personal life. Be as specific as possible. See the following example:

Example: I organized and planned a new company orientation program that involved coordinating six different departments. I had 10 days to structure the program, schedule speakers, and market the program. I used a combination of speakers, multimedia presentations, and interactive discussions to deliver the material. The program exceeded expectations as indicated by follow-up surveys to managers and participants.

1.

2.

3.

4.

5.

6.

7.

8.

9.

10.

©AboutYOU, Inc. 2004

Step II: Analyze Your Accomplishments

The next step is to analyze your accomplishments.

1. Review accomplishment #1 and ask yourself, "What skills were required to accomplish this?" and "How did I achieve the successful outcome I did?" In Figure A.2 put an "X" or a check mark next to the skill that applies. Note: Some of these skills overlap; the overlap is OK because you want to create a robust list of skills.
2. Review the remainder of your accomplishments (#2–#10), checking off those skills that you used in demonstrating that accomplishment.
3. Total the X's or check marks across the columns and put the number in the box marked "Total."
4. See the example in the first column.

Figure A.2 lists some of the skills that have been identified as critical to success in Human Resources.

	Sample	#1	#2	#3	#4	#5	#6	#7	#8	#9	#10	Total
HR Skills													
HR Legislation													
Recruitment and Staffing													
Compensation													
Benefits													
Employee Relations	x												
Organizational Development													
Training	x												
Technology													
Performance Management													
Business Skills													
Business Literacy													
Financial Acumen													
Marketing/Sales													
Measurement	x												
Global Literacy													
Managing Change	x												
Project Management													
Team Leadership													
Time Management	x												
Interpersonal Skills													
Consulting	x												
Persuasion and Influencing	x												
Active Listening													
Empathizing													
Negotiating													
Coaching/Feedback	x												
Analytical Skills													
Problem Solving	x												
Process Improvement													
Systems Thinking													
Visionary and Strategic Analysis													
Applying Technical Solutions	x												

Figure A.2   HR Skills Assessment.

©AboutYOU, Inc. 2005

Step III: Analyze Your Key Skills.

1. Choose the six to eight skills that appear most frequently. Write them below:

2. Do you see any patterns? Which skills emerge most often?

3. Are you using these skills now in your current work? If so, how?

4. What opportunities exist at work or outside work that can allow you to use these skills more often?

5. What skills do you want to enhance? What opportunities exist at work or outside work that may allow you to increase your competency in that area? Write them below or ask a trusted friend, boss, mentor, or coach for ideas.

Sample Page from www.careergames.com

The completely free, interactive web site www.careergames.com allows you to take tests and summarizes the results in each section.

Figure A.3 shows a summary page from the "Hidden Talents" section.

Results for Jennifer

Achieving
Collaborating
Consulting
Creating
Advising
Affirming
Discovering
Managing
Writing
Verbalizing
Communicating
Influencing

Figure A.3 Career Games preferred skills results. Taken from www.careergames.com. Granted by permission of "Cabinet Daniel Porot," 1999, 2000.

Emotional Intelligence Assessment

The concept of Emotional Intelligence was discussed in Chapter 5. This exercise should help you determine areas of Emotional Intelligence in which you are strong and those you may want to improve. Figure A.4 provides a summary of the key components. For more complete definitions, see Figure 5.4 in Chapter 5.

Self Awareness	Emotional Self-Awareness Accurate Self-Assessment Self-Confidence
Self-Management	Emotional Self-Control Transparency Achievement Initiative Optimism
Social Awareness	Empathy Organizational Awareness Service
Relationship Management	Inspirational Leadership Influence Developing Others Change Catalyst Conflict Management Building Bonds Teamwork and Collaboration

Figure A.4 Emotional Intelligence components. *Adapted by permission of Harvard Business School Press. From* Primal Leadership *by Daniel Goleman, Richard Boyatzis, and Annie McKee. Boston, MA, p 39. Copyright © 2002 by Daniel Goleman; all rights reserved.*

Emotional Intelligence Inventory

Refer to Figure A.2 when responding to the questions that follow. These questions are open-ended, and you can answer them best by reflecting on your current and past work experiences.

You can also use them as a vehicle for feedback with your managers, peers, and clients. Try giving them a copy of the questions before you meet. Probe for examples when they provide you with their feedback.

1. In what specific work situations do you demonstrate Emotional Intelligence? What behaviors or actions do you exhibit?

2. Which Emotional Intelligence area(s) do you regard as your strongest? Why? Provide examples.

3. Which Emotional Intelligence area(s) do you regard as your weakest? Why? Provide examples.

4. How do you think your manager would evaluate your Emotional Intelligence? What would he or she say are your stronger and weaker areas? Why?

5. How do you think your peers would rate you? What would they say are your stronger and weaker areas? Why?

6. How do you think your clients would rate you? What would they say are your stronger and weaker areas? Why?

7. What opportunities exist in your work or organization that would allow you to use your Emotional Intelligence strengths to a greater degree?

8. What specific actions can you take to develop your weaker areas? For instance, if "initiative" is your weakest area, commit to make one new suggestion to your boss this week.

9. Summarize what you have learned from this Emotional Intelligence reflection.

10. Determine three to four key actions you can formulate into SMART goals (see Chapter 9).

Values Clarification Exercise

A forced ranking of values can help you clarify your priorities, reinforce the need to make trade-offs and take actions that reflect your priorities. Such a process helps you to satisfy your most important values and achieve greater fulfillment as a result.

Place an "X" or a check mark in the column that most closely describes the strength of each value in Figure A.5. Try to distribute your responses fairly evenly among the four levels of value strength. Be sure to avoid marking an abundance of items "Always Valued."

VALUES	Always Valued	Often Valued	Sometimes Valued	Rarely Valued
PERSONAL GROWTH: Develop my potential and use my talents				
ACHIEVEMENT: Have a sense of accomplishment and mastery				
KNOWLEDGE: Develop and use specific knowledge and expertise				
STATUS: Hold a position of recognized importance in the organization				
COMPETITION: Engage in activities in which people must compete against each other				
CHANGE AND VARIETY: Have job responsibilities with varied tasks				
SERVICE TO SOCIETY: Contribute to a better society				
PHYSICAL STRENGTH: Do work requiring strength, agility, or physical exertion				
INDEPENDENCE: Control my own work/schedule				
LEADERSHIP: Influence others to achieve results				
CREATIVE EXPRESSION: Express my creativity and imagination in my work				
CHALLENGE: Find work that mentally stimulates me				
MONEY: Reap significant financial rewards				
SECURITY: Perform my work without worry about possible unemployment				

Figure A.5 Values clarification assessment.

VALUES	Always Valued	Often Valued	Sometimes Valued	Rarely Valued
MANAGEMENT: Achieve work goals as a result of others' efforts				
WORK WITH OTHERS: Belong to a satisfying work group or team				
POWER: Have control over resources at work				
INTEGRITY: Work ethically and honestly				
BALANCE: Achieve the right proportion between my personal life and professional responsibilities				
FRIENDSHIP: Develop social/personal friendships with work colleagues				
CAREER ADVANCEMENT: Be promotable within the organization				
DETAIL WORK: Deal with tasks that must meet specifications requiring careful and accurate attention to detail				
FAST PACE: Work under time-pressured circumstances with demanding expectations				
HELPING OTHERS: Involve myself in helping other people				
LOCATION: Live in a convenient community				
RECOGNITION: Receive credit for work well done				
EXCITEMENT: Frequent novelty and drama				
MORAL FULFILLMENT: Work contributes to moral ideals				
AESTHETICS: Appreciate the beauty of things and ideas				
HEALTH: Being physically and mentally fit				
POSITIVE ATMOSPHERE: Work in a supportive, pleasing, and harmonious setting				
EFFICIENCY: Being in a time-efficient environment with little bureaucracy				
FAMILY HAPPINESS: Maintain a healthy balance between work and family life setting				
EFFICIENCY: Being in a time-efficient environment with little bureaucracy				
FAMILY HAPPINESS: Maintain a healthy balance between work and family life				

Figure A.5 *Continued*

Here are some steps to take after completing the assessment.

1. Select the top 10 values from the Always Valued column. Go to the Often Valued Column if necessary.
2. Imagine that you have been forced to toss five of those values away. Which must remain with you?
3. Write in your career journal or discuss these with a coach, mentor or trusted friend. Ask them to listen to you as you become clearer on them. Consider the following additional talking or writing prompts:
   a. What do these top values mean to you? Why?
   b. Would you have selected different answers 5 years ago? 10 years ago? What would have been different?
   c. Are you living these top values now in your work and life? How?
   d. How could you make your life more consistent with these values?
   e. What implications do these have for your career planning?

Personal Mission Statement Worksheet

A personal mission statement or philosophy briefly and clearly summarizes your unique purpose. There are no right or wrong answers. Expect to go through several rewrites, but once written, it will serve to guide your career direction.

Here are some prompt questions to help you shape a mission statement:

1. Name a person who has greatly influenced your life. What qualities do you admire most in that person? Which of these qualities do you want in your own life?

2. Refer to the Values Clarification Exercise in this Appendix. What are your top five values? Briefly describe.

3. What do you want to contribute to your family, community, organization, and/or world?

4. What other accomplishments do you want to make in your life?

5. What do you want people to say about you at your 90th birthday?

Sample Mission Statements

The following mission statements were composed by some of our clients in recent years. They may be helpful in composing your own.

1. To live a life of service to my spouse, children, co-workers, customers, and community.

2. To be honest and open when dealing with others.

3. To improve people's lives through more efficient processes and decision making.

4. To use my creative skill to help others realize their own uniqueness.

5. To help me share what I know in order to make a difference in people's lives.

6. To influence people by solving problems in order to make their life better.

Now write a draft of your own mission statement in the blank box in Figure A.6.

Figure A.6   Draft of your mission statement.

©AboutYOU, Inc. 2005

Essential Tips for Networking Interviews

Networking is the deliberate process of exchanging information, resources, support and access. We do this by creating mutually beneficial relationships for personal and professional success.

Why do you need to network?

- To gain information on careers, industries, fields, training, etc.
- To expand your group of contacts, which is the undisputed number-one way of moving your career forward.
- To build your confidence by becoming more comfortable with establishing ongoing relationships and by talking about your assets to others.

These points are applicable to those entering the field and those already employed in HR.

Getting Started

When you're ready to network, start from your own contact base. Who do you know and interact with whom you could tap for names? You likely know someone who knows someone who can lead you to the right person.

Before contacting this new person, it's best to get an introduction. It's even better to have the person who gave you the information call or e-mail giving the contact person a head's up that you will be contacting him or her.

If you must call cold, have your "elevator" speech ready. This is a short "pitch" that basically sells you. It tells someone who you are, what you have been doing and where you have been doing it. It usually ends with the direction you are headed or what your goal is (ex. "interested in learning more about the field of benefits consulting"). Try e-mailing first with a brief introduction and identify what you want (for example, "15 minutes of your time to discuss your perception of the *xyz* field today"). Follow up with a phone call to set up a face-to-face appointment. If you have lunch or coffee, you should pick up the tab. If you can't get an in-person time, then schedule a phone appointment.

Questions to Ask

When you're ready to meet your new contact, be sure to do your homework first. Read up on the area this person works in so you can ask intelligent, well-thought-out questions. Here are some questions you might consider:

1. How did you get started in this career? What was your career path like?

2. What background or skills do you recommend for success in this career direction?

3. What is your typical day like?

4. Is the work environment typically casual or formal? Fast paced or relaxed? What is the balance of team versus independent work?

5. Have you worked in other environments? How would you say they differ?

6. What are the rewards of this work for you? What about the challenges?

7. What would you have done differently if you were entering this field today?

8. How do you see this field changing in the next five years?

9. Do you recommend any professional organizations I should visit or get involved in? (Hint: Ask whether you can come as a guest; in other words, you pay, but this person sponsors you at the next meeting). Do you recommend any web sites to look at?

10. Are there any other people you suggest I speak with?

Developmental Action Planning Exercise

We have continually stressed development planning in this book. Use the tool that you see in Figure A.7 as a starting point. The sample plan shown here is based on a development area that this person has zeroed in on after engaging in self-assessment.

Self – Assessment Area	Improvement Goal	Action Items	Measure(s) of Success	Sources of Support	Desired Completion Date	Actual Completion Date
HR Skills	Become more knowledgeable in national legislation affecting Human Resources.	Research 3 HR Web sites and register to receive email alerts.	Complete research and print findings.	SHRM – national and local chapters www.HR.com	Oct. 1, 2005	
		Attend one professional meeting where the topic is HR legislation.	Register and attend meeting.	Peers and manager (for recommendations)	Nov. 15, 2005	
		Talk with my manager to discuss their view of how this legislation may impact our business.	Schedule meeting and record notes in career journal.	Manager, professional coaches and mentors	December 1, 2005	

Figure A.7   Sample development action plan.

©AboutYOU, Inc. 2005

Appendix B

HR and HR-Related Professional Associations

This appendix provides a sampling of professional associations devoted to HR and related fields. It is by no means an exhaustive list. Associations whose headquarters are in the United States are disproportionately represented. Many of these associations have local chapters in major metropolitan areas.

Academy of Human Resource Development—www.ahrd.org

American Arbitration Association—www.adr.org

American Counseling Association—www.counseling.org

American Payroll Association—www.americanpayroll.org

American Society for Training and Development—www.astd.org

American Staffing Association—www.staffingtoday.org

Association for Quality and Participation—www.aqp.org

College and University Professional Association of Human Resources—www.cupahr.org

Human Resource Planning Society—www.hrps.org

International Association for Human Resource Information Management—www.ihrim.org

International Foundation of Employee Benefit Plans—www.ifebp.org

International Personnel Management Association—www.ipma-hr.org

International Society for Performance and Instruction—www.ispi.org

National Career Development Association—www.ncda.org

National Human Resource Association—www.humanresources.org

National Labor Management Association—www.nlma.org

(The) Organization Development Institute—www.odinstitute.org

Organization Development Network—www.odnetwork.org

Society for Human Resource Management—www.shrm.org

Society for Industrial and Organizational Psychology—www.siop.org

World at Work (formerly the American Compensation Association)—www.worldatwork.org

Appendix C

Interview Guide

Our interviewees were told the following in this order prior to the start of the interview:

- The title, purpose, and target audiences of the book
- The purpose of the interview
- That we did not foresee any risks for their participation, that their participation was entirely voluntary, and that they could terminate the interview at any time for any reason

We then asked the interviewees if they:

- had any questions or needed additional information
- would grant us permission to use their name in the book
- would grant us permission to use the name of his or her organization in the book

We then obtained their verbal informed consent to conduct the interview. What follows is the entire Interview Guide.

There are three groups of questions. Total time will not exceed 30 minutes (unless you wish to speak with me longer).

I.   This first section pertains to career events in your past.

1. Why did you go into HR?

2. How did you get into it?

3. Why have you stayed in it?

4. What has been your biggest challenge as an HR professional?

5. What has been your biggest mistake? 5a. What did you learn from it?

6. What has been your most gratifying experience as an HR professional? 6a. Why was it so?

7. If you could turn the clock back and do one thing differently, what would it be? Why?

8. What was a career defining moment or turning point in your career?

II. This section pertains to your experiences and ideas about career success.

1. What do you believe to be two or three key success factors in your career? 1a. For HR professionals today? 1b. For HR professionals in the next decade?

2. What are two or three major trends in your HR specialty (or specialties if you have more than one or trends in HR generally if you're a generalist)? 2a. How do you keep up with them?

3. How do you keep up with the key issues and trends in your industry?

4. What are two or three key competencies and qualities HR professionals need to possess today?

5. Do you hold any certifications? (e.g., SPHR). 5a. What benefits do you gain from it/them?

6. How do you earn trust and credibility with your clients/customers? 6a. How do you show your value to them? 6b. Can you give an example?

7. What are the best ways for HR people to learn about the organization (e.g., challenges the business faces, culture, power and decision making, what managers worry about)? 7a. Can you give an example of how you did this?

8. How do you measure your success? 8a. How does your boss measure it? 8b. How do your clients/customers measure it?

III. These last few questions pertain to your ideas about Career Development in HR.

   1. What advice do you have for people entering the profession?

   2. What advice do you have for mid-level people in the profession? (mid-level = approximately 6–10 years in HR)

   3. How can HR professionals increase their value/marketability during uncertain economic conditions?

   4. How do you maintain work/life balance?

   5. What have been the most valuable development tools or strategies you have used?

Open-ended question to end interview → Is there anything else you'd like to tell me?

Thank you!

Appendix **D**

Example of HR Career Paths

HR EXPERIENCE NAVIGATOR-GENERALIST

Business Knowledge

HR professionals must understand the business and industry of the company they serve. Key areas of knowledge include applied understanding of the business' value proposition.

LC

*Global accountability
Champion the development of global HR strategy aligned to the needs of the business
Lead major organisational change
Apply knowledge and information about the external environment to integrate all aspects of the business
Seek to develop appropriate organisational culture for the strategy of the business*

| Leadership responsibility outside HR |
| Responsibility for financial management of organisational unit |

SG A,1,2

*Manage HR as a cost service and value
Manage internal and external stakeholders
Champion and contribute to development and improvement of regionally defined HR processes and policies to maximise value added to the business
Apply understanding of business in order to contribute to strategic decision making
Responsible for HR activities at a regional level
Align HR processes with strategic business objectives*

| Responsibility for financial management of organisational unit |

SG 2,3,4

*Understand and manage commercial activities
Understand business operations and how to leverage HR to enhance business performance
Increase international exposure and experience
Contribute to the development and improvement of HR processes to maximise business value
Contribute to organisational change
Responsibility for HR at a local level*

| Cross-functional experience | Cross-business HR experience |
| Managing a significant project across organisational boundaries | Experience of financial management |

SG 4 and below

*Acquire knowledge in HR policies & processes and demonstrate ability to apply knowledge to the specific needs of the business.
Understand the Shell businesses and the environment in which they operate.
Understand the business disciplines & their individual contribution
Understand individual differences and how to use these differences to a positive way
Build personal credibility & broaden network*

| Member of cross functional/ business project team | Experience of process simplification/ rationalisation |
| Experience in an operational environment | Exposure to business undergoing change |

SCALE

| High priority | Medium priority |

HR Delivery	Strategic Contribution	Personal Credibility
Delivery of operational HR activities to businesses in several major categories: Talent Management; Learning&Development; Organisational Development; Performance Management; Managing Employee Relations	HR professionals involved in the business at a strategic level. These activities include managing culture; facilitation of change; strategic decision making.	HR professionals must be credible to both their HR colleagues and business line managers. They need to have effective relationships with both internal and external stakeholders by the establishment of a reliable track record of delivery of results.

HR Delivery

Talent accountability for global business		
HR responsibility for global process/business		
Negotiate collective agreements with staff council/union	Lead major organisational change within HR	Responsible for design & implementation of organisation structure
Work in Corporate Centre/SPS	HR responsibility for setting up zonal/regional business	
Develop & implement HR policies and processes	Talent management experience	
HR responsibility for multiple countries/region	Generalist HR management responsibility for large business unit	Experience of job/work process redesign
Contribute to implementation of new/revised HR policies and processes	Exposure to trade unions, staff councils or industrial relations	Generalist HR management responsibility
Exposure to core HR activities	Recruitment experience	Gain expertise in one HR specialism

Strategic Contribution

Member of Business Leadership Team	HR lead for M&A/major reorganisation	
Member of HR Leadership Team	Lead HR specialist area	Work in Corporate Centre
Member of senior management team	HR responsibility for zonal/regional business	
HR responsibility for business with strategic change	Member of global specialist internal network	Member of HR leadership team
Provide HR input to major organisational change		
Member of local management team		

Personal Credibility

Manage managers	Lead in professional network/ governing body	
External stakeholder management	Attend ELP-AD followed by ELP-LE	
Represent Shell externally	Attend GBLP-AD followed by GBLP-LE	
Key member of professional network/body	Manage virtual team	
Manage people	International experience	
Experience of external HR practices	Represent Shell externally	
Acquire a mentor	Membership of a diverse team	
International experience	Exposure to external HR practices	

		Business Knowledge	
		HR professionals must understand the business and industry of the company they serve. Key areas of knowledge include applied understanding of the business' value proposition.	

LC	Global accountability Champion the development of global HR strategy aligned to the needs of the business Lead major organisational change Apply knowledge and information about the external environment to integrate all aspects of the business Seek to develop appropriate organisational culture for the strategy of the business	Leadership responsibility outside HR	
		Responsibility for financial management of organisational unit	
SG A,1,2	Manage HR as a cost service and value Manage internal and external stakeholders Champion and contribute to development and improvement of regionally defined HR processes and policies to maximise value added to the business Apply understanding of business in order to contribute to strategic decision making Responsible for HR activities at a regional level Align HR processes with strategic business objectives	Responsibility for financial management of organisational unit	
SG 2,3,4	Understand and manage commercial activities Understand business operations and how to leverage HR to enhance business performance Increase international exposure and experience Contribute to the development and improvement of HR processes to maximise business value Contribute to organisational change Responsibility for HR at a local level	Cross-functional experience	Cross-business HR experience
		Managing a significant project across organisational boundaries	Experience of financial management
SG 4 and below	Acquire knowledge in HR policies & processes and demonstrate ability to apply knowledge to the specific needs of the business. Understand the Shell businesses and the environment in which they operate. Understand the business disciplines & their individual contribution Understand individual differences and how to use these differences to a positive way Build personal credibility & broaden network	Member of cross functional/ business project team	Experience of process simplification/ rationalisation
		Experience in an operational environment	Exposure to business undergoing change

	SCALE	
High priority	Medium priority	Depends on specialism

HR Delivery			**Strategic Contribution**			**Personal Credibility**	
Delivery of operational HR activities to businesses in several major categories: Talent Management; Learning&Development; Organisational Development; Performance Management; Managing Employee Relations			*HR professionals involved in the business at a strategic level. These activities include managing culture; facilitation of change; strategic decision making.*			*HR professionals must be credible to both their HR colleagues and business line managers. They need to have effective relationships with both internal and external stakeholders by the establishment of a reliable track record of delivery of results.*	

Talent accountability for global business			Member of Business Leadership Team	HR lead for M&A/major reorganisation		Manage managers	Lead in professional network/ governing body
HR responsibility for global process/business			Member of HR Leadership Team	Lead HR specialist area	Work in Corporate Centre	External stakeholder management	Attend ELP-AD followed by ELP LE
Negotiate collective agreements with staff council/union	Lead major organisational change within HR	Responsible for design & implementation of organisation structure	Member of senior management team	HR responsibility for zonal/regional business		Represent Shell externally	Attend GBLP-AD followed by GBLP LE
Work in Corporate Centre/SPS	HR responsibility for setting up zonal/regional business		HR responsibility for business with strategic change	Member of global specialist internal network	Member of HR leadership team	Key member of professional network/body	Manage virtual team
Develop & implement HR policies and processes	Talent management experience		Provide HR input to major organisational change			Manage people	International experience
HR responsibility for multiple countries/region	Generalist HR management responsibility for large business unit	Experience of job/work process redesign	Member of local management team			Experience of external HR practices	Represent Shell externally
Contribute to implementation of new/revised HR policies and processes	Exposure to trade unions, staff councils or industrial relations	Generalist HR management responsibility				Acquire a mentor	Membership of a diverse team
Exposure to core HR activities	Recruitment experience	Gain expertise in one HR specialism				International experience	Exposure to external HR practices

About the Authors

Photo: Jonathan R. Goldman

BILL KAHNWEILER, Ph.D.

Bill is an Associate Professor and Director of Human Resource degree programs for the Department of Public Administration and Urban Studies at the Andrew Young School of Policy Studies at Georgia State University (GSU). He has been in the field of "people development" for over 30 years and has been a professor at GSU since 1990. Prior to his arrival at GSU, Bill was an organizational and human resources consultant for over ten years in three capacities—internally with General Electric Company, externally with a large, international consulting firm (Hay Management Consultants), and as an entrepreneur running his own consulting business. He also was a Human Resources Development (HRD) professional for the federal prison system, a public high school, and a university, as well as a professor of Counseling Psychology at Miami University of Ohio.

His teaching assignments focus on non-training HRD interventions, including organizational career management, organizational development, and management consulting. In addition, Bill has guided numerous doctoral students to conduct their own research. His teaching style is student-centered; thus, he emphasizes the teaching of and learning from people more than subject matter, per se.

His research interests include: employee involvement in decision making, innovative group career development strategies, consulting competencies for HRD professionals, and effective leadership of HRD functions. He has published over 80 articles in a variety of outlets, from the popular to the scholarly. Bill has been quoted frequently by local and national media on a range of "people issues" in the workplace. He served as editor of the Organizational Development (OD) Journal, a blind, peer-reviewed journal for OD professionals and academics. He also serves as a manuscript reviewer for several other scholarly journals.

Bill was elected to and served on the Board of Directors of The Academy of HRD, the leading professional association devoted to HRD research. He has also served on the boards of several non-profit social service agencies and task forces, with the goal being to improve the lives of people and assist them in reaching their potential.

Bill attempts to walk the HRD talk in his teaching, research, and service. Helping bring out the best in people is at the root of his professional endeavors, be they in the classroom, in the community, or writing at a computer keyboard.

Bill received a B.A. (sociology) and M.A. (counseling) from Washington University in St. Louis. His Ph.D. is in counseling and human systems from Florida State University.

Bill can be contacted at www.myhrsuccess.com.

Photo: Jonathan R. Goldman

JENNIFER B. KAHNWEILER, Ph.D.

Jennifer B. Kahnweiler, Ph.D. is founder and owner of AboutYOU, Inc., a firm specializing in career consulting for professionals and organizations. She has over 25 years' experience in consulting across a wide range of industries and has helped thousands of individuals resolve their career challenges. As an active faculty member of the American Management Association and an instructor at Emory University's Institute for Professional Learning, she delivers many courses in leadership, career development, and communication skills.

Dr. Kahnweiler has been an internal consultant for GE Capital, AGL Resources, and the U.S. Dept. of Education. External consulting assignments have included projects with the Department of Homeland Security, Turner Broadcasting, AT&T, and the Coca-Cola Company. As Vice President of Manchester, an international human resources consulting firm, she delivered and marketed programs to senior executives. Earlier in her career, Jennifer was Director of Career Development and Placement at the University of Cincinnati. Jennifer is an entrepreneur and collaborated with Catalyst to create one of the first firms in the country to offer nationwide career assistance to relocating dual-income families.

As a media expert, Dr. Kahnweiler writes a regular column on work issues for *AARP The Magazine*, which has a circulation of over 28 million readers. She has been a guest host and frequent career expert on JobTalk, a nationally syndicated weekly radio show and has also been interviewed on CNN radio. Jennifer has been published in over 20 trade and professional publications and has been quoted in *The New York Times*, *The Chicago Tribune*, and *The Atlanta Journal-Constitution*.

Dr. Kahnweiler earned her Ph.D. in Counseling and Human Systems from Florida State University. She received her Masters in Counseling and Bachelors in Sociology from Washington University, St. Louis. She holds Master Career Counselor (MCC), National Certified Counselor (NCC), and Licensed Professional Counselor (LPC) certifications, and has served on the board of the National Career Development Association (NCDA) and the SHRMAtlanta Consultant's Forum. She was awarded the Outstanding Career Practitioner of the Year at the 2004 NCDA National Conference in San Francisco. Dr. Kahnweiler currently is on the 2005 NCDA Program Committee, the board of the Georgia Executive Women's Network and is involved in a number of other community projects.

Jennifer can be contacted at www.myhrsuccess.com.

Index